REVISE EDEXCEL GCSE (9—1)
French

REVISION GUIDE

Series Consultant: Harry Smith

Author: Stuart Glover

A note from the publisher

In order to ensure that this resource offers high-quality support for the associated Pearson qualification, it has been through a review process by the awarding body. This process confirms that this resource fully covers the teaching and learning content of the specification or part of a specification at which it is aimed. It also confirms that it demonstrates an appropriate balance between the development of subject skills, knowledge and understanding, in addition to preparation for assessment.

Endorsement does not cover any guidance on assessment activities or processes (e.g. practice questions or advice on how to answer assessment questions) included in the resource nor does it prescribe any particular approach to the teaching or delivery of a related course.

While the publishers have made every attempt to ensure that advice on the qualification and its assessment is accurate, the official specification and associated assessment guidance materials are the only authoritative source of information and should always be referred to for definitive guidance.

Pearson examiners have not contributed to any sections in this resource relevant to examination papers for which they have responsibility.

Examiners will not use endorsed resources as a source of material for any assessment set by Pearson.

Endorsement of a resource does not mean that the resource is required to achieve this Pearson qualification, nor does it mean that it is the only suitable material available to support the qualification, and any resource lists produced by the awarding body shall include this and other appropriate resources.

Difficulty scale

The scale next to each exam-style question tells you how difficult it is.

Some questions cover a range of difficulties.

The more of the scale that is shaded, the harder the question is.

 Some questions are Foundation level.

 Some questions are Higher level.

Some questions are applicable to both levels.

For the full range of Pearson revision titles across KS2, KS3, GCSE, Functional Skills, AS/A Level and BTEC visit:
www.pearsonschools.co.uk/revise

 Pearson

Contents

. . . .

AUDIO

Audio files and transcripts for the listening exercises in this book can be accessed by using the QR codes, hotlinks throughout the book, or going to **www.pearsonschools.co.uk/mflrevisionaudio**.

Listen to the recording

. . . .

A small bit of small print:
Edexcel publishes Sample Assessment Material and the Specification on its website. This is the official content and this book should be used in conjunction with it. The questions in Now try this have been written to help you practise every topic in the book. Remember: the real exam questions may not look like this.

Physical descriptions

Remember to make adjectives agree when you are describing someone.

Mon look

Je suis grand(e) / petit(e).	I am tall / small.
Il / Elle est de taille moyenne.	He / She is of average height.
Je suis mince / gros(se).	I am thin / fat.
J'ai les cheveux courts / longs / mi-longs.	I have short / long / medium-length hair.
J'ai les cheveux roux / noirs / blonds / marron.	I have red / black / blond(e) / brown hair.
Il / Elle a les cheveux raides / frisés / ondulés / en brosse.	He / She has straight / curly / wavy / spiky hair.
J'ai les yeux bleus / noisette / verts / marron.	I have blue / hazel / green / brown eyes.
barbe (f)	beard
lunettes (fpl)	glasses
nez (m)	nose
Il / Elle est beau / belle.	He / She is good-looking.
Je le / la trouve laid(e).	I think he / she is ugly.
Elle est assez jolie.	She is quite pretty.

Irregular adjectives: vieux and beau

 Grammar page 87

	singular		plural	
	masc	fem	masc	fem
old	vieux	vieille	vieux	vieilles
beautiful	beau	belle	beaux	belles

vieil and bel (for nouns starting with a vowel or silent h).

Mon père est assez vieux.

Ma sœur est très belle.

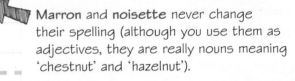 Marron and noisette never change their spelling (although you use them as adjectives, they are really nouns meaning 'chestnut' and 'hazelnut').

Worked example

Écris une description de toi-même. **(20 marks)**

Je suis assez grand mais un peu trop gros. J'ai les yeux bleu-gris et les cheveux mi-longs et blonds. Ma sœur est jolie mais elle est trop mince.

Quand j'étais petite, j'avais les cheveux longs, blonds et frisés, mais à l'âge de treize ans j'ai découvert un nouveau look! Je suis allée chez le coiffeur et je lui ai demandé de me teindre les cheveux en vert. Quand ils sont rentrés à la maison, mes parents étaient vraiment fâchés. Maintenant j'ai un piercing discret que personne ne peut voir!

ming gher

This answer uses modifiers like **assez** and **trop**. It makes the answer easier to read and more interesting.

Aiming higher
- This answer uses three different tenses – imperfect, perfect and present.
- Notice the use of the pronoun **lui**, too. It avoids repeating the noun and helps the text flow.

se teindre les cheveux = to dye one's hair

Now try this

Décris un copain ou une copine. Écris 40–50 mots environ en français.

(16 marks)

Make sure you use:
- modifiers (assez, trop, très)
- correct adjective agreements.

Golden rules
- **Vary your tenses** – your answers will be more interesting if you write about events that happened in the past.
- **Make it stand out** – an unusual twist might make your work stand out from the crowd, e.g. j'ai un piercing discret que personne ne peut voir (I've got a discreet piercing that nobody can see).

1

Character descriptions

You may need to describe someone's personality or to understand descriptions of other people.

La personnalité

Il / Elle a l'air …	He / She looks …
agaçant(e)	annoying
(dés)agréable	(un)pleasant
aimable	friendly
autoritaire	bossy
aventureux / aventureuse	adventurous
bavard(e)	chatty
bête	silly
de bonne / mauvaise humeur	in a good / bad mood
drôle	funny, witty
désordonné(e)	untidy
effronté(e)	cheeky
fou / folle	mad, crazy
gâté(e)	spoilt
gentil(le)	nice, kind
marrant(e)	funny
méchant(e), vilain(e)	mean, nasty
optimiste	optimistic
paresseux / paresseuse	lazy
sage	well-behaved
timide	shy

Object pronouns
Grammar page 92

Using **pronouns** can help you avoid repeating the noun.

me	me	us	nous
you	te	you	vous
him / it	le	them	les
her / it	la		

me, te, le, la + vowel / silent h = m', t', l'

Le sport ne l'intéresse pas.
Sport doesn't interest him.

Russell Howard est marrant mais il est parfois méchant.

Worked example

Mets une croix ✗ dans les trois cases correctes pour décrire Marianne.

(3 marks)

> Marianne est sensible mais pas très intelligente. Elle n'est jamais de mauvaise humeur car elle est vraiment optimiste. Pourtant, elle peut être timide de temps en temps, surtout quand elle sort en groupe.

Intelligente (clever) has **pas** (not) in front of it, so does not apply. De mauvaise humeur (in a bad mood) also doesn't apply as the text says ne … jamais (never). Marrante is not mentioned. So the three correct adjectives are sensible, optimiste and timide.

☒ **A** sensible   ☐ **D** intelligente
☐ **B** de mauvaise humeur   ☒ **E** optimiste
☒ **C** timide   ☐ **F** marrante

EXAM ALERT!

Look out for negatives. Make sure you take them into account when answering questions.

Now try this

Écoute la description d'un copain de Marianne.
Mets une croix ✗ dans les trois cases correctes.

(3 marks)

Julien est …

☐ **A** méchant   ☐ **C** sympa   ☐ **E** bavard
☐ **B** drôle   ☐ **D** effronté   ☐ **F** travailleur

Listen to the recording

Describing family

This page will help you describe your family and to understand descriptions of other people's families.

La famille

beau-père (m)	stepfather
belle-mère (f)	stepmother
confiant(e)	self-confident
demi-frère (m)	half-brother
demi-sœur (f)	half-sister
divorcée	divorced
égoïste	selfish
insupportable	unbearable
jaloux / jalouse	jealous
(vrais) jumeaux (mpl) / (vraies) jumelles (fpl)	(identical) twins
ma sœur cadette	my younger sister
marié(e)	married
mère / père célibataire	single parent
mon frère aîné	my elder brother
séparé(e)	separated

Ma famille

mère	mother
femme	wife
grand-mère	grandmother
père	father
mari	husband
grands-parents	grandparents
grand-père	grandfather
fils	son
fille	daughter

Je suis l'aîné(e).	I am the eldest.
Il / Elle est enfant unique.	He / She is an only child.
Il / Elle m'embête / m'énerve.	He / She annoys me / gets on my nerves.
Elle garde les enfants.	She looks after the children.

Worked example

Read this description of Juliette's family.

Quand j'étais petite, j'habitais avec mes parents à Rennes mais maintenant, j'habite dans la même ville que mon père et ma belle-mère puisque mes parents sont divorcés depuis cinq ans. J'habite aussi avec mon beau-frère cadet qui m'embête parce qu'il est gâté et je le trouve insupportable. Je dois le garder quelquefois le soir et ça, c'est difficile. Je m'entends assez bien avec mon père mais je pense qu'il est un peu égoïste. Quant à ma belle-mère, je crois qu'elle est jalouse quand mon père passe beaucoup de temps avec moi. Pourtant, elle m'aide avec mes devoirs de temps en temps. Je vois rarement ma mère qui habite loin de chez moi en Suisse.

Who does Juliette live with? **(1 mark)**

her dad, stepmother and stepbrother

Reading exam tips

- Comprehension questions on a reading passage usually follow the order of the text.
- Questions in English have to be answered in English – if you give your answer in French it will be marked as wrong, even if it is the correct French word.

This question requires a knowledge not of key words, but of grammar. It is in the **present** tense: Who does Juliette live with? So you must ignore references to the past such as j'habitais (I lived) and focus on maintenant (now): j'habite (I live).

Now try this

You should give two details.

Read the questions carefully and make sure that you answer them in sufficient detail. For example, if the question carries two marks, your answer must contain two elements.

Answer these questions on the text above.
1 How does Juliette describe her stepbrother? **(2 marks)**
2 What does Juliette say about her father's personality? **(1 mark)**
3 Give a positive about Juliette's stepmother. **(1 mark)**
4 Why does Juliette rarely see her mum? **(1 mark)**

Friends

You may be asked questions about friends in your speaking examination, so it is important to practise answering them.

Les copains / copines

ami (m) / amie (f) / copain (m) / copine (f)	friend
bavarder	to chat
coléreux / coléreuse	bad-tempered
compréhensif / compréhensive	understanding
ensemble	together
fidèle	loyal
généreux / généreuse	generous
Il / Elle m'écoute.	He / She listens to me.
Je le / la connais depuis …	I have known him / her for …
Je m'entends bien avec …	I get on well with …
les mêmes centres d'intérêt	the same interests
meilleur(e)	best
Mon meilleur ami / Ma meilleure amie s'appelle …	My best friend is called …
paresseux / paresseuse	lazy
partager	to share
(im)patient(e)	(im)patient
sportif / sportive	sporty
travailleur / travailleuse	hard-working

Remember that when you are describing a friend – whether his / her appearance or character – you must use adjectives that agree with the person described.

Questions about friends

Grammar page 109

It is vital that you understand any questions about your friends, so make sure you know all the question words.

qui	who
que	what
où	where
quand	when
quoi	what
quel(le)	which
qu'est-ce que / qui	what
pourquoi	why
combien de	how many / much
comment	how
à quelle heure	at what time

Comment s'appelle votre ami?
What is your friend called?
Qu'est-ce que vous faites?
What do you do?
Tu as un(e) meilleur(e) ami(e)?
Do you have a best friend?
À ton avis, qu'est-ce que c'est un bon ami?
In your view, what makes a good friend?
Décris un / une de tes copains / copines.
Describe one of your friends.
Pourquoi est-ce que tu t'entends bien avec tes copains?
Why do you get on well with your friends?

Worked example

1 Tu as un(e) meilleur(e) ami(e)?
Oui, elle s'appelle Annette et je la connais depuis cinq ans. Je m'entends bien avec elle parce qu'elle est toujours là pour moi.

2 Selon toi, qu'est-ce que c'est un bon ami?
Un bon ami doit être fidèle et compréhensif. Il est toujours prêt à écouter tes problèmes.

Use adjectives and add a detail wherever you can.

Now try this

Écoute une description d'Aline. Mets une croix ✗ dans les **quatre** cases correctes.

(4 marks)

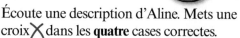
Listen to the recording

- ☐ **A** sportive
- ☐ **B** paresseuse
- ☐ **C** travailleuse
- ☐ **D** compréhensive
- ☐ **E** tolérante
- ☐ **F** généreuse
- ☐ **G** timide
- ☐ **H** coléreuse

You won't always hear the exact word you see in the box, so listen for synonyms (words which mean the same).

Role models

You may need to speak or write about role models or people who inspire you. It's useful to be able to explain why and how they do this.

Les modèles

ado	adolescent
C'est une personne qui …	He / She's a person who …
célèbre	famous
connaissance (f)	acquaintance / friend
idéal(e)	ideal
Il / Elle m'a inspiré(e).	He / She inspired me.
Il / Elle m'inspire.	He / She inspires me.
Je voudrais être comme …	I'd like to be like …
jeunesse (f)	youth (life stage)
mec (m)	guy / dude
personnalité (f)	personality / character
s'entendre avec	to get on with
avoir de l'humour (m)	to have a sense of humour
star (f)	celebrity
trait (m)	(character) trait
vie (f)	life

Aiming higher

Grammar page 94

Try to use relative pronouns **qui** (who, which) and **que** (whom, that, which) as these can add details in a complex way.

Ma cousine, qui fait toujours de son mieux et qui a sa propre entreprise, est mon modèle.

My cousin, **who** always does her best and **who** has her own business, is my role model.

There are other ways to give reasons: parce que (because), car (because), puisque (since) or grâce à (thanks to).

Ma mère m'inspire puisqu'elle a travaillé dur pendant toute sa vie et qu'elle a élevé trois enfants. Elle a réussi grâce à sa personnalité souriante.

My mother inspires me **because** she has worked hard all her life and has brought up three children. She has succeeded **thanks to** her smiling personality.

Worked example

 TRACK 3

Écoute ces deux jeunes qui parlent des stars qui les inspirent.

Mets une croix ✗ dans chaque case correcte.

Listen to the recording

> David Beckham m'inspire parce qu'il a réussi dans la vie grâce à son talent et sa personnalité. Il a gagné beaucoup d'argent, c'est vrai, mais ce qui importe, c'est qu'il est toujours modeste et agréable.

1 Pourquoi est-ce que David Beckham est un modèle selon cet ado? (Donne deux détails.) **(2 marks)**

☒ **A** Il a du talent   ☒ **C** Il est modeste
☐ **B** Il est doué en foot   ☐ **D** Il est riche

> La star qui m'a toujours inspirée, c'est Simon Cowell. Il est célèbre partout dans le monde et ce mec est vraiment cool et dit toujours la vérité.

2 Comment est-ce qu'elle décrit Simon Cowell? (Donne deux détails.) **(2 marks)**

☐ **A** Il est riche   ☒ **C** Il est honnête
☒ **B** Il est cool   ☐ **D** Il est modeste

Read all questions carefully, especially those in French. Pay particular attention to the question words. In Question 1 this is **pourquoi** and in Question 2 this is **comment**.

Now try this

Décris ton modèle. Explique ton choix. Écris 20–30 mots en français.

(12 marks)

Remember to use: adjectives (and make them agree); qui and que; and parce que, puisque and grâce à.

Relationships

In the topics of family and friends you may be asked to express how well or badly you get on with someone. This lets you express and explain your feelings.

Les rapports

amitié (f)	friendship
cadeau (m)	present / gift
chez moi / nous	at home, at my / our house
démodé(e)	old-fashioned
dispute (f)	argument
fiable	reliable
honnête	honest
humeur (f)	mood
pessimiste	pessimistic
petit copain (m) / petite copine (f)	boyfriend / girlfriend
réunion (f)	meeting
seul(e)	alone
soutenir	to support
surnom (m)	nickname
une bonne action	a good deed
vêtements (mpl)	clothes
voisin (m) / voisine (f)	neighbour

Relationship phrases

- Je m'entends mieux avec …
  I get on better with …
- J'ai de bons rapports avec …
  I have a good relationship with …
- Il / Elle ne m'écoute jamais.
  He / She never listens to me.
- On ne se dispute jamais.
  We never argue.
- On se soutient toujours.
  We always support each other.
- Ils / Elles sont vraiment démodé(e)s.
  They are really old-fashioned.

mes copines

Worked example

Écris un blog sur les rapports personnels. **(20 marks)**
- Comment est-ce que tu t'entends avec ta famille?
- Pourquoi?

Je m'entends bien avec ma sœur parce que je la trouve fiable et honnête, alors je peux lui confier mes secrets et on ne se dispute jamais. Par contre, à mon avis mon petit frère est bête et agaçant et il n'aide pas assez chez nous.

En général, j'ai de bons rapports avec mon père car il est compréhensif et me fait rire. Ma mère est très stricte, donc on se dispute, surtout quand je rentre tard le soir ou quand je veux porter des vêtements qu'elle n'aime pas. Par exemple, le week-end dernier, j'allais au cinéma avec mes copines mais ma mère m'a dit de changer de jupe parce que celle que je portais était trop courte!

Make sure that you understand what you are being asked to do and that you answer all parts of the question.

EXAM ALERT!

This can be a tricky topic. Try to:
- use phrases you know, but also use as much complex vocabulary as you can manage
- use a variety of tenses (this student has used the present, **je la trouve**, the imperfect, **j'allais**, and the perfect, **ma mère m'a dit**)
- give opinions and explain or justify them.

Now try this

Tu écris un article pour un journal en ligne. Écris 80–90 mots environ en français. **(20 marks)**

- Comment est-ce que tu t'entends avec les élèves et les profs de ton école?
- Pourquoi?
- Décris un incident récent à l'école.
- Explique ce que tu vas faire l'année prochaine et pourquoi.

When I was younger

You might have to describe what you used to be like or what you used to do when you were younger.

Dans le passé

Quand j'étais petit(e) / plus jeune …	When I was small / younger …
c'était …	it was / used to be …
je faisais …	I used to (do) …
je jouais …	I used to play …
il y avait …	there was / were / used to be …
autrefois	formerly / once
je participais à …	I used to take part in …
j'allais …	I used to go …
il y a cinq / dix ans	five / ten years ago
à l'âge de … ans	at the age of / when I was …
Quand j'avais dix ans …	When I was ten (years old) …

Forming the imperfect

Grammar page 102

To speak about what you were like or did when you were younger, you will often need to use the imperfect tense, so make sure you use it correctly.

First, take the nous form of the present tense and remove the -ons ending:

nous habit~~ons~~.

Then add the following imperfect endings:

je -ais	nous -ions
tu -ais	vous -iez
il / elle / on -ait	ils / elles -aient

habiter / to live

j'habitais	nous habitions
tu habitais	vous habitiez
il / elle / on habitait	ils / elles habitaient

Good news: all verbs except être are regular in the imperfect tense.

Worked example

Lis ce qu'Amélie a écrit sur sa vie d'autrefois.

> Quand j'étais plus jeune, j'habitais une petite maison au bord de la mer avec mes parents mais on a déménagé quand mon frère est né. J'étais plus timide et travailleuse et je lisais beaucoup mais j'étais aussi très contente car ma vie était beaucoup plus simple.

Complète la phrase en mettant une croix ✗ dans la case correcte. **(3 marks)**

1 Amélie habitait …

☐ **A** une grande maison

☐ **B** dans un petit appartement

☒ **C** sur la côte

2 Elle était …

☐ **A** moins timide

☒ **B** plus timide

☐ **C** aussi travailleuse

3 Elle était heureuse parce que / qu' …

☒ **A** sa vie était plus simple

☐ **B** elle lisait beaucoup

☐ **C** elle était pleine de vie

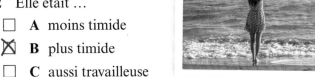

être in the imperfect

The only irregular verb in the imperfect tense is être. The stem is ét- and you add the normal imperfect endings to this stem:

j'étais	I was
tu étais	you were
il / elle / on était	he / she was
nous étions	we were
vous étiez	you were
ils / elles étaient	they were

Look out for synonyms (words which mean the same) – here, au bord de la mer (at the seaside) has the same meaning as sur la côte (on the coast).

Now try this

You might be asked to talk about your life when you were younger. Try this question:

Comment était ta vie quand tu étais plus jeune?

Peer group

It can be important to talk about ways to avoid negative peer pressure, so try to get used to using il faut or on doit followed by an infinitive, meaning 'you must'.

Les pairs

autres (mpl)	others
bande (f)	gang
connaissance (f)	acquaintance
équilibré(e)	well-balanced
être responsable	to be responsible
expérimenter	to experience
fête (f)	party
jeunesse (f)	youth (life stage)
mec (m)	guy / dude / bloke
pairs (mpl)	peers / peer group
piercing (m)	body piercing
pression (f)	pressure
se conformer	to conform
sentiment (m)	feeling
similaire	similar
stress (m)	stress
valeur (f)	value

Avoiding peer pressure

Il faut pouvoir dire non.
You must be able to say no.
On doit être responsable de soi-même.
You must be responsible for yourself.
On ne doit pas changer son attitude sans penser.
You must not change your attitude without thinking.
Il faut être indépendant.
You must be independent.

Il faut se faire de vrais amis, et passer du temps avec eux.
You must make real friends, and spend time with them.

Worked example

Read what Christophe thinks about his peer group.

La vie sociale est importante pour moi, alors je suis membre d'une bande d'ados, mais selon moi c'est bon car on aime les mêmes choses et je trouve mes copains vraiment gentils. Je suis influencé par mes pairs, c'est vrai, mais c'est une influence positive. Mes amis et moi avons fait du bénévolat ensemble dans une association qui aide les animaux en danger et nous allons organiser une nouvelle équipe de rugby pour les moins de douze ans dans notre ville.

1 What does Christophe think about his gang?
(1 mark)
They are (really) kind.

2 Describe something good which the gang has already done. **(1 mark)**
voluntary work for a charity helping animals in danger

3 What are they planning for the future? **(1 mark)**
organising a rugby team for under 12s in their town

Take care to identify the correct tenses. Be aware of clues in the text. For example you can see **nous avons fait** in the text, which would lead you to the answer to question 2 – something they have done. Similarly, **nous allons** + the infinitive indicates the future, so this would point you towards the answer to question 3.

Now try this

Listen to Céline talking about peer pressure.

Put a cross ✗ in the three **correct** boxes of the topics she mentions.

Listen to the recording

☐ **A** vandalism   ☐ **D** stealing
☐ **B** smoking   ☐ **E** alcohol
☐ **C** drugs   ☐ **F** mugging

(3 marks)

Listen not just for the French for these words but also for anything related to them.

Money

Money plays a part in many of the topics, especially those associated with work. Revising the near future will help you talk about what you are going to do with money.

L'argent

argent liquide (m)	cash
carte bancaire (f)	bank card
carte de crédit (f)	credit card
chèque de voyage (m)	traveller's cheque
billet (de 10€) (m)	(10€) note
pièce (de 2€) (f)	(2€) coin
euro (m)	euro
centime (m)	cent
livre (f)	pound (sterling)
monnaie (f)	change (coins)
changer de l'argent	to change money
dépenser de l'argent	to spend money
toucher un chèque	to cash a cheque
taux de change (m)	exchange rate
faute (f)	mistake
problème (m)	problem
compte (m)	account

Near future

Grammar page 103

Use part of aller (to go) + infinitive to say what you are going to do soon.

Nous allons chercher une banque.
We are going to look for a bank.
Ils vont mettre de l'argent de côté.
They are going to save some money.

Je vais changer de l'argent.
I am going to change some money.

Worked example

Listen to these three short passages and decide where they are taking place. Put a cross ✗ next to each correct answer. **(3 marks)**

Listen to the recording

Papa, tu as de la monnaie pour le parking?

1 ☐ **A** in a bank   ☒ **C** in a car park
  ☐ **B** at the post office

Je peux payer mes achats par carte de crédit?

2 ☒ **A** in a shop   ☐ **C** at home
  ☐ **B** at school

Je peux changer de l'argent ici?

3 ☐ **A** in the street   ☒ **C** in a bank
  ☐ **B** in a café

Remember to include all relevant details in your answers. Listen carefully, as all three questions are covered in a short passage of French!

Listening strategies

- The listening passages in the exam are not very long, so make sure you really concentrate on every word to find the answers.
- Jot down any answers you are unsure of in pencil on the first listening, then check them to confirm or change them on the second listening.
- The recording will carry on to the next activity after the second listening, so make sure you are not still trying to change answers then.
- Don't confuse similar words such as monnaie (change) and porte-monnaie (purse – literally 'change-carrier').

Now try this

Listen to Bernard talking about money. Answer the questions in English.

Listen to the recording

1 What has Bernard just done? **(2 marks)**
2 Why has he done this? **(1 mark)**
3 What does he hope to do soon? **(1 mark)**

Customs

French customs can be different from those in England. You might need to know about some of these in your exam.

Les coutumes

à l'heure	on time
assister à	to attend / be present at
culturel(le)	cultural
en retard	late
(in)formel(le)	(in)formal
joue (f)	cheek
poignée de main (f)	handshake
ponctualité (f)	punctuality
présentation (f)	introduction
s'embrasser	to kiss
saluer	to greet
se présenter	to introduce oneself
vie familiale (f)	family life

Use tu when: Use vous when:

Use tu when:
- you are being friendly or informal
- you are talking to your own family or friends
- you are talking to people roughly your own age or younger.

Use vous when:
- you are being polite or formal
- you are speaking to someone you don't know
- you are addressing someone much older than you
- you are referring to more than one person.

Worked example

Read what Jamal says about French life.

> Je suis arrivé en France il y a quelques années et j'ai remarqué plein de différences entre ma vie et celle des Français. La vie familiale est importante et on mange souvent en famille. De plus, les Français sont vraiment contents quand j'essaie de parler français. Je trouve un peu bizarre qu'on salue avec une poignée de main parce que c'est trop formel, à mon avis, mais ça me plaît quand on s'embrasse deux ou trois fois sur les joues.

1 Give three examples of differences Jamal noted in French customs. **(3 marks)**

The French often eat together as a family.
They like visitors to try to speak French.
They greet each other with a handshake.

2 What does he like about French greetings? **(1 mark)**

that people kiss each other on the cheek (two or three times)

Think about this in your role plays – you will need to address officials and employees as **vous** in role plays but use **tu** with French-speaking friends. A good way to get this right is to listen to the way the teacher doing the role play addresses you!

Remember that **ça me plaît** is a way of saying that Jamal likes what follows, so this section will provide the answer to question 2.

Remember to give sufficient detail in your answers.

Remember that in question 1 you must use the more formal register **vous** but in question 2 you need the informal **tu**. In the role play exam you will only need to cover one topic (and register) at a time.

Now try this

You will often need to ask a question as part of a role play.
Have a go at these two questions on different topics using the key words provided.
1 Tu parles avec un(e) employé(e) dans un office de tourisme: recommandation bon hôtel?
2 Tu parles à ton ami(e): activités week-end?

Everyday life

When you talk about everyday life, you might need to sequence your ideas and actions.

La vie quotidienne

après	after
avant	before
d'habitude	usually
de temps en temps	from time to time
déjeuner	to have lunch
deux / trois fois par semaine	twice / three times a week
devoirs (mpl)	homework
dîner	to have dinner
en général / généralement	in general
normalement	normally
quitter	to leave
rentrer	to go home
tous les jours / chaque jour	every day
vie (f)	life

Before and after

- avant de + infinitive = before doing something

  Avant d'aller au collège je mange du pain grillé.

  Before going to school I eat some toast.

- après avoir + past participle = after having done something

  Après avoir mangé mon petit déjeuner je suis allé au collège.

  After having eaten breakfast I went to school.

Worked example

Écoute Marine qui parle de sa vie de tous les jours.

Complète les phrases en mettant une croix ✗ dans les cases correctes.

Listen to the recording

1 La vie de Marine est … **(1 mark)**

- ☐ **A** très compliquée
- ☒ **B** pas très compliquée
- ☐ **C** très intéressante

2 Elle va à son petit job … **(1 mark)**

- ☐ **A** avant le lycée
- ☐ **B** le mercredi
- ☒ **C** deux fois par semaine

3 Elle se relaxe … **(1 mark)**

- ☒ **A** après avoir fini son travail scolaire
- ☐ **B** rarement
- ☐ **C** avec sa famille

4 Elle s'endort … **(1 mark)**

- ☐ **A** avec difficulté
- ☒ **B** sans problème
- ☐ **C** devant sa télé

D'habitude, le matin je prends des céréales et un jus d'orange – si je ne suis pas trop pressé!

Ma vie n'est pas très compliquée. En fait, elle est assez simple. Après une journée fatigante au lycée, je rentre, épuisée. Le mardi et le jeudi, je travaille dans un petit magasin tout près de ma maison, mais normalement, après avoir fait mes devoirs, je me détends devant un écran, soit celui de mon ordi, soit celui de ma télé. De temps en temps, je sors avec mes copines, mais en général, le sommeil me vient facilement.

Listen out for the part of the text that refers to each question. As the questions come in order, it is easier than you think. Just listen for key words – here, **pas très compliquée** for 1, **mardi et jeudi** for 2, **après avoir fait mes devoirs** for 3 and **le sommeil … facilement** for 4.

Now try this

Décris ta vie de tous les jours.

Remember to add as much detail as you can, offer and justify opinions and perhaps use different tenses.

11

Meals at home

When you write or speak about eating at home, you can make longer sentences by using connectives.

Les repas à la maison

casse-croûte (m)	snack
céréales (fpl)	cereals
fait(e) maison	home-made
jambon (m)	ham
Je ne bois / mange pas de ...	I don't drink / eat ...
Je ne mange rien.	I don't eat anything.
Je suis trop pressé(e).	I'm in too much of a hurry.
légumes (mpl)	vegetables
pain (m)	bread
petit déjeuner (m)	breakfast
plat cuisiné (m)	ready meal
plateau (m)	tray
repas du soir (m)	evening meal
steak haché (m)	hamburger
viande (f)	meat

de la salade

des frites

de la viande

Worked example

Décris ce que tu manges normalement chez toi.

> Mon casse-croûte préféré c'est le croque-monsieur. C'est un sandwich grillé. Je le fais moi-même. On fait un sandwich avec du jambon et du fromage, puis on le fait griller. Je le mange avec du ketchup!
>
> Chez nous, on mange quand on a faim! Par exemple, hier ma sœur a mangé du steak haché avec des pommes de terre à quatre heures en rentrant de l'école, mais moi, je suis allé à mon club alors je ne suis pas arrivé à la maison avant cinq heures et demie et il ne restait plus rien dans le frigo. Donc j'ai dû manger un plat cuisiné du congélateur parce que mes parents n'étaient pas allés au supermarché.

Aiming higher

This is a good response but to get a higher mark it would need to use more than one tense.

Aiming higher

This response deserves a higher grade because it uses **connectives** such as quand, avec, donc, parce que. It also includes the **perfect** tense of a modal verb (j'ai dû manger) and an **imperfect** tense (il ne restait plus rien), as well as the present tense and a variety of structures.

Now try this

Alex, ton ami(e) français(e), t'a envoyé un email sur ce que tu manges chez toi. Écris une réponse à Alex. Tu dois faire référence aux points suivants:
- ce que tu manges normalement
- ce que tu as mangé hier soir à la maison
- ton opinion sur les repas chez toi
- ce que tu vas manger demain.

Écris 80–90 mots environ en français.

(20 marks)

Here are some connectives you could use:

et	and	parce que	because
ou	or	(même) si	(even) if
mais	but	alors	then
donc	so / therefore	aussi	also
car	because	quand	when

Food and drink

Food and drink in different French-speaking countries can be very different.

À manger et à boire

(pâté de) foie gras (m)	goose liver pâté
agneau (m)	lamb
apéritif (m)	drink before a meal
baguette (f)	baguette
Bon appétit!	Enjoy your meal!
champagne (m)	champagne
crudités (fpl)	raw vegetables
épicé(e)	spicy
fruits de mer (mpl)	seafood
goûter	to taste
pâtisseries (fpl)	pastries
plat (m)	dish
tartine (f)	slice of bread (with butter / jam, often for breakfast)
végétarien(ne)	vegetarian

Using on

The French often use the word **on** to translate 'you', 'we', 'they' or even 'people' in English. The direct translation is 'one' but that sounds posh in English. On is not considered posh and it is used all the time. It uses the same part of the verb as il and elle. Try to use it yourself in speaking and writing. For example:

En France, on mange beaucoup de viande.
In France, people eat lots of meat.
Au Maroc, on mange plein de plats épicés.
In Morocco, they eat lots of spicy dishes.
On va souvent en France.
We often go to France.

Worked example

En France on mange beaucoup de légumes.

Lysette parle de ses vacances au Maroc.

Je viens de rentrer de vacances au Maroc. On était chez des copains de ma sœur. Ce qui m'a plu le plus, c'était la cuisine traditionnelle marocaine. Puisque j'adore essayer des plats régionaux, j'ai bien mangé. Un soir on est allés chez une copine et on a mangé un tagine à l'agneau, au citron et aux figues, que j'ai trouvé vraiment délicieux.

Malheureusement ma sœur l'a trouvé trop épicé et elle a dû boire beaucoup d'eau minérale. Ma mère n'est pas venue avec nous parce qu'elle ne mange jamais de viande.

1 What does Lysette enjoy trying? **(1 mark)**
regional dishes

2 What was in the tagine she found delicious?
(3 marks)
lamb, lemon and figs

3 What did Lysette's sister think of the dish?
(1 mark)
too spicy

4 What did she have to do? **(3 marks)**
drink lots of mineral water

EXAM ALERT!

If you see a word that might be a cognate (word that looks the same in French and English) or near cognate and you think you might be able to guess its meaning, it is better than leaving a blank! Here **figues** looks like 'figs', and that's what it means!

Now try this

Lis le texte encore une fois. Qui parle? Lysette, sa sœur ou sa mère?
1 Je suis végétarienne. **(1 mark)**
2 Je n'aime pas la cuisine épicée. **(1 mark)**
3 Le tagine m'a beaucoup plu. **(1 mark)**

Shopping

Shopping is a part of everyone's life and is a topic which you need to be familiar with. It may involve descriptions of items, so be careful with adjectives.

Faire des achats

achats (mpl)	purchases
bijouterie (f)	jeweller's
bonnet (m)	woolly hat / beanie
cadeau (m)	present / gift
carte de crédit (f)	credit card
ceinture (f)	belt
confiserie (f)	sweet shop
écharpe (f)	scarf
faire du lèche-vitrine	to window shop
fermé(e)	closed
librairie (f)	bookshop
magasin de vêtements	clothes shop
maquillage (m)	make-up
ouvert(e)	open
payer	to pay for
sac à dos (m)	rucksack
soldes (mpl)	sale

Using the adjective 'new'

Grammar page 87

nouveau (new) = irregular adjective
used in front of noun: un nouveau livre (a new book).

singular		plural	
masc	fem	masc	fem
nouveau	nouvelle	nouveaux	nouvelles

nouvel (for masculine nouns starting with a vowel or silent h)

un nouveau collier	a new necklace
un nouvel accessoire	a new accessory
une nouvelle bague	a new ring

When 'new' means 'different', e.g. you want a new glass to replace a dirty one, use autre (other): Est-ce que je peux avoir un autre verre? Can I have a different glass?

Worked example

Read the text and answer the question below.

Le bonnet MP3

C'est le nouvel accessoire indispensable pour les jeunes, les fanatiques de la mode et de la bonne musique. Vous pouvez tout simplement relier votre lecteur MP3 au récepteur fourni dans votre bonnet. Puis mettez le récepteur dans votre poche ou votre sac et écoutez vos chansons favorites – sans fil. La transmission du récepteur au bonnet est efficace jusqu'à 12 mètres. L'émetteur ainsi que le récepteur fonctionnent chacun avec deux piles AAA (non incluses).

Name **two** types of people who might buy this product.

(2 marks)

young people and music fans

Reading strategies

In questions aimed at higher grades there will be some vocabulary you won't have revised. Here are some strategies to help you.

- **Read** the questions in English to find out more information.
- **Cognates** and near cognates will help: indispensable, fanatique, musique, accessoire, but be careful: piles = batteries (not piles!).
- **Context** – the text is about an MP3 player and earphones, so the chances are un récepteur is some sort of receiver (it isn't crucial to know which sort exactly).

Now try this

Answer the questions in English.

1 What do you have to do to make the device work? **(1 mark)**
2 Which two places are suggested for placing the receiver? **(1 mark)**
3 How close must the receiver be to the earphones? **(1 mark)**
4 How many batteries come with the hat? **(1 mark)**

Watch out – a tricky question!

Shopping for food

You may need to use quantities when you are shopping for food, so make sure you know them!

Faire les courses

un kilo de	a kilo of
un litre de	a litre of
un morceau de	a piece of
un paquet de	a packet of
un peu de	a little of / a bit of
un pot de	a jar of
un tiers de	a third of
une boîte de	a box / can of
une bouteille de	a bottle of
une douzaine de	a dozen
une tranche de	a slice of
champignon (m)	mushroom
chou (m)	cabbage
fraise (f)	strawberry
œuf (m)	egg
pain au chocolat (m)	chocolate pastry
pêche (f)	peach
pomme (f)	apple
pomme de terre (f)	potato
yaourt (m)	yoghurt

Quantities

After quantities de does not change to agree with the noun. It stays as de. Before a vowel, it becomes d'.

assez de	enough
beaucoup de	lots of
moins de	less
pas mal de	quite a lot of
plein de	lots / plenty of
plus de	more

Elle a assez de bananes.
She's got enough bananas.
Tu as trop d'argent.
You have got too much money.
Il y a plein de pommes.
There are plenty of apples.

Worked example

Écoute Amandine et son père qui parlent de ce qu'ils doivent acheter. Complète la liste en français.

Listen to the recording

Amandine:	Nous avons besoin d'un litre de lait, je crois … euh … non, attends … deux litres, c'est ça.
Papa:	D'accord, et aussi d'un kilo de fraises et d'une douzaine d'œufs.
Amandine:	D'accord, mais il nous faut aussi un pot de miel et … euh … voyons … ah non, on a assez de bananes.
Papa:	On y va, alors.

fraises	frites
deux litres	bananes
miel	une douzaine

....2 litres.... de lait   (1 mark)

Un kilo de ....fraises....   (1 mark)

....une douzaine.... d'œufs   (1 mark)

Un pot de ....miel....   (1 mark)

More listening strategies

- Don't be too hasty in writing down your answers – things sometimes change, so you need to listen until the end!

- If you do change your mind about an answer, make sure you cross it out completely and write the correct answer clearly instead.

- When speaking normally, especially in dialogues, people often use 'thinking' noises, but don't be put off by them! You can use your own 'thinking' noises to gain time in your speaking assessment.

Euh …	Er …
Ah …	Er …
Attends / attendez …	Er, wait …

Now try this

Translate these sentences into French.

1 I would like a packet of biscuits.
                                                     (2 marks)
2 We have enough vegetables.   (2 marks)
3 There are lots of peaches.   (2 marks)

Social media

The vocabulary and phrases here will help you talk about social media and understand and express opinions on the subject.

Les réseaux sociaux

blog (m)	blog
courrier électronique / email (m)	email
cyber harcèlement (m)	cyber bullying
écran (m)	screen
effacer	to delete
en ligne	online
forum (m)	chatroom
logiciel (m)	software
numérique	digital
ordinateur (m)	computer
page d'accueil (f)	homepage
page web (f)	web page
site web (m)	website
surfer	to surf
tchatter	to chat
télécharger	to download

Expressing opinions

Use these different phrases to avoid being repetitive.

À mon avis, il ne faut pas passer trop de temps en ligne.
In my opinion, you shouldn't spend too much time online.

Selon mon frère, le logiciel est nul.
According to my brother, the software is rubbish.

Je trouve que les réseaux sociaux sont utiles.
I find that social networks are useful.

Je pense que Facebook est le moyen le plus efficace de rester en contact avec mes amis.
I think that Facebook is the most effective way to stay in contact with my friends.

Worked example

Salut! C'est Luc. Je mets mes photos sur Instagram parce que c'est plus facile et plus simple que Snapchat, mais ma sœur a créé une page Facebook pour ses photos.

Vrai ou faux?
Luc préfère Snapchat pour ses photos. **(1 mark)**
faux

La sœur de Luc met ses photos sur Facebook.
(1 mark)
vrai

Aiming higher

Don't just express an opinion; add a reason or justification.

À mon avis, il ne faut pas passer trop de temps en ligne parce qu'on doit aussi être actif.

In my opinion, you shouldn't spend too much time online because you should also be active.

Don't be fooled by words that appear in the text and in the question. That doesn't necessarily mean that the statement is true!

Now try this

Answer these questions, which might be asked on the topic of social media. Give your opinion and reasons where you can.

1 Que penses-tu des réseaux sociaux?
2 Tu passes combien de temps en ligne chaque jour? Pourquoi?
3 Quel est ton réseau social préféré? Pourquoi?

Technology

We all use technology a lot in everyday life; here are some French technical terms to learn.

La technologie

charger	to load
effacer	to delete
fichier (m)	file
harcèlement (m)	bullying / harassment
Internet (m)	internet
mot de passe (m)	password
sauvegarder	to save
sécurité (f)	security
site web (m)	website
surfer	to surf
taper	to type
tchatter (en ligne)	to chat (online)
télécharger	to download

Comparatives

You often want to be able to compare two things in French. To do this, you use:

plus (more)
moins (less) } + adjective + que (than / as)
aussi (as)

Mon ordi est plus cher que le tien.
My computer is more expensive than yours.
Elle tape aussi vite que moi.
She types as quickly as me.

As in English, you can also use comparatives without que (than).
Les articles sont moins chers sur Internet.
Things are cheaper on the internet.
Here, the comparison is implied: ... que dans les magasins (... than in the shops).

Worked example

Réponds à ces questions en français.

1 Quels sont les avantages de faire des achats en ligne?
Il est souvent moins cher de faire des achats en ligne et les sites web sont toujours disponibles. On n'a pas besoin de quitter la maison et tout est vite livré.

2 Comment as-tu utilisé la technologie le week-end dernier?
J'ai tchatté avec mes copains en Afrique sur Internet et j'ai aussi téléchargé plusieurs chansons formidables.

3 Que penses-tu du cyber harcèlement?
C'est vraiment nul. J'ai une copine qui a été harcelée en ligne il y a quelques mois et c'était très désagréable.

Il est souvent moins cher de faire des achats en ligne.

Always add details: use adverbs, e.g. **souvent** (often), **toujours** (always) and **vite** (quickly), and negatives, e.g. **on n'a pas besoin**, if you can.

Make sure you use the perfect tense, e.g. j'ai tchatté / j'ai téléchargé (I chatted / I downloaded).

Give an opinion and try to either justify it or give an example to back it up. Use any chance you have to vary tenses; here you can use the perfect a été harcelée (was bullied) and the imperfect c'était (it was).

Now try this

You see this advertisement online:

> Téléchargez de la musique sur notre site web. C'est gratuit!

How much does it cost to download music from this site? **(1 mark)**

Internet advantages and disadvantages

Try to memorise as many of the phrases on this page as you can, so that you'll be able to talk about internet pros and cons.

Aspect positif et aspect négatif d'Internet

Internet, c'est un moyen pratique de …
The internet is a good way of …

s'informer.   keeping up to date.

acheter des billets de train / cinéma.
buying train / cinema tickets.

rester en contact avec ses amis.
keeping in touch with friends.

jouer à des jeux.   playing games.

Internet, c'est dangereux / mauvais quand on …
The internet is dangerous / bad when you …

ne surveille pas les enfants.
don't keep an eye on children.

passe tout son temps libre devant l'écran.
spend all your free time in front of a screen.

donne ses coordonnées sur un forum.

Je fais des recherches pour mes devoirs.
I do research for my homework.

Opinion phrases

Add an opinion phrase wherever possible to personalise your work.

À mon avis, les parents doivent savoir avec qui leurs enfants communiquent en ligne.
In my opinion, parents should know who their children are communicating with online.

Selon moi, on ne doit pas rester en ligne après huit heures du soir.
According to me, you shouldn't stay online after 8 p.m.

Personnellement je trouve que sur Internet, les livres coûtent moins cher.
Personally, I find that books cost less on the internet.

J'envoie un email à mon cousin au Maroc.
I'm sending an email to my cousin in Morocco.

Worked example

 SPEAKING

Tu aimes utiliser Internet?

> J'utilise Internet pour faire des recherches pour mes devoirs, pour faire des achats, pour contacter mes amis … pour tout.

Weaknesses in this sample answer are:
- it does not give an opinion
- there is only one tense
- and it simply lists activities.

Aiming higher

> Selon moi, Internet est un moyen rapide d'accéder à toutes sortes d'information, mais on ne doit pas oublier les inconvénients. Personnellement, je pense que le problème le plus grave, c'est qu'il y a des gens qui harcèlent les autres en ligne. La semaine dernière, on a piraté l'ordinateur de mon frère et un inconnu a fait des achats avec sa carte de crédit. Il dit qu'il ne fera plus d'achats en ligne. Ça, c'est dommage.

Aiming higher

To give a better answer, you need to:
- use a wide range of appropriate and interesting vocabulary
- use a wide range of structures, including some complex items
- express and explain a range of ideas and points of view.

il y a des gens qui harcèlent
= there are people who harass

Now try this

 SPEAKING

Réponds aux questions en français.
1 Comment est-ce que tu utilises Internet?
2 Selon toi, quels sont les avantages et les inconvénients d'Internet?

Arranging to go out

Vocabulary associated with arranging to go out is important when you are listening to what other people are planning or suggesting.

Organiser une sortie

aller à la piscine	to go to the swimming pool
aller au centre sportif	to go to the sports centre
aller au cinéma	to go to the cinema
faire du bowling	to go bowling
faire du VTT	to go mountain biking
faire mes devoirs	to do my homework
garder mon petit frère	to look after my little brother
Je dois …	I have to …
Je peux / Je ne peux pas …	I can / can't …
On va au stade?	Shall we go to the stadium?
ranger ma chambre	to tidy my room
Tu veux / Vous voulez …?	Do you want to …?
Tu veux sortir?	Do you want to go out?
Tu viens / Vous venez?	Are you coming?

Suggesting an activity

Listen for **si** at the start of a sentence, with the verb in the imperfect tense, as this can be used to suggest an activity in spoken French. It means 'What if / How about?'

Si on allait en ville?
What if we went into town?
Si tu amenais ta sœur?
How about bringing your sister?

Si on jouait au foot?

Si on faisait du vélo?

Worked example

Listen to these young French people talking about where they're going. Put a cross ✗ in the **three** correct boxes.   **(3 marks)**

Listen to the recording

> Tu veux aller à la patinoire ce soir?
>
> Si on allait à la piscine?
>
> Tu veux faire du VTT cet après-midi?

- ☒ **A** going swimming
- ☐ **B** going bowling
- ☐ **C** going to the theatre
- ☒ **D** going to the ice rink
- ☐ **E** going to the shops
- ☒ **F** going mountain biking

There are two main ways to say 'we' in French: **nous** and **on**. You can use either, but don't mix the two in the same sentence.

Learning vocabulary

To prepare for your listening exam, you need to learn lots of vocabulary.

- **Look** at and learn the words.
- **Cover** the English words.
- **Write** the English words.
- **Look** at all the words.
- **See** how many you have got right.

For an extra challenge, cover the **French** words and repeat the stages above.

Now try this

Listen to the recording. Answer the questions **in English**.

Listen to the recording

1 Where is Lucas invited to go?
    (1 mark)
2 What activity is suggested?
    (1 mark)
3 Why can't he go?   **(1 mark)**

Hobbies

You might well have a writing or speaking question about your hobbies, so make sure you're prepared for it!

Les passe-temps

J'aime ...

nager / danser
faire les magasins
jouer de la guitare / du piano
jouer aux échecs / sur mon ordinateur
aller au théâtre
aller au club des jeunes
sortir avec mes copains

I like ...

swimming / dancing
shopping
playing the guitar / the piano
playing chess / on my computer
going to the theatre
going to the youth club
going out with my friends

J'aime lire.

J'aime écouter de la musique.

J'aime regarder la télé.

Likes and dislikes

Use these verbs with the infinitive to talk about your likes and dislikes: adorer, aimer, détester, préférer.

J'adore danser.
I love dancing (to dance).
Je déteste jouer de la batterie.
I hate playing the drums.
Je préfère retrouver mes amis.
I prefer meeting my friends.
Ce qui me plaît, c'est d'aller en ville avec mes copains.
What I like is going into town with my friends.

Make sure you use the correct accents on Je préfère!

Worked example

Écris un email à un nouveau correspondant sur tes passe-temps. Écris 80–90 mots en français.   **(20 marks)**

J'aime écouter de la musique et sortir avec mes copains. Je n'aime pas le sport et je déteste aller au théâtre.

Aiming higher

Ma passion, c'est la musique, surtout la musique classique. Je joue du piano depuis presque dix ans et je trouve ça vraiment relaxant. En plus, le week-end dernier je suis allée à un concert avec ma meilleure amie, Alice. Quand j'étais plus jeune je faisais de la natation trois fois par semaine, mais maintenant je préfère danser avec mes copines parce que c'est beaucoup plus amusant. De temps en temps je lis des romans ou des magazines afin de me détendre un peu. Dimanche prochain j'irai au théâtre en ville avec ma sœur car nous aimons regarder des pièces comiques ensemble.

In this answer, four tenses are used, reasons are given for opinions and more complex constructions are used (e.g. **depuis** + the present tense).

How to develop more complex sentences

Sentences can be developed with words like surtout (especially), presque (nearly), vraiment (really), quand (when), mais (but), parce que (because), de temps en temps (from time to time), ou (or), afin de (in order to) and car (because).

Now try this

Écris un blog sur tes passe-temps. Il faut parler de:
• ce que tu as fait le week-end dernier
• comment tu l'as trouvé
• ce que tu vas faire le week-end prochain et pourquoi.

Écris 80–90 mots en français.

(20 marks)

Make sure that you cover all the aspects of the question and that you use appropriate tenses to talk about the past and future.

Music

Many young French-speaking people like British and American music. Don't be surprised if they write or talk about singers and bands that you like too!

La musique

Mon chanteur préféré / ma chanteuse préférée, c'est …	My favourite singer is …
J'écoute …	I listen to …
Je suis fana de …	I'm a fan of …
musique pop / rock	pop / rock
musique folk / jazz	folk / jazz
musique classique	classical music
Je joue du piano / de la guitare.	I play the piano / guitar.
célébrité (f)	celebrity
chanson (f)	song
groupe (m)	group / band
musicien (m) / musicienne (f)	musician
orchestre (m)	orchestra
chanter	to sing
écouter la radio	to listen to the radio
télécharger	to download

'This' and 'that'
Grammar page 90

Remember that the words for this / that / these / those are adjectives in French and they need to agree with the word they describe:

masc sg	fem sg	masc pl	fem pl
ce	cette	ces	ces

Add -ci to the noun when you use ce / cette / ces to make it mean 'this' or 'these', e.g. ce groupe-ci (this group), ces musiciennes-ci (these musicians), and add -là to make it mean 'that' or 'those': cette musique-là (that music), ces chanteurs-là (those singers).

Worked example

Lis ce courrier électronique de Maryam.

> Hier soir je suis allée voir Ed Sheeran en concert avec quelques amis. Il était formidable et l'ambiance était géniale. Je me suis très bien amusée et j'ai même dansé. Il a chanté ma chanson favorite, alors je n'oublierai jamais cette soirée-là. Ce serait mon rêve d'aller voir ma chanteuse favorite, Taylor Swift, en concert dans un proche avenir!

Complète chaque phrase en utilisant un mot de la case. Attention! Il y a des mots que tu n'utiliseras pas.

concert	copains	préférée	nul
super	chanté	dansé	chanteur

1 Maryam est allée voir un concert avec des
   …copains… **(1 mark)**
2 Elle a trouvé le concert …super… **(1 mark)**
3 Maryam a même …dansé… **(1 mark)**
4 Elle voudrait bientôt aller voir sa chanteuse
   …préférée… **(1 mark)**

Now try this

Fill in the gaps with an appropriate word from the box.

Hier j'ai assisté à un concert de musique
……………… . C'était vraiment
……………… car les membres du
groupe ne savaient pas jouer de leurs
……………… . **(3 marks)**

super	pop	chanter
nul	amis	instruments

EXAM ALERT!

You must include words which make sense in the gaps. For example in question 1 the word has to be a plural noun, as **des** comes before the gap. The only possible answer is therefore **copains**.

Sport

When you talk about sports, you need to use jouer or faire. Make sure that you get the à / au / à l' / aux and du / de la / de l' / des parts right.

Faire du sport

Je joue / jouais …	I play / used to play …
au basket / tennis	basketball / tennis
Je fais / faisais …	I do / used to do …
des arts martiaux	martial arts
du vélo	cycling
de la danse	dancing
de l'aérobic	aerobics
de l'aviron	rowing
de l'équitation	horseriding
de l'escalade	rock climbing
du patin à roulettes	rollerskating
de la voile	sailing
du ski nautique	waterskiing
des sports d'hiver	winter sports
une / deux fois par semaine	once / twice a week
tous les samedis	every Saturday

To play / do sports

- jouer + à + sport / game:
  Je joue au football.
  I play football.
  Je joue aux cartes.
  I play cards.
- faire + de with other sports:
  Je fais de la natation. I swim.

Je fais du ski.

Je joue au rugby.

Worked example

You must be able to identify when an activity happened, is happening or will happen.

Read the passage about Sophie's interest in sport. Answer the questions in English.

Je suis très sportive. Quand j'étais petite, je jouais souvent au basket: je m'entraînais trois fois par semaine et le week-end on jouait contre d'autres équipes. Une fois, on a gagné le championnat régional. C'était incroyable. Maintenant, ce que je préfère, c'est le judo et j'en fais tous les soirs sauf le jeudi, mais je fais aussi de la planche à voile, ce qui me plaît beaucoup. Cet hiver, je vais faire du ski pour la première fois et j'aimerais bien essayer le tir à l'arc car c'est un sport différent.

1 What did Sophie use to do three times a week when she was younger? **(1 mark)**
basketball training

2 How does she describe winning the local championship? **(1 mark)**
incredible

3 When does she currently do judo? **(1 mark)**
every evening except Thursday

4 What other sport does she currently do? **(1 mark)**
windsurfing

5 What sport would she like to try? **(1 mark)**
archery

Past, present and future

- For 'past' activities you need to look for words in the imperfect or perfect tense (étais, past participles).
- For 'present' you need present tense verbs with words such as maintenant (now) or d'habitude (usually).
- For 'future' look for the near future (je vais + infinitive), future tense (je ferai) or the conditional (je voudrais).

Now try this

Réponds aux questions en français.
1 Qu'est-ce que tu aimes comme sport?
2 Tu aimerais essayer quel sport à l'avenir? Pourquoi?

Reading

Read as many different types of text as you can, including novels, non-fiction, cartoons, magazines and web pages.

La lecture

fana de	fanatical about
temps libre (m)	free time
roman (m)	novel
loisirs (mpl)	leisure
lire	to read
journal (m)	newspaper
bande dessinée (f)	comic
dessin animé (m)	cartoon (film)
magazine (m)	magazine
actualités (fpl)	news
livre (m)	book

Irregular past participles

Grammar page 100

Lire (to read) is one of the verbs that has an irregular past participle in French (lu). It's really important to remember some of the others, too. Here are the most useful ones.

avoir	➡ eu		faire	➡ fait
être	➡ été		mettre	➡ mis
voir	➡ vu		dire	➡ dit
lire	➡ lu		écrire	➡ écrit
devoir	➡ dû		rire	➡ ri
vouloir	➡ voulu		boire	➡ bu
pouvoir	➡ pu		prendre	➡ pris
savoir	➡ su		comprendre	➡ compris
connaître	➡ connu		conduire	➡ conduit
courir	➡ couru		ouvrir	➡ ouvert

Je suis fana de bandes dessinées.

Worked example

LISTENING TRACK 11

Listen to the recording

Listen to these four young French people talking about what they read. Complete the sentences in English.

Marine: Moi, j'aime lire des bandes dessinées.

Lionel: Je n'aime pas trop la lecture mais je lis les actualités en ligne.

Marianne: Moi, je préfère lire des magazines.

Mohammed: Je lis des romans de temps en temps mais je ne lis jamais le journal.

aime lire gives you the clue as to what to listen for.

actualités is news, so it's what comes next that you need to listen for.

préfère lire is the clue here.

listen for **ne ... jamais** (never).

1 Marine likes reading .....comics..... **(1 mark)**
2 Lionel reads the news ......online...... **(1 mark)**
3 Marianne prefers reading ...magazines... **(1 mark)**
4 Mohammed never reads a newspaper **(1 mark)**

Now try this

LISTENING TRACK 12

Listen to the recording

Écoute Anne qui parle de la lecture. Qu'est-ce qu'elle aime lire? Mets une croix ✗ dans les trois cases correctes. **(3 marks)**

☐ **A** les romans d'aventure   ☐ **D** les magazines de sport

☐ **B** les journaux en ligne   ☐ **E** les romans d'espionnage

☐ **C** les livres sur les animaux   ☐ **F** les bandes dessinées

Films

Practise describing the films you like and past / future visits to the cinema for both speaking and writing questions. Here are some details to help you.

Les films

acteur (m) / actrice (f)	actor
film d'aventures (m)	adventure film
film comique (m)	comedy
film d'espionnage (m)	spy film
film de science-fiction (m)	sci-fi film
film de suspense (m)	thriller
film romantique / d'amour (m)	romance
film principal (m)	feature film
réduction (f)	reduction
salle complète (f)	sold out
séance (f)	showing
soir (m)	evening
les effets spéciaux (mpl)	special effects
vedette (f)	film star
énerver	to annoy
version originale (VO) (f)	original version (i.e. not dubbed)

avoir expressions

avoir faim / soif	to be hungry / thirsty
avoir raison / tort	to be right / wrong
avoir besoin de	to need
avoir peur	to be afraid
avoir l'air	to look (angry, sad, etc.)
avoir lieu	to take place
avoir envie de	to feel like (doing something)

J'ai peur des films d'horreur.
I am afraid of horror films.

Worked example

Regarde la photo. Réponds aux questions.   **(24 marks)**

1 Décris-moi la photo.
Il y a des gens qui regardent un film au ciné. Je pense que c'est un film comique parce que tout le monde rit.

2 Moi j'aime les films comiques. Et toi?
Je les aime aussi car ils me font rire.

These answers use parts of verbs other than **je** (I). Using **ils**, for example, shows that you can handle different parts of the verb.

3 Parle-moi d'un film que tu as vu au cinéma récemment.
Le week-end dernier je suis allé regarder un film d'espionnage au ciné avec mes copains. On s'est bien amusés car le film était fascinant.

EXAM ALERT!

Note how this student expands answers by adding opinions and then makes the sentences more complex by giving a reason for or explaining the opinion.

4 Tu préfères regarder des films au ciné ou chez toi? Pourquoi?
Je préfère regarder des films chez moi car on peut bavarder sans déranger tout le monde et c'est plus pratique et moins cher.

The student uses the present, perfect and imperfect tenses, along with at least five opinions and reasons.

5 Quel est le prochain film que tu voudrais voir?
Je voudrais voir le nouveau film de James Bond parce que j'aime bien les films d'action.

Now try this

Regarde encore une fois la photo ci-dessus.

Écris une description de la photo et exprime ton opinion sur le cinéma. Écris 20–30 mots en français.
(12 marks)

TV

If you talk or write about TV, you need to be able to describe the types of programme you watch.

La télévision

actualités / informations / infos (fpl)	news
comédie dramatique (f)	drama
comédie de situation (f)	sitcom
dessin animé (m)	cartoon
documentaire (m)	documentary
feuilleton (m)	soap
jeu télévisé (m)	game show
météo (f)	weather forecast
mon émission préférée	my favourite programme
policier (m)	detective programme
pub (f)	adverts
série (f)	series
télévision câblée (f)	cable television
télévision satellite (f)	satellite television
chaîne (de télévision) (f)	television channel
poste de télévision (m)	television set
télécommande (f)	remote control

Pronouncing préféré(e)(s)

Préféré(e)(s) is often mispronounced. Pull your lips into a smile and keep them there as you say all three syllables.

Une de mes émissions préférées, c'est …
One of my favourite programmes is …

Coping with role plays

☑ You must use the points below each question to help you prepare what to say.

☑ You don't need to add details when you are doing a role play. Just stick to the essentials.

☑ The teacher will speak first.

☑ Do not simply repeat the prompts.

☑ Sometimes a symbol will indicate the type of information you need to give. Where you see:
- **!** you must respond to something you have not prepared.
- **?** you must ask a question.

☑ The instructions will always be in French and will give you at least a few basic items of vocabulary.

☑ Revise question words before the role play, but remember that est-ce que … ? can be used to ask a question if no specific question word is required. For example, *Est-ce que tu aimes … ?* (do you like …?) or just *Tu aimes … ?*, raising your voice at the end to make it sound like a question.

Worked example

You are discussing TV with a French friend. You must:

Use the points below to help you prepare what to say.

La télé: Tu discutes de la télé avec un(e) ami(e) français(e).

1 quand tu regardes la télé
Tu regardes beaucoup la télé?
Je regarde la télé le soir.

2 émission préférée
Ah bon, qu'est-ce que tu préfères regarder?
Mon émission préférée c'est X Factor.

3 !
Pourquoi tu aimes ce programme?
J'aime la musique.

4 télé avec qui
D'accord. Avec qui aimes tu regarder la télé?
Je regarde la télé avec ma famille.

5 ? émission détestée
Il y a une émission que tu détestes?
Je n'aime pas les documentaires. **(10 marks)**

Now try this

Translate these sentences into French.
1 I prefer watching documentaries.
               (2 marks)
2 Yesterday I watched a cartoon with my brother. **(3 marks)**
3 Tomorrow I am going to watch my favourite soap opera. **(3 marks)**

Celebrations

In France, people observe many of the same celebrations we do – but they also have some special celebrations that we are less familiar with.

Les fêtes

Bon anniversaire!	Happy birthday!
divertissement (m)	entertainment
fête (f)	celebration / party
fête nationale (f) / le quatorze juillet (m)	Bastille Day / 14 July
fêter / célébrer	to celebrate
feux d'artifice (mpl)	fireworks
fiançailles (fpl)	engagement
jours fériés (mpl)	public holidays
mariage (m)	wedding / marriage
noces (fpl)	marriage ceremony / wedding
plaisir (m)	pleasure / amusement
spectateur (m) / spectatrice (f)	viewer / audience member
Toussaint (f)	All Saints' Day

Using pouvoir

You might need to understand passages where people are saying what they (or someone else) can do. The verb pouvoir (to be able) is frequently used. It is often followed by a verb in the infinitive.

Je peux aller en ville?
Can I go into town?
On peut y faire du shopping.
You can go shopping there.
Nous pouvons regarder un spectacle.
We can watch a show.
Ils peuvent aller au cinéma.
They can go to the cinema.

On peut visiter le château.

Worked example

Le quatorze juillet est un jour férié en France. La fête nationale a été instituée en 1880 et on célèbre la prise de la Bastille, une prison à Paris, en 1789. Ce jour-là, il y a un défilé militaire sur les Champs-Élysées. Il y a des spectacles nocturnes partout en France et on peut voir des feux d'artifice dans plusieurs villes. On organise également des bals, souvent le 13 juillet, veille de la fête nationale, ce qui permet aux gens de continuer à célébrer jusqu'au petit matin!

With more difficult passages like this one, you don't have to understand every word to be able to get the correct answer.

Look for clues and try to work out the meaning of words you don't know. For example, here you may not know the word **défilé** but it has the adjective **militaire** after it and you might work out that it is a parade from the context: if the military is involved in a celebration in Paris, a parade is the most likely reason. Similarly, **feux d'artifice** might be worked out from **spectacles nocturnes** and the fact that it is a celebration.

Answer these questions in English.

1 In what year was the first Bastille Day holiday?
(1 mark)
1880

2 What happens on the Champs-Élysées? **(1 mark)**
a military parade

3 What happens in many towns? **(1 mark)**
firework displays

4 Why are some events scheduled for 13 July?
(1 mark)
to allow celebrations to go on into the early hours

Now try this

Translate this passage into English.
(7 marks)

En France, le premier novembre est une fête religieuse populaire. Toutes les écoles sont fermées et tout le monde passe la journée en famille. On pense aux membres de la famille qui sont morts et on va à l'église où on apporte beaucoup de fleurs. Le soir, on prend souvent un grand repas ensemble.

Festivals

Although some French festivals are the same as ours, they are often celebrated differently.

On célèbre!

Bonne année!	Happy New Year!
Carême (m)	Lent
festival (m)	festival
Fête des mères (f)	Mother's Day
Fête des rois (f)	Epiphany (6th Jan)
Jour de l'an (m)	New Year's Day
Noël (m)	Christmas
nouvel an (m)	new year
Pâques	Easter
réveillon (m)	overnight party
Saint Sylvestre (f)	New Year's Eve
traditionnel(le)	traditional
veille de Noël (f)	Christmas Eve
vendredi saint (m)	Good Friday

La fête des rois est une fête importante en France où on mange des galettes.

Worked example

Lis ce texte. Mets une croix ✗ dans les quatre cases correctes. **(4 marks)**

> De nos jours, il y a plein de marchés de Noël en France mais l'un des plus anciens est celui qui a lieu à Strasbourg, dans l'est de la France, depuis plus de quatre siècles. Le marché a eu lieu pour la première fois quand la ville faisait partie de l'Allemagne. La fête dure cinq semaines et attire tous les ans plus de deux millions de visiteurs, y compris des touristes britanniques. La cathédrale impressionnante domine le marché qui est devenu l'événement le plus populaire de la région.

Don't pick an answer just because the same word appears in the sentence and the passage. For example, **touristes britanniques** appears in a sentence and the passage but that sentence is incorrect. On the other hand, **un mois** does not appear in the passage, yet it is a key word as **cinq semaines** (five weeks) in the text equates to **plus d'un mois** (more than a month) in the sentence.

☐ **A** Il n'y a pas beaucoup de marchés de Noël en France.

☒ **B** Le marché de Strasbourg existe depuis plus de 400 ans.

☐ **C** Strasbourg a toujours été en France.

☐ **D** Deux mille touristes britanniques visitent le marché tous les ans.

☒ **E** Le marché de Strasbourg a lieu chaque année.

☐ **F** Le marché a lieu en Bretagne.

☒ **G** La fête dure plus d'un mois.

☒ **H** Il y a une cathédrale à Strasbourg.

Now try this

Listen to Thomas talking about Mother's Day in Quebec.

Listen to the recording

Complete the sentences in English. Remember that where there are two marks for a question, two elements will be needed.

1 In Canada Mother's Day is always on
.... **(2 marks)**

2 Last year Thomas gave his mother
.... on Mother's Day.
(1 mark)

3 His little sister made a ....
(1 mark)

4 His brother .... **(2 marks)**

Holiday preferences

Expressing opinions, however simple, is really important, and when you are talking about holidays, you are bound to have some opinions!

Les vacances que j'aime

C'est / C'était ...	It is / It was ...
chouette / génial	great
fantastique / formidable	brilliant
intéressant	interesting
ennuyeux	boring.
Ce que j'aime,	What I like is
c'est de me faire bronzer.	sunbathing.
Ce n'est pas mon truc.	It's not my thing.
Le plus important,	The most important
c'est de faire du sport.	thing is to do sport.
Quand j'étais petit(e),	When I was young,
ça allait.	it was OK.
J'adore être en plein	I love being outdoors,
air, même quand il pleut.	even when it's raining.
Ce que j'aime le plus,	What I like the most
c'est d'aller à la piscine.	is going to the pool.

Expressing likes and dislikes

adorer	to love
aimer	to like
préférer	to prefer
je n'aime pas	I dislike
détester	to hate

+ infinitive

J'adore faire du camping.   I love camping.

Je préfère aller à la campagne.
I prefer going to the countryside.

Worked example

WRITING

Écris un blog au sujet de vacances désastreuses.   **(20 marks)**

Je suis allé en Italie dans un camping. C'était horrible. Il a fait mauvais et c'était ennuyeux. J'ai joué aux cartes et c'était nul.

This covers the topic but is limited and has no real development. Vocabulary is simple and repetitive (e.g. c'était). The only word used to join ideas is et.

Aiming higher

D'habitude, nous passons les vacances dans un petit hôtel au bord de la mer dans l'ouest de la France, mais cette année, mon père a décidé de faire du camping parce que c'est moins cher. Les vacances étaient affreuses parce qu'il a plu presque tout le temps. En plus, je ne pouvais pas dormir à cause des jeunes d'à côté qui faisaient la fête et il y avait plein d'insectes partout et je déteste ça. Mes parents étaient déçus aussi car la piscine couverte du camping était fermée et on a dû aller à la ville la plus proche pour se baigner. Je ne ferai plus jamais de camping.

Aiming higher

The answer covers the question in detail, using present, imperfect and perfect tenses and even a future tense at the end. The student has added details, along with opinions, and used different parts of the verb (nous, on, ils, je, il). Negatives, adjectives (with correct agreement) and connectives also feature, along with interesting and varied vocabulary, which makes the answer very impressive.

Now try this

LISTENING TRACK 14

Listen to these young French people talking about their holiday preferences.
Complete each sentence in English.

1 Corinne likes going ....   **(1 mark)**
2 Yvon prefers holidays that are ....   **(1 mark)**
3 Carole hates going ....   **(1 mark)**
4 Denis likes going ....   **(1 mark)**

Hotels

You need to be prepared to discuss where you stay on holiday – and to give your opinion of hotels you've been to!

Loger dans un hôtel

ascenseur (m)	lift
escalier (m)	staircase
avec douche / bain	with shower / bath
salle de bains (f)	bathroom
clef / clé (f)	key
premier / deuxième étage (m)	first / second floor
rez-de-chaussée (m)	ground floor
liste des prix (f) / tarif (m)	price list
réception (f)	reception
parking (m)	car park
porte d'entrée (f)	entrance
jardin (m)	garden
salle de jeux (f)	games room
climatisation (f)	air conditioning
donner sur la plage	to look onto the beach
fonctionner / marcher	to work

Negatives

Grammar page 106

Ne or n' (before a vowel) comes before the verb

ne ... pas = not
ne ... plus = no longer
ne ... jamais = never
ne ... personne = nobody
ne ... guère = hardly
ne ... que = only
ne ... rien = nothing
ne ... ni ... ni = neither ... nor ...

La climatisation ne marchait pas.
The air conditioning wasn't working.

Worked example

  READING

Read the text. Answer the questions below.

> Après avoir lu toutes les brochures des hôtels dans le Midi, Lila avait choisi un petit hôtel familial qui donnait sur la plage. Il y avait une piscine et une salle de jeux pour les enfants, et pour les grands-parents, il y avait la climatisation et un ascenseur. Mais, en arrivant toute la famille a été vraiment déçue. L'hôtel était en construction donc la famille ne pouvait ni voir la plage ni dormir la nuit à cause du bruit. Il n'y avait rien à faire pour les enfants et la climatisation ne marchait pas. La famille ne retournera jamais à cet hôtel.

1 How did Lila choose her holiday accommodation? **(1 mark)**

read all the brochures of hotels in the area

2 Name one facility for the young and one for the old that made the hotel suitable. **(2 marks)**

swimming pool / air conditioning

3 What couldn't the family see and why? **(2 marks)**

the beach because the hotel was still being built

4 What wasn't working? **(1 mark)**

air conditioning

5 What will the family not do? **(1 mark)**

go back to that hotel

Brochures is a cognate (word which is the same in both languages) meaning 'brochures' but you also need to understand **après avoir lu toutes les brochures**. So be careful to look on each side of a cognate to make sure that you have fully worked out the meaning.

Construction is a cognate but you need to work out that in combination with **en** it means 'under construction'; **voir la plage** after the negative **ni** gives the location for the answer to Question 3.

EXAM ALERT!

If a question is in the negative, the construction **ne ... ni ... ni** will help point you towards the key word / information that you need.

Now try this

 SPEAKING

Réponds aux questions en français.
1 Quels sont les avantages des hôtels?
2 Comment serait l'hôtel de tes rêves?

Campsites

You might read or hear descriptions of French campsites, which are often large and well equipped.

Au camping

camper	to camp
faire du camping	to go camping
aire de jeux (f)	play area
bloc sanitaire (m)	shower block
randonnée (f)	hike
lieu (m)	place
parc d'attractions (m)	amusement park
camping (m)	campsite
caravane (f)	caravan
emplacement (m)	pitch
sac de couchage (m)	sleeping bag
eau potable (f)	drinking water
en plein air	outside
location de vélos (f)	bike hire
colonie de vacances (f)	summer camp

Alternatives for aller

Try to vary not only the tenses of verbs, but also the verbs themselves.

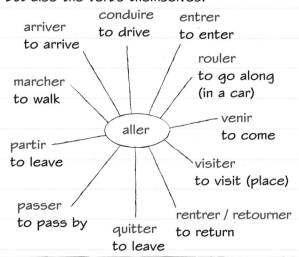

arriver — to arrive
conduire — to drive
entrer — to enter
rouler — to go along (in a car)
marcher — to walk
aller
venir — to come
partir — to leave
visiter — to visit (place)
passer — to pass by
quitter — to leave
rentrer / retourner — to return

Worked example

Simon parle de vacances passées dans un camping en France. Mets une croix ✗ dans les trois cases correctes.

> L'année dernière, pour la première fois, j'ai passé l'été dans une colonie de vacances dans un camping énorme dans le sud de la France. Il a fait beau et tout le monde s'est bien amusé. Il y avait plus de cent jeunes, des garçons et des filles, et les moniteurs étaient, pour la plupart, agréables et gentils. Le premier jour, un petit groupe a loué des bicyclettes et nous avons fait une balade dans la région, ce qui m'a plu car le paysage était pittoresque et nous avons pu remarquer des oiseaux et beaucoup de petits animaux de campagne. Je me suis fait de bons amis et j'espère retourner là-bas l'année prochaine.

Look for clues in the text – there are positives **beau**, **amusé**, **bons** which suggest that Simon did like his holidays. Similarly, **moniteurs** are described as **agréables** and **gentils**, so **impolis** is incorrect.

Look for linked words in the text. **Balade** and **bicyclette** mean that **a fait du vélo** is correct. In the same way, **paysage pittoresque** is similar to **campagne très belle**, so this is also correct.

- ☒ **A** Simon a aimé les vacances.
- ☐ **B** Les moniteurs en colonie étaient plutôt impolis.
- ☒ **C** Simon a fait du vélo.
- ☐ **D** Simon va en colonie tous les ans.
- ☒ **E** Simon a trouvé la campagne très belle.
- ☐ **F** Il n'y avait que des garçons au camping.

Now try this

Translate this short passage into English. **(7 marks)**

> J'aime faire du camping parce que la nature me plaît et que j'adore être en plein air. Malheureusement ma famille préfère loger dans un hôtel ou un gîte, alors d'habitude on ne fait pas de camping. Quand je serai plus âgé, je vais faire du camping avec mes copains au pays de Galles et ce sera génial.

Accommodation

It is always good to use different tenses when you discuss holiday accommodation.

Le logement

héberger	to accommodate
loger	to stay
réserver	to book
appartement loué (m)	rented flat
auberge de jeunesse (f)	youth hostel
chambre d'hôte (f)	bed and breakfast
gîte (m)	holiday home
hôtel (m)	hotel
chez des copains	at friends' house
confortable	comfortable
complet / complete	full
spacieux / spacieuse	spacious
en été	in summer
en hiver	in winter
en automne	in autumn
au printemps	in spring

aller voir = to visit (person)
visiter = to visit (place)

Aiming higher

Use tense markers together with a range of tenses to aim for a higher grade.

☑ **Present**

toujours	always
d'habitude	usually

Cette année on va dans un camping.
We are going to a campsite this year.

☑ **Past**

il y a longtemps	a long time ago
l'été dernier	last summer

Avant on louait un gîte.
Before we used to rent a holiday home.

☑ **Future**

l'année prochaine	next year
dans quelques semaines	in a few weeks' time

À l'avenir je réserverai une chambre à l'avance.
In future I will reserve a room in advance.

Worked example

Vous allez passer vos vacances en France. Vous écrivez au bureau de tourisme dans la ville où vous allez séjourner.

Écrivez un email de 40–50 mots avec les informations suivantes:
- quand vous allez arriver en France
- le nombre de personnes dans votre famille
- le genre de logement que vous préférez
- pourquoi vous avez cette préférence.

(16 marks)

Monsieur, Madame,

Je vais passer mes vacances dans votre ville en juillet. Nous sommes cinq (deux adultes et trois enfants) et nous cherchons un logement pour quinze jours. Je préfère louer un appartement dans une résidence avec piscine car je suis sportif.

Cordialement

Now try this

Écoute ces jeunes qui parlent du logement pour les vacances. Mets une croix ✗ dans les cases correctes.

Listen to the recording

1 Caroline préfère loger …
- ☐ dans un hôtel
- ☐ dans un camping
- ☐ dans une auberge de jeunesse

(1 mark)

2 Chloé a passé les vacances …
- ☐ dans une caravane
- ☐ dans un appartement
- ☐ chez sa tante **(1 mark)**

3 Éloïse a trouvé son hôtel …
- ☐ confortable
- ☐ bien équipé
- ☐ sale **(1 mark)**

4 Ramona a passé … au camping.
- ☐ une semaine
- ☐ deux semaines
- ☐ un mois **(1 mark)**

Holiday destinations

It's important to practise saying where you go on holiday and why.

Les destinations

Je vais en Espagne / France.	I go to Spain / France.
Je suis allé(e) …	I went …
à l'étranger	abroad
dans une station de ski	to a ski resort
dans une station balnéaire	to a beach resort
sur la côte	to the coast
au bord de la mer	to the seaside
bois (m)	wood
colline (f)	hill
ferme (f)	farm
lac (m)	lake
montagne (f)	mountain
pays (m)	country
rivière (f)	river
C'est près de Nantes.	It's near Nantes.
C'est loin de la côte.	It's far from the coast.

How to say 'to'

masc	fem	plural
au or à l'	à la or à l'	aux

J'adore passer les vacances au bord de la mer.
I love spending the holidays by the sea.
Je suis allé(e) à l'étranger.
I went abroad.
J'aime passer les vacances à la campagne.
I like holidaying in the country.

Literary extracts

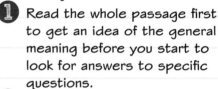

1. Read the whole passage first to get an idea of the general meaning before you start to look for answers to specific questions.
2. Sometimes, this general meaning and context will help you work out the meaning of tricky words.

Worked example

Tous les ans Papa et Maman se disputent beaucoup pour savoir où aller en vacances, et puis Maman se met à pleurer et elle dit qu'elle va aller chez sa maman, et moi je pleure aussi parce que j'aime bien Mémé, mais chez elle il n'y a pas de plage, et à la fin on va où veut Maman et ce n'est pas chez Mémé.

Hier, après le dîner, Papa a dit:
– Écoutez-moi bien! Cette année, je ne veux pas de discussions, c'est moi qui décide: Nous irons dans le Midi. J'ai l'adresse d'une villa à louer à Plage-les-Pins. Trois pièces, eau courante, électricité. Je ne veux rien savoir pour aller à l'hôtel et manger de la nourriture minable.

– Eh bien, mon chéri, a dit Maman, ça me paraît une très bonne idée.

(adapted from *Le Petit Nicolas en vacances* by J.-J. Sempé and R. Goscinny, 1962)

Read the **first paragraph** of the text. Answer the following questions in English.

1. What happens every year? **(1 mark)**
Mum and Dad argue about where to go on holiday

2. What does Mum end up doing? **(2 marks)**
crying and saying she is going to her mum's

3. Why does Nicolas not want to go to his gran's? **(1 mark)**
there is no beach

4. Where does the family end up going? **(1 mark)**
wherever Mum wants

Now try this

Read the rest of the passage. Answer these questions in English.
1 What type of accommodation has Dad found in the South of France? **(1 mark)**
2 Give three features of the accommodation. **(3 marks)**

3 What reason does Dad give for not wanting to stay in a hotel? **(1 mark)**
4 Where do you think the family will go on holiday? **(1 mark)**

Travel

Travel is a topic which lends itself to discussions of plans and aspirations.

On voyage

quartier (m)	area / part of town
traversée (f)	crossing
permis de conduire (m)	driving licence
vol (m)	flight
pièce d'identité (f)	identity document
voyage (m)	journey / trip
voyager	to travel
station de ski (f)	ski resort
circulation (f)	traffic
séjourner	to stay
séjour (m)	stay
vacances de neige (fpl)	winter / skiing holiday

Talking about the future

Grammar page 103

When you want to discuss your plans you have a number of options. You can use:

aller + the infinitive:
Je vais voyager.   I'm going to travel.

the future tense:
J'irai en Allemagne.   I'll go to Germany.

the conditional:
Je voudrais aller en Chine.
I'd like to go to China.

espérer:
J'espère visiter les États-Unis.
I hope to visit the USA.

compter:
Je compte faire du tourisme.
I plan to go sightseeing.

rêver:
Je rêve d'aller en Australie.
I dream of going to Australia.

Worked example

  SPEAKING

Réponds à ces questions sur les voyages.

1 À l'avenir, tu voudrais voyager? Pourquoi?

J'aimerais voyager partout dans le monde parce qu'il est important de découvrir des cultures différentes et d'essayer la cuisine d'autres pays. En plus, je voudrais améliorer ma connaissance de la façon de vivre des autres afin d'élargir mes horizons. Si j'avais beaucoup d'argent, j'irais en Chine ou en Australie car ce sont des pays lointains.

2 Comment seraient tes vacances de rêve? Pourquoi?

Mes vacances idéales seraient sans doute à l'étranger, peut-être en Amérique du Sud, avec mes meilleurs copains. Puisque je parle l'espagnol couramment, je pourrais communiquer facilement avec les gens là-bas. Je logerais dans un hôtel cinq étoiles et je bronzerais tous les jours avant de prendre un repas délicieux le soir.

Improving your answers

- Try to use varied vocabulary: améliorer and élargir are interesting verbs which demonstrate your grasp of French.
- Use advanced constructions, for example avant de + infinitive (before doing), en plus (furthermore), puisque (seeing that).
- Include adverbs, e.g. couramment.
- Vary your tenses if possible – here the conditional tense coupled with difficult verbs demonstrates the student's fluency.
- Make your structure clear. This student's answers make a clear point and explain or elaborate immediately afterwards.

Now try this

  TRACK 16

Listen to these people talking about travel. Complete the answers in English.

1 Jérôme would like to travel .... **(1 mark)**

2 Assiom wants to go to .... **(1 mark)**

because .... **(1 mark)**

3 Léo hopes to visit .... **(1 mark)**

Listen to the recording

Holiday activities

It is good to be able to talk about what you do, did or will do on holiday as well as where you go, went or are going.

Activités de vacances

On peut ...   You can ...

faire de l'escalade   faire du patin à glace   se détendre

faire du vélo   faire de la natation   faire de la voile

faire du ski   faire une promenade   jouer au tennis

How to say 'this' and 'these'   Grammar page 90

ce	this + masculine nouns
cet	this + any masculine noun starting with a vowel or silent h
cette	this + feminine nouns
ces	these + **all** plural nouns

Cet été je vais en France.
I am going to France this summer.
Cette visite guidée est chère.
This tour is expensive.
Ces jeunes ont pris des cours de tennis.
These youngsters had tennis lessons.

Worked example

Read this information about holiday activities. Put a cross ✗ in the boxes where the statements are correct.

(5 marks)

La municipalité a décidé d'organiser tout un programme d'activités pour les jeunes de tout âge cet été. Il y a des visites guidées de la vieille ville et une grande variété d'activités sportives au stade municipal. En cas de mauvais temps, et pour ceux qui préfèrent rester à l'intérieur, il y a la possibilité d'essayer une nouvelle langue ou d'apprendre à faire de la cuisine italienne ou chinoise à la maison des jeunes. Chaque après-midi au musée, il y a des cours sur l'histoire et la vie culturelle de la région. Au théâtre Racine, les petits peuvent regarder des dessins animés tous les jours à partir de 11 heures.

☒ **A** The town has organised a range of activities.
☐ **B** The events are taking place in December.
☐ **C** There are no outdoor events.
☒ **D** You can learn a new language.
☐ **E** You can learn to cook French specialities.
☒ **F** There are activities for very young children.
☒ **G** You can learn about history in the afternoon.
☒ **H** There are lots of sporting activities available.
☐ **I** If you want to see films, you should go to the youth club.

Most of A–I refer to material in the text, but only five are accurate. You have to be able to appreciate ideas rather than just have a simple knowledge of vocabulary. Think about why the statements below are incorrect.
B is false as the programme is for the summer (**cet été**).
C is wrong as guided visits of the town (and activities at the stadium) will be outdoors.
E is incorrect as Italian and Chinese cooking (**cuisine italienne ou chinoise**) is being taught.
I is wrong because, although the youth club is mentioned, the films (**dessins animés**) are at the theatre (**au théâtre**).

Now try this

Regarde bien cette photo.
1 Décris-moi la photo.
2 Moi j'aime faire du ski. Et toi?
3 Tu préfères les vacances d'été ou d'hiver? Pourquoi?
4 Moi je suis allé en France l'année dernière. Et toi?
5 Mes vacances de rêve seraient au Canada. Et toi?

Holiday plans

Make sure you know the future tense in order to talk about holiday plans. Mix it up by using the nous form as well as the je form.

Projets de vacances

pendant les grandes vacances	in the summer holiday(s)
les vacances de neige	winter sports holiday
l'été (m) / l'hiver (m) prochain	next summer / winter
demain	tomorrow
après-demain	the day after tomorrow
le lendemain	the next day
louer	to rent
passer la journée	to spend the day
port de pêche (m)	fishing port
court de tennis (m)	tennis court
terrain de golf (m)	golf course

The nous form in the future

Near future
Nous allons voyager en Afrique.
We are going to travel across Africa.

Future tense
Nous irons en Autriche.
We will be going to Austria.
Nous aurons une chambre dans un hôtel.
We will have a room in a hotel.

Nous ferons de la planche à voile.
We will go windsurfing.

Worked example

Translate this passage into French.   **(12 marks)**

> I normally go on holiday abroad with my family but next summer my sister and I are hoping to spend a month in Canada at our uncle's house. We will go shopping in Montreal and we will visit the mountains, where we'll go walking. My sister would like to go skiing.

Normalement je passe mes vacances à l'étranger avec ma famille mais, l'été prochain, ma sœur et moi, nous espérons passer un mois au Canada chez notre oncle. Nous ferons des achats à Montréal et nous irons à la montagnes où nous ferons de la randonnée. Ma sœur voudrait faire du ski.

EXAM ALERT!

There are many things for you to consider when you are translating a passage like this, but perhaps the most important is to realise that a word-for-word translation will not work.

Translating go

This is not always part of aller – 'go walking' and 'go skiing' are translated using the verb faire.

Now try this

Lis ce texte. Réponds aux questions en français.

Gisèle parle de ses projets de vacances.

1 Comment sait-on que Gisèle n'est jamais allée au Japon?   **(1 mark)**
2 Décris l'hôtel où la famille logera.   **(2 marks)**
3 Pour qui va-t-elle acheter des souvenirs?
(1 mark)

> Ma famille et moi, nous irons au Japon pour la première fois en août et j'attends les vacances avec impatience. Nous logerons dans un hôtel chic et cher à Tokyo et mon père a réservé deux chambres avec balcon et jacuzzi. Nous achèterons des cadeaux pour le reste de ma famille et mes copains.

Holiday experiences

Talking about past holidays is important – and you will need to know winter holiday vocabulary as well as summer holiday words.

Souvenirs de vacances

en hiver	in winter
vacances d'hiver (fpl)	winter holidays
stage de ski (m)	skiing course
l'hébergement (m)	accommodation
société (f)	company
nourriture (f)	food
suffisant(e)	sufficient / enough
J'ai fait …	I did …
C'était …	It was
Les vacances étaient …	The holidays were …
On avait faim …	We were hungry …
Nous sommes sortis …	We went out …
Nous avons choisi …	We chose …
Nous avons partagé …	We shared …

J'ai fait du snowboard.

Perfect tense: être verbs

Grammar page 101

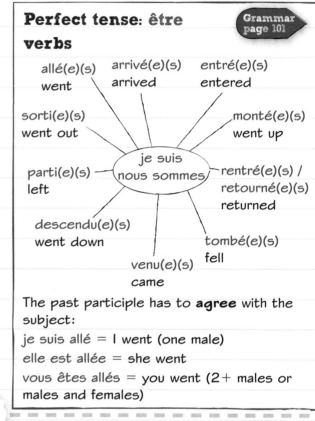

allé(e)(s) went
arrivé(e)(s) arrived
entré(e)(s) entered
sorti(e)(s) went out
monté(e)(s) went up
je suis nous sommes
parti(e)(s) left
rentré(e)(s) / retourné(e)(s) returned
descendu(e)(s) went down
tombé(e)(s) fell
venu(e)(s) came

The past participle has to **agree** with the subject:

je suis allé = I went (one male)

elle est allée = she went

vous êtes allés = you went (2+ males or males and females)

Worked example

READING

Read the text and answer the question in English about Baptiste's holiday.

L'année dernière, en hiver, j'ai fait un stage de ski UCPA avec mon meilleur copain Brice. L'UCPA est une société qui organise des vacances sportives.

Nous avons choisi un stage de ski à La Plagne dans les Alpes. C'était un stage pour les ados de 13 à 17 ans. L'hébergement était dans un chalet énorme. Nous avons partagé notre chambre avec deux autres garçons qui faisaient le même stage.

La nourriture était suffisante mais nous sommes souvent sortis le soir pour aller à la pizzeria parce qu'on avait une faim de loup après la journée sur les pistes.

1 When exactly was the holiday? **(1 mark)**
last winter

2 Who is Brice? **(1 mark)**
Baptiste's best friend

3 For whom was the holiday intended? **(1 mark)**
for teenagers aged 13–17

4 Why did they often go out to eat? **(2 marks)**
they were very hungry after a day's skiing.

Now try this

LISTENING TRACK 17

Écoute ces trois jeunes qui parlent des vacances récentes. Mets une croix ✗ dans la case correcte.

Listen to the recording

1 Marc a fait …
☐ du ski nautique
☐ de la voile
☐ du ski **(1 mark)**

2 Laure est sortie souvent …
☐ à la patinoire
☐ au stade
☐ au restaurant **(1 mark)**

3 Jacques a joué …
☐ au tennis de table
☐ au snooker
☐ au tennis **(1 mark)**

Question 4 is worth two marks – make sure you include more than one detail.

Transport

Knowing the various forms of transport and the vocabulary that goes with them can be really helpful.

Le transport

en voiture

en train

en bateau

en métro

en autobus
(arrêt d'autobus
= bus stop)

en car

en / à bicyclette /
vélo

en avion

en camion

à pied

Worked example

READING

Read this passage about Gabrielle's family holiday. Finish the sentences in English.

> L'année dernière nous sommes allés en Angleterre. Nous avons décidé de voyager en voiture et nous sommes partis de bonne heure. Après avoir pris le bateau à Calais, nous avons continué le voyage de Douvres à Londres en voiture. Comme mon père ne voulait pas conduire dans une grande ville qu'il ne connaissait pas, nous avons loué des vélos pour nous balader. Le soir, on a pris le métro ou un taxi. Un jour, nous avons fait une visite guidée en car à Windsor où nous avons vu le beau château.

1 They travelled to Calais by ......car....... **(1 mark)**

2 Because Dad didn't want to drive in London they
   .hired bikes. **(1 mark)**

3 In the evening they travelled by underground
   or ....taxi....... **(2 marks)**

4 They went to Windsor by .....coach.... **(1 mark)**

En or à

For most means of transport the French use en + the word for the means of transport without the le, la or l'. However, it is à pied and either en or à vélo / bicyclette.

This is a straightforward passage but lots of different types of transport are mentioned. You need to be quite sure that you get the right one each time. One means of transport (boat) is mentioned in the text but does not provide an answer. Be careful too with car – it looks like 'car' in English but it actually means 'coach' (or 'bus'). Always watch out for words that **look the same** in both languages but have **different** meanings.

Now try this

SPEAKING

Réponds aux questions en français.
1 Tu préfères quel moyen de transport? Pourquoi?
2 Tu aimes voyager en avion? Pourquoi (pas)?

Directions

You might need help finding your way, so you will need to understand directions.

Les directions

 Tournez à gauche.
Turn left.

Tournez à droite.
Turn right.

 Allez tout droit.
Go straight on.

 Au coin, tournez à droite.
Turn right at the corner.

 Traversez le pont.
Cross the bridge.

> Don't confuse **tout droit** (straight on) with **à droite** (on the right).

 Traversez la rivière.
Cross the river.

 Allez tout droit aux feux.
Go straight on at the lights.

Allez jusqu'au carrefour.
Go to the crossroads.

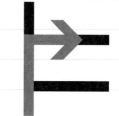 Prenez la deuxième rue à droite.
Take the second road on the right.

 Prenez la première rue à gauche.
Take the first road on the left.

Worked example

Dans la rue en France.

Vous êtes dans une grande ville en France. Vous voulez de l'aide.

1   votre nationalité
Vous êtes de quelle nationalité?
Je suis britannique.

2   Logement où
Vous logez où?
Je loge dans un hôtel en ville.

3   !
Qu'est-ce que vous cherchez?
Je cherche l'office de tourisme.
C'est à gauche.

4   distance
C'est loin d'ici?
Non, c'est là-bas.

5   ? stade
Il y a un stade en ville?
Oui, en face de l'office de tourisme

(10 marks)

EXAM ALERT!

Using **j'ai** and **je suis**: it's easy to get these two verbs confused under pressure. Remember **j'ai** is 'I have' and **je suis** is 'I am'. **But** you use j'ai with ages and some other French expressions (e.g. **j'ai faim** – I'm hungry).

Thinking on the spot: try not to panic if you cannot remember a particular word. Try to find a different way of saying something which might be OK. Here, remember any place to stay will do. You don't have to try to say something truthful!

Asking a question: there is often more than one way to ask a question. Here you could ask for directions to the stadium or simply ask if there is one.

Now try this

Écoute ces conversations dans une rue en France.
Mets une croix ✗ dans la case correcte.

1 ☐ ←   ☐ ↑   ☐ →

2 ☐   ☐   ☐

3 ☐   ☐   ☐   **(3 marks)**

Holiday problems

All kinds of problems can occur on holiday – including problems with travel or accommodation.

Les problèmes en vacances

retard (m)	delay
place (f)	seat
en panne	broken down
manquer le train	to miss the train
embêtant	annoying
Il y a du monde.	It's busy / crowded.
se plaindre	to complain
déçu(e)	disappointed
Je suis désolé(e).	I'm sorry.
gendarmerie (f) / commissariat (m)	police station
C'était le comble.	It was the last straw.
faute (f)	mistake
réparation (f)	repair
endommagement (m)	damage
vol (m)	theft
remplacer	to replace

Adverbs

Grammar page 91

Adverbs describe verbs: 'walk **quickly**', 'read **slowly**'.
Here are some useful adverbs.

- vite quickly
- vraiment truly, really
- mieux better
- bien well
- lentement slowly
- adverbs
- mal badly
- rapidement rapidly
- seulement only
- heureusement happily, fortunately

Worked example

LISTENING TRACK 19

Écoute Sandrine qui parle de ses récentes vacances.

Listen to the recording

Nous avons eu plein de problèmes pendant nos vacances en Belgique. Le voyage de Nice à Bruxelles était un vrai cauchemar. Notre vol est parti avec cinq heures de retard, ce qui était très embêtant. Une fois arrivés, on a eu du mal à trouver un taxi mais nous sommes enfin arrivés à l'hôtel. Mon père était déçu car nos chambres étaient trop petites et il y avait toujours du monde dans les rues devant et derrière l'hôtel, et nous n'avons pas pu dormir à cause du bruit.

Mets une croix ✗ dans les quatre cases correctes.

(4 marks)

- ☐ **A** La famille de Sandrine est allée en France.
- ☐ **B** L'avion est parti à l'heure.
- ☒ **C** Il était difficile de prendre un taxi.
- ☒ **D** Ils ont passé les vacances dans un hôtel.
- ☐ **E** Le père de Sandrine était content du logement.
- ☒ **F** Les rues près de l'hôtel étaient animées.
- ☐ **G** L'hôtel était un peu isolé.
- ☒ **H** Ils n'ont pas bien dormi.

In listening tasks, try to work out the meanings of the eight statements. Look for any cognates or clues from words you know. For example, look at why some of these answers are wrong:

- The key phrase in statement B is à l'heure (on time); retard in the text means this is wrong.
- Content in statement E is the exact opposite of the word in the text – déçu – so this is not correct.

Now try this

READING

Read this passage about travel problems and answer the questions in English.

Je suis arrivé à la gare en avance mais j'ai dû faire la queue à la caisse. Le train est arrivé à l'heure précise mais il y avait du monde et je ne pouvais pas trouver de place, alors j'étais debout pendant tout le voyage.

1 What problem was there at the station? **(1 mark)**
2 When did the train arrive? **(1 mark)**
3 What could the writer not find? **(1 mark)**

Asking for help

Things can sometimes go wrong – and it's even worse when you're on holiday.

Demander de l'aide

agent de sécurité (m)	security guard
parapluie (m)	umbrella
argent (m)	money
perdre	to lose
oublier	to forget
J'ai dû aller au commissariat.	I had to go to the police station.
laisser	to leave (something behind)
triste	sad
C'est / C'était dommage.	It is / was a pity.
traumatisé(e)	shocked
en cuir	leather
trouver	to find
échanger	to exchange
J'ai perdu mon portable.	I've lost my mobile.

Saying 'it' or 'them'

Grammar page 92

masculine = le

feminine = la —— it   them ——— plural = les

(both change to l' before a vowel)

Je peux le / la changer?   Can I change it?
Je peux les changer?   Can I change them?

In the perfect tense, put the word for 'it' or 'them' before the part of avoir and make the past participle agree if you need to:
J'ai acheté une écharpe.   I bought a scarf.
but Je l'ai achetée.   I bought it.

Mes clés! Je les ai oubliées dans ma voiture.

Worked example

LISTENING TRACK 20

Listen to these people who need help. Answer the questions in English.

Listen to the recording

1 On m'a volé mon portable dans la rue.

2 J'ai acheté une veste ici hier. Je peux l'èchanger? Elle ne me va pas.

3 J'ai laissé mon portefeuille dans un train il y a deux heures. Vous l'avez trouvé?

4 Je suis tombée en traversant la rue et j'ai mal au dos.

Where are these people? Put a cross ✗ in the **four** correct boxes.   **(4 marks)**

☒ **A** at the hospital
☐ **B** at the cinema
☒ **C** at the station lost property office
☐ **D** at the tourist office
☒ **E** in a clothes shop
☒ **F** at the police station
☐ **G** in a café
☐ **H** at a football ground

Listening for clues

Short passages in French will be over very quickly and you might not be able to understand everything. When this happens, listen for clues.

In tasks like this one, look at the eight options first. Then listen for words connected with a hospital, cinema, lost property office, etc. For example, mal (hurt) is associated with a hospital and acheté (bought) with a shop. On the other hand, there is no mention of films, drinks, information or football.

Now try this

SPEAKING TRACK 21

This is part of a role play in a clothes shop to which you are returning an item. Listen to the recording and answer in the pauses.

Listen to the recording

Vous voulez échanger un article que vous avez acheté récemment.

1 Échanger robe / chemise?   4 ? autre article
2 Raison   5 ? prix
3 !

Eating out in a café

Learn as many words for food and drink as you can, especially snacks at a café.

Manger au café

beurre (m)	butter
bifteck (m)	steak
confiture (f)	jam
crêpe (f)	pancake
croissant (m)	croissant
croque-monsieur (m)	cheese and ham toastie
gâteau (m)	cake
miel (m)	honey
pain (m)	bread
pâtes (fpl)	pasta
café (m)	coffee
chocolat chaud (m)	hot chocolate
eau minérale (f)	mineral water
jus de fruit (m)	fruit juice
lait (m)	milk
limonade (f)	lemonade
thé (m)	tea

Talking about food flavours

In French you can't just say 'a milky coffee'; you have to use a form of à.

un café au lait   a milky coffee

masculine	feminine	plural
au	à la	aux
à l' after vowel or silent h	à l' after vowel or silent h	

un café au lait

une glace à la fraise

des crêpes aux pommes

Worked example

 TRACK 22

Écoute Joël qui est au café. Qu'est-ce qu'il commande? Mets une croix ✗ dans les quatre cases correctes.   **(4 marks)**

Listen to the recording

☐ **A** un café
☐ **B** une crêpe
☐ **C** des pommes   ☒ **G** de l'eau minérale
☐ **D** du beurre   ☒ **H** un croissant
☒ **E** de la confiture   ☐ **I** du miel
☒ **F** un chocolat chaud   ☐ **J** du lait

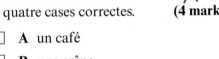
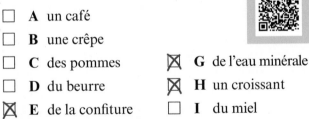

Waitress:	Un café au lait, monsieur?
Joël:	Euh … non, un chocolat chaud et un verre d'eau minérale, je crois.
Waitress:	Très bien, et avec ça?
Joël:	Une crêpe aux pommes, s'il vous plaît.
Waitress:	Ah, désolée, il n'en reste plus.
Joël:	Alors un croissant.
Waitress:	Avec du beurre et du miel?
Joël:	Seulement avec de la confiture.
Waitress:	D'accord, monsieur.

Listening strategies

- People sometimes **change their minds**, so don't assume they are ordering every item of food you hear mentioned.
- Make sure you listen to the **whole dialogue** and check what the person actually orders. It might not be what they originally wanted, or they might be offered something which they don't want.
- Listen for phrases such as *je regrette* (I'm sorry), which might tell you that something is not available, or *non, merci*, which tells you they do not want what is on offer.

Now try this

 TRACK 23

Écoute Delphine et Marcus. Qu'est-ce qu'ils veulent? Mets une croix ✗ dans chaque case correcte.

Listen to the recording

Delphine
☐ **A** un thé   ☐ **C** une glace au citron
☐ **B** du lait   ☐ **D** une glace à la fraise

(2 marks)

Marcus
☐ **A** un coca   ☐ **C** un gâteau
☐ **B** du chocolat   ☐ **D** une glace à la vanille

(2 marks)

Eating out in a restaurant

Manger au restaurant

assiette (f)	plate
couteau (m)	knife
cuillère (f)	spoon
fourchette (f)	fork
verre (m)	glass
nappe (f)	tablecloth
serviette (f)	napkin
entrée (f)	starter
plat principal (m)	main course
dessert (m)	dessert
boisson (f)	drink
carte (f)	menu
menu (à prix fixe) (m)	fixed-price menu
plat (du jour) (m)	dish (of the day)
plats à emporter (mpl)	takeaway
pourboire (m)	tip
service compris	service included
self-service / self (m)	self-service restaurant
snack (m)	snack bar

Saying 'there'

Grammar page 93

Use **y** to say 'there' in French and to replace **à** + noun after a verb.

Je vais au café.	I'm going to the café.
➡ J'y vais.	I'm going there.
Je joue au football.	I play football.
➡ J'y joue.	I play it (football).

Idioms with y

Il y a deux cafés.	There are two cafés.
Il y a trois jours.	Three days ago.
On y va!	Let's go!
Allons-y!	Let's go!
Ça y est.	That's it!

Nous y allons pour des fêtes. We go there for parties.

Worked example

Lis ce texte au sujet d'une soirée au restaurant pour Sylvie et sa famille. Réponds aux questions.

Samedi soir, je suis allée au restaurant avec ma famille pour fêter l'anniversaire de ma mère. Nous avons réservé une table pour 20 heures mais nous avons dû attendre une demi-heure au bar. J'ai commandé un steak-frites mais tout était froid. Les autres repas étaient délicieux et chauds! Pourtant, le service était très lent et ma mère a trouvé les serveurs impolis, surtout quand un garçon lui a demandé son âge. Par contre, la patronne du restaurant était gentille et nous a offert une bouteille de vin, ce qui m'a beaucoup plu.

1 Pourquoi est-ce que Sylvie est allée au restaurant? **(1 mark)**
pour fêter l'anniversaire de sa mère

2 Ils ont dû attendre combien de minutes dans le bar? **(1 mark)**
30

3 Quel repas n'était pas délicieux? **(1 mark)**
le steak-frites / le repas / celui de Sylvie

4 Comment était le service? **(1 mark)**
lent

5 Pourquoi est-ce la mère de Sylvie a pensé que les serveurs étaient impolis? **(1 mark)**
Un serveur lui a demandé son âge.

6 La bouteille de vin a coûté combien? **(1 mark)**
C'était gratuit.

Now try this

Alex, ton ami français, t'a envoyé un email au sujet d'une soirée récente au restaurant.
Écris une réponse à Alex en français (80–90 mots). Tu dois faire référence aux points suivants:

- où tu es allé(e)
- ton opinion sur le repas
- pourquoi tu vas au restaurant en famille
- tes projets pour ton prochain repas au restaurant.

(20 marks)

Buying gifts

It can be nice for your friends and family to know that you thought of them while you were on holiday, so why not buy them a present?

Les cadeaux

cadeau (m)	present / gift
souvenir (m)	souvenir
cher / chère	expensive
soldes d'été (mpl)	summer sales
vêtements (mpl) (de marque)	(designer) clothes
à la mode	fashionable
taille (f)	size
écharpe (f)	scarf
ceinture (f)	belt
marque (f)	brand / make / label
maquillage (m)	make-up
bijoux (mpl)	jewellery
achats (mpl)	purchases
montre (f)	watch

Avez-vous du maquillage moins cher?

Asking questions

You might need to ask questions in shops when you are looking for presents. To ask questions in French you can:

1 Raise your voice to turn a statement into a question. ▾
Vous vendez des ceintures?
Do you sell belts?

2 Put Est-ce que at the start of a question.
Est-ce que vous avez des vêtements de marque?
Do you have any designer clothes?

3 Swap the subject and verb round and add a hyphen. (Note that this only works when the subject is a pronoun.)
Avez-vous des écharpes?
Do you have scarves?
Also add -t- between two vowels:
Ton copain aime-t-il les écharpes?
Does your friend like scarves?

Worked example

Situation: au magasin de souvenirs.

Vous voulez acheter un cadeau pour votre mère.

1 vous êtes en vacances
Je peux vous aider?
Je suis en vacances.

2 cadeau pour qui?
Ah oui. Vous voulez acheter un cadeau pour qui?
C'est pour ma mère.

3 !
Ah bon, vous avez déjà choisi un cadeau?
Oui, j'ai choisi ce bracelet en or, s'il vous plaît.

4 ? deuxième achat
Avez-vous aussi une ceinture noire en cuir?
Voilà une belle ceinture. Vous l'aimez?

5 ? prix
Oui. C'est combien?
Cent euros.   **(10 marks)**

Role play

As the instructions will be in French, you need to use your preparation time carefully.

- There will be some helpful vocabulary in the questions – read them carefully.
- ? means you need to ask a question. You can use some of the ideas above.
- ! means you have to respond to something you aren't expecting, so you will have to listen closely.
- It's always good to be polite, so use merci, s'il vous plaît and monsieur / madame.

Now try this

Listen to this conversation in a souvenir shop.

What is the customer buying?
          (3 marks)

Listen to the recording

Opinions about food

Food can certainly divide opinions but it's always good to express your opinions in French.

Ce que j'aime manger

J'adore l'ail.	I love garlic.
Je déteste les spaghettis.	I hate spaghetti.
Je trouve les pizzas malsaines.	I think pizzas are unhealthy.
malade	ill
bien cuit(e)	well cooked, well done
escargots (mpl)	snails
plein de goût	tasty
amer / amère	bitter
goûteux / goûteuse	tasty
dégoûtant(e)	disgusting
délicieux / délicieuse	delicious
(trop) épicé(e)	(too) spicy
salé(e)	salty
sucré	sweet

Time adverbs

Add time expressions wherever you can.

tous les jours	every day
quelquefois	sometimes
de temps en temps	now and again
souvent	often
toujours	always
ne … jamais	never
rarement	seldom
une fois par semaine	once a week

Je mange toujours des repas légers.
I always eat low-fat meals.

Quelquefois je mangeais au snack.
I sometimes used to eat at the snack bar.

Worked example

Alex, ton ami français, t'a envoyé un email sur ce qu'il aime manger.

Écris une réponse à Alex. Tu dois faire référence aux points suivants :
- ce que tu aimes manger
- ce que tu n'aimes pas manger et pourquoi
- un repas dégoûtant que tu as mangé récemment
- ce que tu vas manger ce soir.

Écris 80–90 mots environ en français.   **(20 marks)**

J'aime manger du poulet car le goût me plaît et j'en mange souvent à la cantine. Pourtant, je ne mange jamais de curry parce que je trouve ça trop épicé. La semaine dernière, je suis allé à un nouveau restaurant en ville où j'ai pris du poulet-frites avec des petits pois, mais le repas était dégoûtant. Ce soir, mon frère va préparer un bon repas car nous allons célébrer l'anniversaire de ma petite sœur. Nous mangerons son plat favori, du steak-frites.

Je ne mangerai jamais d'escargots.
I will never eat snails.

Writing a good short answer in French

You don't have much space to impress in a short task like this.
- Focus on being accurate. Just use words you know are right.
- Try to vary your vocabulary a little (e.g. use *car* as well as *parce que* for 'because').
- Give opinions, however simple (it could be *j'aime*, *je n'aime pas*, *je déteste* or *c'est super*) but try to vary them (*je trouve ça* + adjective, *ça me plaît*).
- Give reasons (*c'est trop épicé*).
- Make sure you cover every bullet point.

Now try this

Réponds aux questions en français.
1 Qu'est-ce que tu préfères manger?
2 Qu'est-ce que tu préfères boire?

 Remember to give reasons for your preferences.

Weather

Using weather phrases in your written and spoken tasks, particularly about holidays, can be impressive – especially when you use a variety of tenses.

La météo

Il pleut.   Il neige.   Il y a du soleil.

Il y a du brouillard.   Il fait froid.   Il fait chaud.

chaleur (f)	heat
ciel (m)	sky
éclaircie (f)	sunny interval
nuage (m)	cloud
orage (m)	thunderstorm
pluie (f)	rain
vent (m)	wind
couvert	overcast
ensoleillé	sunny

Different tenses

Present:

Il y a du vent.   It is windy.
Il fait chaud.   It is hot.

Past (imperfect):

Il y avait du vent.   It was windy.
Il faisait chaud.   It was hot.

Future:

Il y aura du vent.   It will be windy.
Il fera chaud.   It will be hot.

Conditional:

Il y aurait du vent.   It would be windy.
Il ferait chaud.   It would be hot.

Il va pleuvoir.   It's going to rain.

Worked example

Read the weather report and answer the question below.

> Hier il faisait froid et il y avait du brouillard, mais aujourd'hui, dans l'ouest, il y a du soleil et la température est de 15 à 19 degrés. Dans l'est le temps est aussi ensoleillé et il ne pleut pas. L'après-midi, les nuages arriveront du nord et il y aura du vent dans toute la région. Pendant la nuit, on risquera d'avoir des orages, surtout dans le nord. Demain la matinée sera caractérisée par des vents forts mais l'après-midi, il y aura des éclaircies et il fera moins froid.

lundi		nuageux et froid
mardi		froid avec de la pluie
mercredi		ensoleillé

True or false? It rained yesterday.

false   **(1 mark)**

- Use your knowledge of **tenses** to help you answer this question – you are looking for past tense markers, such as **hier** (yesterday), or past tense verbs, such as **faisait** (was).
- Next, look for a mention of rain (**pluie / il pleut**). If you can't find those words, you know there was no rain yesterday.
- Remember:
  est (m) = east   nord (m) = north
  ouest (m) = west   sud (m) = south

Now try this

Put a cross ✗ by the four correct statements, according to the forecast in the weather report.

- ☐ **A** It was foggy yesterday.
- ☐ **B** It is overcast in the west today.
- ☐ **C** There is no rain in the east.
- ☐ **D** There will be storms in the afternoon.
- ☐ **E** It might snow during the night.
- ☐ **F** Tomorrow morning will be windy.
- ☐ **G** It will be stormy on Tuesday.
- ☐ **H** The best day of the week is Wednesday.   **(4 marks)**

Tourism

Le tourisme

se détendre	to relax
se reposer	to rest
s'amuser	to have a good time
monument (m)	monument
musée (m)	museum
galerie d'art (f)	art gallery
château (m)	castle
architecture (f)	architecture
s'installer	to settle in
cathédrale (f)	cathedral
tour (f)	tower
jardin zoologique (m)	zoo
palais (m)	palace
hôtel de ville (m)	town hall
office de tourisme (m)	tourist office

Reflexive verbs

Grammar page 98

Some verbs need an extra me, te, se, nous, vous:

je + me	nous + nous
tu + te	vous + vous
il(s) / elle(s) + se	

Je m'amuse.　　I have a good time.

Elle ne s'ennuie pas.
She isn't / doesn't get bored.

Reflexive verbs take être in the perfect tense. The past participle has to agree with the subject:

Elle s'est trompée.	She's made a mistake.
Elles se sont reposées.	They rested.
Ils se sont relaxés.	They relaxed.

Elle s'est installée sur un banc dans la galerie d'art.
She sat down in the art gallery.

Aiming higher

This is quite a complex piece of French but it is the answer to the 'why' question in this task. The fact that her grandparents have only lived in Marseille for a month is the reason she doesn't know the city well.

Worked example

Read what Suzanne says about her holiday.

Je viens de passer du temps dans le sud de la France, à Marseille, chez mes grands-parents. Ils y habitent depuis seulement un mois et c'était une ville que je ne connaissais pas. J'ai fait plein de visites. J'ai admiré le château d'If et la belle cathédrale dont l'architecture est superbe. Je me suis vite installée dans un café chic au vieux port d'où je pouvais voir passer tous les touristes.

Mon grand-père, qui s'intéresse à l'histoire, est allé au musée de la marine et il s'est bien amusé, pendant que moi, j'ai profité de son absence pour passer des heures au musée d'arts africains.

Answer these questions in English:

1 Where did Suzanne stay while she was in Marseille? **(1 mark)**
at her grandparents'

2 Why was she not familiar with the city? **(1 mark)**
Her grandparents have only lived there for a month.

3 Where did she go to watch the tourists? **(2 marks)**
to a café in the old port / harbour

4 Where did her grandfather spend some time? **(1 mark)**
at the maritime museum

5 Which museum did Suzanne visit? **(1 mark)**
the African art museum

Answering 'why?' questions

These questions can be difficult as you sometimes need to provide quite a long answer. It will normally also include a verb and an explanation, especially if more than one detail is requested. Look at the number of marks available as this will indicate the amount of detail needed to answer the question properly.

Now try this

Réponds aux questions en français.

1 Tu aimes faire du tourisme? Pourquoi (pas)?

2 Qu'est-ce qu'il y a pour les touristes dans ta région?

Describing a town

Using modal verbs can help you describe any town – including your own, or one you have visited.

Description d'une ville

banlieue (f)	suburb
bâtiment (m)	building
boîte de nuit (f)	nightclub
déchets (mpl)	rubbish
département (m)	administrative district
embouteillage (m)	traffic jam
endroit (m)	place
fleurs (fpl)	flowers
historique / moderne	historic / modern
industriel(le)	industrial
pittoresque	picturesque
touristique	touristy

Modal verbs

Grammar page 99

Modal verbs are followed by another verb in the infinitive.

pouvoir   to be able to / can
vouloir   to want to
devoir   to have to / must

On ne peut pas interdire les voitures.
You can't ban cars.

On devrait installer des bancs.
They should install benches.

Je voudrais avoir un cinéma de 8 salles.
I would like to have an 8-screen cinema.

Il y a des fleurs partout.
There are flowers everywhere.

Worked example

 TRACK 25

Murielle discusses her town.

Listen to the recording

> Ma ville est vraiment propre et il y a très peu de déchets et de graffitis. Il y a des fleurs partout mais on devrait installer des bancs pour s'asseoir. On a une grande gamme de magasins qui sont ouverts jusqu'à 21 heures, même le dimanche, mais à mon avis, il faut faire plus de promotions afin d'attirer les clients.

Answer the questions by putting a cross ✗ next to the correct answer.

1 What improvement does she suggest for the town centre? **(1 mark)**

- ☒ **A** have benches for people to sit on
- ☐ **B** have flowers everywhere
- ☐ **C** clean up the streets

2 What does Murielle think would encourage more shoppers at the shopping centre? **(1 mark)**

- ☐ **A** more shops to open on Sunday
- ☒ **B** shops to organise more promotions
- ☐ **C** shops to stay open later

Here, in both questions all three of the options are mentioned somewhere in the text, so your job is to work out the precise meaning. For example, the town is described as **propre** (clean) and there are already flowers everywhere so the last two options in question 1 can be ruled out. Similarly in question 2, the shops are already open late, even on Sundays, so neither of those alternatives can be correct.

Now try this

 TRACK 26

Écoute André qui parle de sa ville. Mets une croix ✗ dans chaque case correcte.

Listen to the recording

1 Pour résoudre le problème de la circulation, il faut:

- ☐ **A** interdire les voitures
- ☐ **B** augmenter le prix pour stationner en ville
- ☐ **C** améliorer les transports en commun **(1 mark)**

2 Pour les jeunes on devrait:

- ☐ **A** construire un nouveau centre sportif
- ☐ **B** proposer des tarifs réduits pour enfants et ados
- ☐ **C** ouvrir un bowling **(1 mark)**

In difficult listening tasks like this one you have to understand in detail how adjectives, intensifiers, negatives and tenses are used.

Countries

Travelling abroad is often a good way to discover new cultures and have different experiences.

Les voyages partout dans le monde

Allemagne (f)	Germany
Angleterre (f)	England
Autriche (f)	Austria
Belgique (f)	Belgium
douanes (fpl)	customs
Écosse (f)	Scotland
Nouvelle-Zélande (f)	New Zealand
séjour (m)	stay
séjourner	to stay (for a holiday)
Suède (f)	Sweden
Suisse (f)	Switzerland

Je voudrais aller en France.

How to say 'to' or 'in' a country

Most countries in French are feminine and you use en to say 'to' or 'in' the country:

Je suis allé en Espagne.   I went to Spain.

Elle a passé une   She spent a week
  semaine en Italie.   in Italy.

Some countries are masculine in French and 'to / in' is au:

Je vais au Canada.   I'm going to Canada.

Elle habite au Portugal   She lives in Portugal.

Other masculine countries include le Japon (Japan), le Mexique (Mexico), le pays de Galles (Wales), le Maroc (Morocco).

Some countries are plural in French and 'to / in' is aux:

Je voudrais aller aux États-Unis.
I'd like to go to the USA.

Elle aimerait aller aux Pays-Bas.
She'd like to go to the Netherlands.

Worked example

Listen to these young people talking about holidays abroad. Where did they go?   **(4 marks)**

Listen to the recording

1 Luc	Germany
2 David	Scotland
3 Chantal	Japan
4 Hélène	USA

1 Moi, l'année derniére, je suis allé an Allemagne.

2 Au lieu d'aller en Espagne comme d'habitude, nous avons fait du camping en Écosse.

3 Moi, je voulais aller en France, mais j'ai dû aller au Japon avec ma famille.

4 J'ai passé un mois intéressant aux États-Unis.

You have to listen just as carefully to easier listening passages. Here you are just being asked to identify a country, which should present no problems – as long as you have learned the words for all the countries most often needed! But take care: in each of numbers 2 and 3, two countries are named but only one is the right answer. In 3, for example, Chantal says where she **wanted** to go (France) but the task asks you where she **went** (Japan).

Remember that you will need to cover all the bullet points.

Now try this

Écrivez un article intéressant sur des vacances à l'étranger que vous avez passées récemment.

Vous devez faire référence aux points suivants:
• ce que vous pensez des vacances en général
• pourquoi vous êtes allé(e) à votre destination

• les activités les plus intéressantes que vous avez faites
• projet pour l'avenir.

Justifiez vos idées et vos opinions. Écrivez 130–150 mots en français.   **(28 marks)**

Places to visit

You may need to talk about places you've been to on holiday.

Les attractions touristiques

bar (m)	bar
discothèque (f)	disco
site touristique (m)	tourist attraction
tranquille	quiet
centre commercial (m)	shopping centre
grand magasin (m)	department store
centre sportif (m)	sports centre
parc d'attractions (m)	theme park
visite guidée (f)	guided tour
boîte de nuit (f)	nightclub
commerce (m)	shop / business
marché (m)	market
piscine (en plein air) (f)	(open-air) swimming pool
place (f)	square
port (m)	harbour

Modifiers

assez	quite
beaucoup	much / a lot
trop	too (much)
encore	more
un peu	a bit
très	very
plus	more
moins	less
plutôt	rather
vraiment	really

Il y a beaucoup de choses à visiter en Bretagne.
There are many things to visit in Brittany.
Les bars sont trop bruyants le soir.
The bars are too noisy in the evenings.

Worked example

Janine a écrit sur une visite à Futuroscope.

> Je viens de visiter le parc d'attractions Futuroscope. C'était un monde inimaginable où l'atmosphère était toujours fantastique, avec des aventures palpitantes, des sensations inoubliables et des spectacles vivants. Ce que j'ai apprécié le plus, c'était le spectacle nocturne où les lumières ont illuminé le ciel. Mon frère cadet a préféré le théâtre 3D, mais mon père était heureux car l'entrée était gratuite pour les moins de 16 ans.

Mets une croix ✗ dans chaque case correcte.

1 Janine a trouvé l'atmosphère au parc … **(1 mark)**

☐ **A** décevante ☐ **C** triste

☒ **B** géniale ☐ **D** oubliable

2 Janine a préféré … **(1 mark)**

☐ **A** les aventures ☒ **C** l'activité de nuit

☐ **B** le théâtre 3D ☐ **D** le bowling

3 Son père était content car … **(1 mark)**

☐ **A** il a aimé les lumières

☐ **B** il avait acheté les billets en avance

☒ **C** il n'a pas dû payer des billets pour ses enfants

☐ **D** il a gagné de l'argent

Questions in French

Be careful with tasks like this where the questions contain so much French. The reading assessment requires understanding of the questions as well as of the passage in which you find the answers, so don't just skim the questions.

For question 2, make sure that you get the right person's opinion. Here you need to find Janine's favourite attraction, not her little brother's!

Question 3 is tricky – lumières is in the text but has nothing to do with the answer. Not paying and gratuite need to be linked.

Now try this

Listen to Martin discussing places to visit in the town where he lives. Which places does he recommend?

Listen to the recording

Find the **three** correct answers.

☐ **A** main square
☐ **B** zoo
☐ **C** park
☐ **D** church
☐ **E** indoor pool
☐ **F** outdoor pool **(3 marks)**

Describing a region

Not everyone lives in a lively, bustling town, so be prepared to describe the region where you live and understand other people's descriptions, too.

Description d'une région

espace vert (m)	green space
pittoresque	picturesque
ferme (f)	farm
Il n'y a rien à faire.	There's nothing to do.
isolé(e)	isolated
île (f)	island
rivière (f) / fleuve (m)	river
distractions (fpl)	things to do
équipements (mpl)	facilities
inconvénient (m)	disadvantage
montagne (f)	mountain
village (m)	village

Singular and plural

Grammar page 87

Il y a une piscine municipale.
There is a / one public swimming pool.

Il y a plusieurs piscines.
There are several swimming pools.
Les piscines sont fantastiques.
The swimming pools are great.

- Nouns and adjectives ending -al / -au / -eau: plural = -x

	singular	plural
animal	un animal	des animaux
office	un bureau	des bureaux

Worked example

Réponds aux questions.

1 Qu'est-ce qu'il y a pour les jeunes dans ta région?
À vrai dire, il n'y a rien à part des champs et des collines où on peut se promener s'il fait beau. Même dans le village, il n'y a qu'un petit magasin et une église. Il n'y a ni cinéma ni centre sportif dans la région et pour s'amuser, il faut aller à la ville la plus proche qui se trouve à dix kilomètres de chez moi.

2 Tu aimes ta région? Pourquoi (pas)?
J'aimais ma région quand j'étais petit mais maintenant, je la trouve trop isolée surtout car la plupart de mes copains habitent assez loin de chez nous et les bus ne sont pas fréquents. À l'avenir, je voudrais habiter dans une grande ville.

Practising for general conversation

1 Practise answering similar questions on a variety of topics before your speaking test as this will give you more self-confidence.

2 Listen carefully to the question asked and don't be afraid to ask for something to be repeated if you aren't sure of the meaning. It may be rephrased for you.

3 Try to give full answers. However, only add details if you are confident you can do so accurately. Choose details you can add without running the risk of making errors.

Now try this

Regarde cette photo.

1 Décris-moi la photo.
2 Moi, j'aime habiter en Angleterre. Quelle est ton opinion?
3 Tu préfères habiter en ville ou à la campagne? Pourquoi?
4 Tu voudrais habiter où à l'avenir? Pourquoi?
5 Où habitais-tu quand tu étais petit(e)?

Subjects

You need to be able to talk about your school subjects, give your opinions and justify them.

Les matières

J'apprends / J'étudie ...   I learn / I study ...
J'aime / Je préfère ...   I like / I prefer ...
Je n'aime pas ...   I don't like ...

 l'allemand (m)   la physique (f)

 l'anglais (m)   les maths (fpl)

 l'espagnol (m)   l'informatique (f)

 le français (m)   la géographie (f)

la biologie (f)   l'histoire (f)

 la chimie (f)   l'EPS / éducation
                           physique (f)

Negative sentences

After the negative ne ... pas, use de before the noun.

Je ne fais pas de gymnastique.
I don't do gymnastics.

Je n'ai pas de cours le mercredi.
I don't have lessons on Wednesdays.

depuis + present tense

depuis + present tense = how long you have been doing something

J'apprends le français depuis quatre ans.
I have been learning French for four years.

> EPS 'e' is pronounced 'uh': 'uh pay ess'.
> EMT – 'uh em tay'. (This is DT in English.)
> Subject names are often abbreviated:
> techno, info, bio, géo.

Worked example

SPEAKING

Regarde cette photo.

1 Décris-moi la photo.
Il y a quatre élèves dans une classe ou dans la bibliothèque. Tout le monde fait du travail scolaire et ils ont l'air heureux.

2 Quelle est ta matière préférée? Pourquoi?
Moi, je préfère l'anglais parce que c'est une matière utile et intéressante. La lecture me plaît, alors je lis beaucoup même quand je suis chez moi.

3 Les maths, c'est une matière utile? Quelle est ton opinion?
À mon avis c'est important, mais je ne suis pas fort(e) en maths. J'ai toujours trouvé cette matière compliquée, pourtant je fais des progrès en travaillant dur.

4 Tu as laissé tomber quelles matières?
J'ai laissé tomber le dessin, car je ne suis pas du tout créatif / créative, et aussi la géo parce que c'était assez ennuyeux.

5 Tu veux continuer tes études de français?
Je ne sais pas ce que je voudrais étudier plus tard dans la vie, mais je vais continuer mes études de français car j'adore les langues.

(24 marks)

Vocabulary from the question

- The question can offer useful vocabulary, which you can copy, use and adapt. In question 2 the student heard *ta matière préférée* and adapted this to *je préfère*.

- In the perfect tense you can often use the past participle you hear but remember to change the part of *avoir* or *être*. In question 4 the student heard *tu* as *laissé tomber* and replied with *j'ai laissé tomber*.

- After *c'est* or *c'était*, the adjective is always masculine, even if the original subject was feminine.

- If you can, it's good to adapt what you hear. In question 5, *tu veux continuer* was adapted in the reply as *je vais continuer* rather than the more obvious *je veux continuer*.

Now try this

LISTENING TRACK 29

Listen to Lucas, Manrouf and Kévin talking about their school subjects. Which subject is each discussing, and why do they either like or dislike it?

(6 marks)

Listen to the recording

School life

Discussing how things are at school can divide opinions.

La vie au collège

J'ai trop de devoirs. I have too much homework.

Je déteste les contrôles. I hate tests.

Les examens sont durs. Exams are hard.

Les arts ménagers, c'est nul. Cookery is rubbish.

Il est faible en dessin. He is weak at art.

La journée scolaire est longue. The school day is long.

Le professeur est sympa. The teacher is nice.

Mes notes sont bonnes. My marks are good.

J'aime les langues étrangères. I like foreign languages.

J'adore l'étude des médias. I love media studies.

Je suis fort(e) en maths. I am strong in maths.

Le prof de sciences physiques explique bien.
The chemistry and physics teacher explains it well.

> Les maths, ça m'énerve!
> Maths drives me mad!

'First', 'second', 'third'

premier is the only ordinal number to change in the feminine form:

	masculine	feminine
1st	premier	première
2nd	deuxième	deuxième
3rd	troisième	troisième

le premier cours the first lesson
la première leçon the first lesson

Je suis en …
I am in …

sixième Yr 7
cinquième Yr 8
quatrième Yr 9
troisième Yr 10
seconde Yr 11
première Yr 12
terminale Yr 13

Worked example

 LISTENING TRACK 30

Écoute ces jeunes qui parlent de la vie au collège.

Que pensent-ils? Choisis entre:

- opinion positive
- opinion négative
- opinion positive et négative. **(4 marks)**

Listen to the recording

1 Quand j'étais en sixième, j'étais vraiment content car tout le monde était gentil.

opinion positive

2 Moi, j'aime bien mon collège, pourtant les profs sont quelquefois sévères, ce qui ne me plaît pas.

opinion positive et négative

3 Je suis faible en maths et en français et on nous donne beaucoup trop de devoirs, alors je ne peux pas sortir le soir.

opinion négative

4 Je trouve toutes mes matières intéressantes sauf l'anglais, qui m'embête.

opinion positive et négative

Positives and negatives

It's often quite easy to pick out positive phrases in a listening task (j'aime, j'adore, super, intéressant, fantastique, marrant) and negative ones, too (je n'aime pas, je déteste, nul, ennuyeux).

Be on the lookout for more complex ways of expressing likes and dislikes:

La géo m'énerve.
Geography gets on my nerves.

Le français me passionne. I love French.

La techno m'embête.   IT annoys me.

L'histoire me plaît.
I like history (literally 'history pleases me')

L'EPS me déplaît.
I don't like PE. (literally 'PE displeases me')

Now try this

 LISTENING TRACK 31

Écoute trois autres jeunes et écris **opinion positive**, **opinion négative** ou **opinion positive et négative**.

Listen to the recording

1 …………………………

2 …………………………

3 …………………………   **(3 marks)**

School day

Everyone has an opinion about their school day. Be ready for the chance to express yours!

La journée scolaire

commencer	to begin
finir	to finish
durer	to last
fréquenter l'école	to attend school
le matin	in the morning
l'après-midi	in the afternoon
cours (m) / leçon (f)	lesson
récréation / récré (f)	break
heure du déjeuner (f)	lunch break
retenue (f)	detention
pas d'école	no school
trimestre (m)	term
grandes vacances (fpl)	summer holidays
rentrée (f)	start of the new school year

Third person plural

The third person singular (he / she) and plural (they) of most verbs sound the same but are **spelled differently:**

singular (he / she)	plural (they)
elle commence	elles commencent
il rentre	ils rentrent

Irregular third person plural forms:

aller	to go	ils / elles vont	they go
avoir	to have	ils / elles ont	they have
être	to be	ils / elles sont	they are
faire	to do	ils / elles font	they do

Les cours finissent à quatre heures.
Lessons finish at four o'clock.

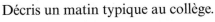

Worked example

Décris un matin typique au collège. **(20 marks)**

Le matin, les cours commencent à huit heures et demie et finissent à une heure. Il y a une récréation à dix heures et demie. Chaque cours dure une heure. Nous avons quarante minutes pour le déjeuner.

This answer is adequate but there are no opinions, no interesting details, and just one tense.

Le matin, on commence assez tôt, à huit heures trente. Puisque j'habite très loin de mon collège, je dois y aller en car de ramassage, ce qui m'énerve car je trouve le voyage barbant et monotone. Après être arrivée à l'école, je vais directement à la salle de classe où je retrouve mes copains. On a quatre cours d'une heure, mais il y a une récré de trente minutes entre le deuxième et le troisième cours. Normalement je bavarde avec mes amis mais hier, je suis allée à la bibliothèque parce que je devais finir mes devoirs d'anglais. À une heure, on déjeune et moi j'apporte tous les jours des sandwichs car les repas à la cantine sont nuls.

Look how this student has included much more detail with longer sentences (she uses connectives: **puisque, mais, ce qui, car, où, parce que**), opinions and justifications (**m'énerve, barbant** and **monotone, nuls**), time phrases and adverbs (**assez tôt, très loin, normalement, tous les jours**) as well as different tenses (present, perfect and imperfect) and complex constructions (**après être arrivée**).

Now try this

 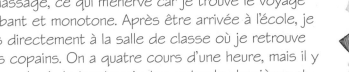

Décris un après-midi typique au collège. **(20 marks)**

Reuse or adapt some of the things in the 'aiming higher' answer above.

Comparing schools

You might need to compare schools in your own area, or French and English schools.

Une comparaison des collèges

brevet (m)	exam taken at 15
bac (m)	exam taken at 18
diplôme (m)	qualification
bulletin scolaire (m)	school report
école (f)	school
collège (m)	secondary school
maternelle (f)	nursery school
lycée d'enseignement professionel / LEP (m)	vocational school
école privée (f)	private school
lycée (m)	sixth form
échouer à un examen	to fail an exam
passer un examen	to sit an exam
réussir un examen	to pass an exam
moins / plus difficile	less / more difficult

Adjective agreements

Grammar page 87

singular		plural	
masc	fem	masc	fem
court	courte	courts	courtes
long	longue	longs	longues
actif	active	actifs	actives

La journée est plus longue.
The day is longer.
Les grandes vacances sont moins longues.
The summer holidays are shorter.

Les cours sont intéressants.

Worked example

 SPEAKING

Fais-moi une comparaison des collèges anglais et français.

En France, en général, les collèges sont plus grands que les collèges en Angleterre. Il y a plus d'élèves et plus de profs. Je préfère aller au collège en Angleterre parce qu'en France, on doit aller à l'école le samedi matin. Je détesterais ça!

Aiming higher

En Angleterre, je trouve que c'est mieux parce que la journée scolaire est moins longue qu'en France. Selon moi, les élèves français commencent trop tôt. Mais en Angleterre, il faut porter un uniforme et à mon avis c'est stupide. En France, c'est mieux, on porte ce qu'on veut. L'année dernière, je suis allée voir mon correspondant à Lille et je l'ai accompagné au collège.

To improve your answer:
• Include lots of opinions.
• Do not repeat nouns if you can help it. Use pronouns instead as this is more natural. But take care as object pronouns come before the verb in French. Here **je l'ai accompagné** (I accompanied him) is not just more natural, it also shows off what you know in French!

Remember to give your opinion, and try to use a simple conditional expression:
Je détesterais ça! (I would hate that!)

Now try this

 READING

Lis ce que dit Rina sur son lycée en France. Mets une croix ✗ dans chaque case correcte.

Moi, je ne suis pas du tout contente car je vais passer un examen de maths demain et j'ai peur de ne pas y réussir. L'année prochaine je ne resterai pas ici au lycée car mon père m'a dit que je peux aller à une école privée qui se trouve près de l'université. Je suis tout à fait ravie de ça!

1 Rina est mécontente car …
☐ **A** elle a échoué à un examen
☐ **B** elle va bientôt passer un examen
☐ **C** elle a réussi à un examen   **(1 mark)**

2 L'année prochaine Rina voudrait …
☐ **A** continuer ses études à son lycée
☐ **B** aller à la fac
☐ **C** changer d'école   **(1 mark)**

3 Rina pense qu'elle va être …
☐ **A** triste
☐ **B** très contente
☐ **C** fatiguée   **(1 mark)**

Describing schools

You can describe schools in terms of what they look like, but also by expressing opinions about them.

Au collège

niveau (m)	level
couloir (m)	corridor
rentrée (f)	first day back at school
laboratoire (m)	laboratory
bibliothèque (f)	library
mixte	mixed
cour (f)	playground
résultat (m)	result
hall (de l'école) (m)	(school) hall
école publique (f)	state school
succès (m) / réussite (f)	success
sécher les cours	to skip lessons
enseigner	to teach

Using qui and que
Grammar page 94

These words are used to link two parts of a sentence or two clauses, so that the sentence is longer and more complex.

qui = who / that / which

que = whom / that / which

Je vais à un collège qui est situé au centre-ville. I go to a school which / that is situated in the town centre.

C'est le prof que j'aime le plus. He / She's the teacher (whom) I like best.

Even when we might miss out who, whom, that or which in English, you have to use them in French:

La matière scolaire que je préfère, c'est l'anglais. The school subject (which / that) I prefer is English.

Worked example

Read the three descriptions of schools and then the statements in English below. Who made each statement – Dominique (D), Édouard (E) or François (F)?

Dominique: Mon collège est grand et moderne. Il y a environ mille cinq cents élèves. J'aime mon collège car il est bien équipé, même s'il n'y a pas de piscine.

Édouard: Mon collège, qui se trouve dans une très petite ville à la montagne, est assez vieux. Les bâtiments sont un peu démodés et à mon avis on n'a pas assez d'ordinateurs.

François: Je vais à mon collège depuis seulement un mois mais je l'aime parce que les profs sont travailleurs et intelligents et tous les élèves peuvent réussir s'ils travaillent dur.

1 My school is not well equipped. **(1 mark)**

E

2 I recently moved schools. **(1 mark)**

F

3 You cannot go swimming at my school. **(1 mark)**

D

4 I think my school is quite old-fashioned. **(1 mark)**

E

5 Hard work is usually rewarded at my school. **(1 mark)**

F

Answering questions based on more than one text

- Read and check **all** the texts before trying to answer the question.
- Beware of negatives! For example, bien équipé appears in the first text, but question 1 asks whose school is **not** well equipped. In 3, on the other hand, both **cannot go swimming** and pas de piscine are in the negative.
- Look for different ways of saying the same thing, such as **recently** and depuis seulement un mois.
- Check all your answers at the end by looking back at the texts.

Now try this

Karine parle de quoi? Mets une croix ✗ dans les trois cases correctes. **(3 marks)**

Listen to the recording

☐ **A** la récré
☐ **B** les bâtiments
☐ **C** le sport
☐ **D** les devoirs
☐ **E** les contrôles
☐ **F** les copains

55

School rules

The rules at each school may be different but everyone will have an opinion about them.

Le règlement scolaire

Il faut ...	You have to ...
bien se tenir en classe	behave well in class
éteindre son portable	switch off your mobile
être poli(e) / respectueux/euse	be polite / respectful
écouter les profs	pay attention to the teachers
Il est interdit de ...	You are not allowed to ...
courir dans les couloirs	run in the corridors
fumer (dans les vestiaires)	smoke (in the changing rooms)
mâcher du chewing-gum	chew gum
porter des boucles d'oreilles	wear earrings
utiliser son portable en classe	use your mobile in class

Il faut + infinitive

il faut + infinitive = **have to / must** do something.

Il faut être à l'heure.
You have to / must be on time.

il ne faut pas + infinitive = **must not** do something.

Il ne faut pas fumer.   You mustn't smoke.

- Other ways of saying you are **not allowed** to do something:

Il est défendu de courir dans les couloirs.
It is forbidden to run in the corridors.

Il est interdit de dire des gros mots.
Swearing is not allowed.

Il est interdit de courir dans les couloirs.

Worked example

Which sign matches which person?   **(5 marks)**

A Il est interdit de mâcher du chewing-gum en classe.

B Aujourd'hui il n'y a pas d'école à cause de la grève.

C Les élèves doivent arriver à l'heure à tous les cours.

D Il faut enlever ses chaussures en entrant dans la grande salle.

E Rencontre parents-professeurs, à 18 heures le mardi 4 février.

F Le bureau de l'école est fermé jusqu'à midi.

In short texts like these, one word or a short phrase can be the key to finding the correct answer (e.g. arriver à l'heure in C). Likewise, don't just look for a word in the text and the same one in the sentence (e.g. fermé in F goes with (iii) as it refers to le bureau but you might think it goes with (i) because that option also has the English word 'closed').

(i) Raphaël's school is closed today. B
(ii) Lilou must get to lessons on time. C
(iii) The school office is closed. F
(iv) Pupils must take their shoes off in the hall. D
(v) Baptiste's parents are due at school this evening. E

Reading exam tip

Look through all the questions and do the ones you're confident about first. Then come back to the others. Never leave a gap – always have a go, even if you're not sure.

Now try this

 Remember to give your reasons!

Réponds aux questions en français.
1 Que penses-tu du règlement de ton collège? Pourquoi?
2 Qu'est-ce que tu aimerais changer à ton école?

Problems and pressures

Academic and social pressures can be issues at school. You may need to be able to speak about these and understand other students' issues.

Les problèmes scolaires

absent(e)	absent
conseiller (m) / conseillère (f) d'orientation	careers adviser
vestiaires (mpl)	changing rooms
progrès (m)	progress
l'enseignement moral et civique (EMC) (f)	personal, social, health and economic (PSHE) education
bulletin scolaire (m)	school report
remplaçant(e) (m / f)	supply teacher
emploi du temps (m)	timetable
redoubler	to repeat a year
pression (f)	pressure
injuste	unfair
fiche de travail (f)	worksheet
pensionnat / internat (m)	boarding school
rédaction (f)	essay
réunion (f)	meeting
punition (f)	punishment

Using the perfect tense

Grammar
page 100

When you want to talk about things that happened in the past, you normally use the perfect tense in French.

Remember that this has two parts – a part of avoir (in most cases) or être (in a few cases) and a past participle: for example elle a mangé or elle est allée (remember that the participle must agree after part of être).

It is useful to remember that the French perfect tense translates a number of tenses in English:

nous avons travaillé we worked / we have worked / we did work

Je suis allée en ville.

J'ai bien travaillé en classe.

Worked example

Listen to Séverine talking about problems at her school and answer the questions in English.

Listen to the recording

> J'ai peur de rater mes examens. J'ai fait beaucoup de révisions, je suis très travailleuse et mes profs croient que j'aurai de bons résultats, mais je n'arrive jamais à me souvenir de tous les détails quand je passe un examen. Je ne peux rien dire à mes parents parce qu'ils pensent que je vais réussir sans problème.

1   What is Séverine's concern?   **(1 mark)**

that she is going to fail her exams

2   Why does she have reason to be optimistic?

(3 marks)

She has done a lot of revision. She is hardworking. Her teachers think she'll get good grades.

3   Why can't she speak to her parents?   **(1 mark)**

They think she'll pass easily.

Listening for negatives and opinions

- Negatives completely change the meaning of a verb, so you really do have to make an effort to identify them in listening tasks. It's not just ne … pas that you have to be aware of; in this text you heard ne … jamais (never) and ne … rien (nothing).

- Listen carefully for opinions and the person who expresses them. In this text Séverine is worried but her teachers are confident of her success, as are her parents; if you didn't listen carefully, you might confuse these opinions.

Now try this

Séverine's friend, Allyah, is also worried.

1 What is she concerned about?   **(1 mark)**

2 What solution has been proposed?

(2 marks)

Listen to the recording

Primary school

Talking about what you used to do at primary school and comparing it to your current school life is a good way of introducing the imperfect tense.

L'école primaire

instituteur (m) / institutrice (f)	teacher (primary)
Quand j'étais petit(e) …	When I was small …
j'allais à l'école à pied	I walked to school
j'avais un petit cartable	I had a small school bag
je mangeais à la cantine	I ate at the canteen
on s'amusait plus	we had more fun
on avait moins de contrôles	we had fewer tests
on faisait des promenades en été	we used to go for walks in the summer

Imperfect tense

Grammar page 102

Imperfect tense = what **used to** happen

Je jouais au foot.
I used to play football.
Quand j'avais huit ans.
When I was eight.
On dessinait.
We used to draw.

Je jouais au foot dans la cour de récréation.
I played football in the playground.

Les profs n'étaient pas sévères.
The teachers weren't strict.

On chantait et dessinait tous les jours.
We used to sing and draw every day.

Worked example

Lisez ce texte écrit par Raphaël.

> Quand j'étais à l'école primaire, je faisais toujours ce que les instituteurs me demandaient. Pourtant, mon frère Marc était moins sage et une fois, mes parents ont dû aller afin de parler à son institutrice qui n'était pas contente.
>
> On chantait en classe et on s'amusait mieux. Je jouais au foot mais maintenant je n'y joue plus, car je n'ai pas de temps à cause du travail scolaire et de mon petit job. Heureusement, mon frère s'est beaucoup calmé et maintenant il un bon élève.

Mets une croix ✗ dans les quatre cases correctes.

(4 marks)

☐ **A** Raphaël joue toujours au foot.
☒ **B** Raphaël était un bon élève.
☐ **C** Marc était un élève sage.
☒ **D** Raphaël a trouvé l'école primaire plus amusante.
☒ **E** Marc est plus calme ces jours-ci.
☐ **F** Raphaël n'était pas content à l'école primaire.
☒ **G** Raphaël passe beaucoup de temps à travailler.
☐ **H** Marc a un petit job

Finding information

In more difficult passages of French you will need to display good comprehension skills including an ability to draw conclusions. In the text the fact that Raphaël always did what his primary school teachers asked meant that the student correctly concluded that he was a good pupil. Likewise the fact that Raphaël now has lots of school work and has a part-time job means that he could be accurately said to be spending lots of time working.

Now try this

Réponds aux questions en français.

1 Ton école primaire était comment?
2 Tu as préféré le collège ou l'école primaire? Pourquoi?

Success at school

It's always nice to celebrate success at school!

La réussite à l'école

chorale (f)	choir
réussir	to succeed
note (f)	mark / grade
contrôle (m)	test / assessment
épreuve (f)	test
exercice (m) / pratique (f)	exercise / practice
examen (m)	exam
oral (m)	oral
bloc-notes (m)	note pad
diplôme (m)	qualification
année scolaire (f)	school year
fort(e) en	good at
commerce (m)	business studies
perfectionner	to improve (knowledge / skills in)

How to say 'my'

'My' has three forms in French mon, ma and mes.

Because it is an adjective, it needs to agree with the word it describes.

Use mon with masculine words: mon collège (my school).

Use ma with feminine words: ma classe (my class).

Use mes with plural words: mes examens (my exams).

Remember that feminine words starting with a vowel or silent 'h' use mon and not ma: mon école (my school).

'Your' (ton, ta, tes) and 'his / her' (son, sa, ses) follow the same rules.

Worked example

Lis le texte et mets une croix ✗ dans les cases correctes.

> Salut, je m'appelle Sunita. Mon petit ami Jules est très doué. Il a de bonnes notes dans toutes les matières et il est extrêmement fort en maths. Je dois avouer que j'en suis jalouse parce que moi, je suis une élève moyenne.
>
> Ma mère dit que j'ai d'autres talents. Par exemple, je suis forte en sport et je fais partie de la chorale de l'école, mais je voudrais de meilleures notes, surtout en français car pour moi, c'est la matière la plus importante.

1 Jules est …
☐ **A** fort   ☒ **C** intelligent
☐ **B** beau   **(1 mark)**

2 Il est très doué en …
☐ **A** français   ☐ **C** EMT
☒ **B** maths   **(1 mark)**

3 Sunita …
☐ **A** est forte en français   ☒ **C** chante bien
☐ **B** n'est pas sportive   **(1 mark)**

4 Elle aimerait réussir surtout en …
☐ **A** sport   ☒ **C** français
☐ **B** maths   **(1 mark)**

Sorting out questions in French

You will often be faced with questions in French in reading tasks and it's really important to read them as carefully as you read the text itself.

- Look at each question in turn. Don't be tempted to move on to the next one before you have tried to understand the first.
- You might see the same word occurring in more than one question, so make sure you know where it is relevant. For example, français appears once only in the text but in questions 2, 3 and 4. It is only relevant in question 4.
- Make a note of words that have more than one meaning. For example, fort usually means 'strong' but in the context of subjects it means 'good'.

Je suis fort en rugby.

Now try this

Écoute Anila qui parle de la réussite scolaire. Anila a réussi en quelles matières?
Mets une croix ✗ dans les trois cases correctes.

Listen to the recording

☐ **A** anglais   ☐ **D** musique
☐ **B** EPS   ☐ **E** commerce
☐ **C** dessin   ☐ **F** art dramatique

(3 marks)

School trips

You may need to talk about trips you've been on with your school – to France or elsewhere.

Les visites scolaires

visiter	to visit
groupe scolaire (m)	school group
voyager	to travel
ma classe de français	my French class
lendemain (m)	next day
participer à	to participate in / go on
sortie (f)	outing
excursion (f)	excursion / outing
organiser	to organise
parc d'attractions (m)	theme park
partir	to leave
sortir	to go out
louer	to hire

The imperative

When you want to tell someone to do something you need to use the 'imperative' form of the verb, which is basically either the tu or the vous part of the verb in the present tense (without the tu or the vous).

- With verbs ending in -re or -ir, the tu part of the verb doesn't change: Écris! Write! Finis tes devoirs! Finish your homework!
- With -er verbs, including aller, you leave off the final s: Mange! Eat! Va! Go!
- The vous part of the verb never changes: Allez! Go! Écoutez! Listen!

Worked example

Regarde la photo et réponds aux questions en français.

(24 marks)

1 Décris-moi la photo.

Sur la photo il y a un groupe d'élèves dans un bus. Je crois que c'est en été car ils portent des vêtements légers.

2 Moi, j'aime les visites scolaires. Quel est ton avis?

J'aime les visites scolaires parce que j'adore sortir avec mes copains. Pourtant, je n'aime pas les visites au musée car je trouve ça ennuyeux. Quand j'étais à l'école primaire, j'ai visité un musée romain et c'était nul.

3 Décris une visite scolaire récente.

Le mois dernier, je suis allé au théâtre avec ma classe d'anglais. On a vu une pièce de Shakespeare et c'était très bien. Cependant, le trajet était très long et on est rentré tard.

4 Est-ce que ton école organise beaucoup de visites scolaires? Pourquoi (pas)?

À mon avis, le collège n'organise pas assez de visites, mais je sais qu'elles coûtent cher, surtout quand on va à l'étranger.

5 Que pensent tes parents des visites scolaires?

Ils pensent que les visites scolaires sont intéressantes et importantes car on peut s'informer sur toutes sortes de sujets.

Giving extra information

- Use your own experiences to give examples as this enables you to use different tenses (here a perfect and imperfect) and varied connectives (here quand and car).
- Give opinions and points of view using expressions like je crois que (answer 1), à mon avis (answer 4) or ils pensent que (answer 5). The last one lets you give other people's point of view.

Now try this

Read the passage written by Dalila and put a cross ✗ in the box beside the three correct statements.   **(3 marks)**

> Ma classe de français a visité Disneyland à Marne-la-Vallée il y a deux mois. Nous y sommes allés le vendredi matin et nous avons passé deux nuits là-bas. Le samedi, j'ai fait tous les manèges, ce qui m'a plu, et le soir, nous avons vu un spectacle en plein air avec un feu d'artifice. Le lendemain matin, nous avons fait une excursion à Paris où j'ai fait une promenade en bateau.

☐ **A** Dalila went to Paris with her French friends.

☐ **B** She travelled by car.

☐ **C** She went on all the rides.

☐ **D** She went for two months.

☐ **E** She watched fireworks.

☐ **F** She went on a boat trip.

School activities

It's good to be able to explain why you take part in events at school.

Les activités scolaires

pièce (f)	play
profiter au maximum d'un	to get the most out of a
spectacle musical (m)	musical production
oublier	to forget
inoubliable	unforgettable
incroyable	incredible
fier / fière de	proud of
accomplissement (m)	accomplishment
faire partie de	to be part of
concours (m)	competition
mémorable	memorable
se détendre	to relax
délégué(e) (m/f)	delegate / representative

Present participles

These are words which end in -ing in English, e.g. going, doing.

In French they always end in -ant. Normally you take the nous part of the present tense, drop the nous, cross off the -ons and add -ant:

~~nous~~ travaill~~ons~~ ➡ travaillant

Common exceptions to the rule are étant (being) and ayant (having).

Present participles are often used with en to mean 'on / in / while / by doing something'.

En participant à la chorale, cela fait du bien à notre corps. By participating in a choir, you do your body good.

Worked example

 LISTENING TRACK **36**

Listen to these young French people talking about school activities. Put the correct number in the box. **(4 marks)**

Listen to the recording [QR code]

Be careful! Four of the answers shown are not needed.

1 Je viens de participer à un spectacle musical au lycée. J'ai chanté et dansé et c'était génial.

2 Moi, j'ai joué dans un tournoi pour l'équipe de rugby de mon collège.

3 J'ai gagné le concours de talent de mon école et je suis très heureuse.

4 Moi, j'ai fait de l'athlétisme pour mon collège mais malheureusement on a perdu.

☐ **A** debating contest	☐ **E** choir
1 **B** school musical	☐ **F** school football team
4 **C** school athletics	2 **G** school rugby team
☐ **D** school play	3 **H** school talent contest

Listening for the key word

In some listening tasks, recognising one key word can give you the answer and the rest does not all need to be understood.

In this task you really only need to identify musical, rugby, talent and athlétisme to answer the questions.

Of the four words, talent is the most difficult as it is pronounced differently in the two languages. Not all cognates are easy to identify in French. For example, le théâtre is easy to understand in a reading task but much more difficult in a listening question as it is pronounced so differently from 'theatre'.

Watch out! In this task the words are relatively easy to spot, but they won't always be!

Now try this

 WRITING

Translate the following into French.
1 I play football for my school. **(2 marks)**
2 I sing in the choir. **(2 marks)**
3 I would like to participate in a play. **(3 marks)**

4 My basketball team won a match yesterday. **(3 marks)**
5 There is a music festival in school every year and it's great. **(3 marks)**

Exchanges

Going on a school exchange is a productive and often quite inexpensive way of improving your French.

Les échanges scolaires

échange (m)	exchange
correspondant(e)	pen friend
améliorer	to improve
culture (f)	culture
goûter	to taste
nouveau / nouvelle	new
apprécier	to appreciate
différence (f)	difference
entre	between
vie (f)	life
la vie quotidienne	daily life
tous les jours	every day
famille (f)	family
foyer (m)	home

Structuring a sequence

You can make what you say and write in French more interesting by adding a sequence. For example, you could use days of the week, particularly if you are on an exchange.

Vendredi, je suis allé en ville avec mon correspondant puis samedi, nous avons visité Paris.

You could also use expressions like plus tard (later), le lendemain (the next day) or avant-hier (the day before yesterday).

Be careful when you split the day up – there is no French word for 'in':

le matin	in the morning(s)
l'après-midi	in the afternoon(s)
le soir	in the evening(s)

Le matin, nous avons mangé un casse-croûte.

Worked example

 TRACK 37

Listen to Benjamin giving reasons why he might go on a school exchange to England.

Fill in the gaps in English. **(4 marks)**

Listen to the recording

> 1 Je peux me faire de nouveaux amis pendant un échange scolaire.
>
> 2 Je voudrais visiter un autre pays.
>
> 3 On peut apprécier un style de vie différent.
>
> 4 J'aimerais bien améliorer mes compétences en langue.

1 I can ..make new friends..

2 I'd like to visit ..another country..

3 You can appreciate a different ..lifestyle..

4 I'd really like to improve my ..language skills..

Working out meaning from context

Even if you cannot recall the meaning of a word you see or hear in French or if you don't know it, you can make an informed guess at the answer by looking at the context in which it is used. In tasks where you have to complete a sentence in English, make sure that what you write actually fits in and makes sense (even if it's a guess!). Say the sentence back to yourself at the end to check.

In question 4, if you did not understand **mes compétences en langue**, you might have recognised **langue** and remembered that it means 'tongue', which gives you a clue that it has something to do with language.

Now try this

  SPEAKING

Réponds aux questions en français.

1 Tu as déjà participé à un échange scolaire?

2 C'était comment?

Remember to listen out for the tense in the question, so you can match it.

Future plans

Using the conditional is a good way of expressing what you want to do in the future.

Projets d'avenir

Je voudrais ...	I would like to ...
réussir à mon brevet	pass my (GCSE) exams
entrer en première	go to the sixth form
continuer mes études	continue studying
étudier la sociologie	study sociology
préparer le bac	study for (A level) exams
aller à l'université	go to university
chercher un emploi	look for a job
faire du bénévolat	do volunteering
faire un apprentissage	do an apprenticeship
prendre une année sabbatique	do a gap year
gagner de l'argent	earn some money
aller voir le conseiller / la conseillère d'orientation	go and see the careers adviser
réussir	be successful

Conditional tense

Grammar page 104

To say what you **would like** to do, use a conditional verb + infinitive.

Je voudrais ...	I would like to ...
J'aimerais ...	I would like to ...
Je préférerais ...	I would prefer to ...
Je pourrais ...	I could ...

J'aimerais voyager à l'étranger.
I would like to travel abroad.
Je voudrais être médecin.
I would like to be a doctor.

Je voudrais étudier
l'anglais et l'histoire
à l'université.

Worked example

WRITING

Écris au sujet de tes études à l'avenir.

> Ensuite je voudrais aller en première et préparer mon bac. Après le bac, j'aimerais bien trouver un emploi. J'aimerais aller à l'université mais je crois que cela coûte trop cher.

This answer uses the **present** tense and the **conditional**, but with a limited range of vocabulary – a few **adjectives** would have improved the work. Using the conjunction **mais** (but) is a good way to join sentences and make the text flow better.

ning
gher

> Je voudrais réussir mon bac et aller à l'université. Je préférerais étudier à Paris parce que j'ai beaucoup de copains qui y habitent et j'adore la ville. En ce moment, je pense que j'aimerais prendre une année sabbatique pour faire du bénévolat en Afrique. Ça m'intéresserait beaucoup car j'aimerais bien aider les gens, surtout les enfants.

This account is a coherent piece of writing using different tenses and a variety of structures. It avoids overusing **parce que** by including the alternative **car**. The construction **qui y habitent** (who live there) is a good use of a relative pronoun with the pronoun **y** (there).

These are students' first paragraphs of their answers – your answers would need to be longer.

Now try this

LISTENING TRACK 38

Listen to three French teenagers talking about their plans.

Answer the questions in English.

Listen to the recording

1 What does Marianne want to do next year? **(1 mark)**
2 What are Salomon's plans for his future studies? **(2 marks)**
3 For how long does Romain plan to do an apprenticeship? **(1 mark)**

Languages beyond the classroom

Knowing more than one language can be very useful, not just for specific jobs but also in life.

Parler d'autres langues

savoir (parler)	to know (how to speak)
langue (f)	language
profession (f)	profession
interprète (m)	interpreter
métier (m)	job
étranger / étrangère	foreign
comprendre	to understand
entreprise (f)	company
communiquer	to communicate
pays (m)	country
monde (m)	world
utiliser	to use

Questions about languages

You might need to talk about your future and how languages, particularly French, might play a role in it. In speaking tasks you might have to answer questions like these, so be prepared!

- À l'avenir, tu voudrais habiter à l'étranger?
- Est-ce que tu aimerais travailler en Europe?
- À mon avis, parler d'autres langues, c'est important. Quel est ton avis?
- Tu connais quelqu'un qui sait parler une autre langue?

Il n'y a pas qu'en France qu'on parle le français.

Worked example

Lis cet article sur l'acteur Bradley Cooper.

> Bradley Cooper n'est pas un Américain typique puisqu'il sait parler une autre langue et ça, c'est assez rare. Au cours de ses études d'anglais à l'université de Georgetown, le jeune Bradley a décidé d'améliorer ses compétences afin de mieux communiquer avec les gens des pays francophones. Il a donc commencé à suivre des cours de français et il a fait d'énormes progrès. En plus, après avoir passé six mois à Aix-en-Provence comme étudiant, il a réussi à parler couramment le français. Maintenant, il est souvent interviewé en français et il est devenu l'acteur américain le plus populaire en France. Il a de nombreux amis français.

Understanding a text

This sort of text needs to be read all the way through as the statements you need to assess can apply to the passage in general or to particular parts of it. Once you have got the general meaning, then look at the detail more carefully.

Remember to look for synonyms such as l'université and la fac or bien connu and populaire.

Mets une croix ✗ dans les quatre cases correctes.

- ☐ **A** Bradley Cooper est un Américain typique.
- ☐ **B** Il ne parle qu'une langue.
- ☒ **C** Il a étudié l'anglais à la fac.
- ☒ **D** Il a voulu pouvoir parler aux gens d'autres pays.
- ☐ **E** Bradley ne parle plus le français.
- ☒ **F** Il a fait des études en France.
- ☒ **G** Bradley est bien connu en France.
- ☐ **H** Sa petite amie est française. **(4 marks)**

Now try this

Réponds aux questions en français.
1 Quels sont les avantages d'apprendre une langue étrangère?
2 Que penses-tu des cours de langues au collège?

Looking to the future

Using the future tense will allow you to discuss your plans and how you will build working relationships.

À l'avenir

Quand je quitterai le collège ...	When I leave school ...
Après avoir quitté le collège ...	After I have left school ...
je chercherai un emploi	I will look for a job
j'étudierai l'économie à l'université	I will study economics at university
je ferai un apprentissage	I will do an apprenticeship
j'apprendrai les techniques de constructions	I will learn building skills
je voyagerai	I will see the world
je commencerai ma carrière	I will start my career
j'aurai ma propre entreprise	I will have my own firm
travail (m) en équipe	team work
entreprendre un projet	to take on a project
partager les profits	to share the profits

Future tense

Grammar page 103

Learn and use the following future tense verbs and phrases. The first one is a regular -er verb, the rest are irregular.

je jouerai	I will play
j'irai	I will go
j'aurai	I will have
je serai	I will be
je ferai	I will make / do
je verrai	I will see

Je ferai le tour du monde.

Je serai footballeur professionnel.

Worked example

WRITING

Traduis le texte ci-dessous en français.

> My friend Sophie is very intelligent. She would like to go to university and later she is going to travel abroad because she likes visiting other countries. After leaving school I would prefer to look for a job in a hospital because I like team work. My dream would be to go around the world before returning to England, where I will live.

Mon amie Sophie est très intelligente. Elle voudrait aller à la fac et plus tard, elle va voyager à l'étranger parce qu'elle aime visiter d'autres pays. Après avoir quitté le collège, je préférerais chercher un emploi dans un hôpital puisque j'aime le travail en équipe. Mon rêve serait de faire le tour du monde avant de retourner en Angleterre, où j'habiterai.

Translating words ending in '-ing'

Translating words ending in '-ing' can be tricky as there are so many ways of doing so.

1. If the '-ing' word comes after 'on', 'in', 'by' or 'while', you can usually use a present participle preceded by en: en travaillant dur (by working hard).

2. If it follows a verb such as 'like', 'hate', 'try', you need to use an infinitive: elle aime visiter (she likes visiting).

3. If it follows 'before', use avant de + the infinitive: avant de retourner (before returning).

4. If it follows 'after', use the infinitive of avoir or être with the appropriate past participle: après avoir quitté le collège (after leaving school) après être arrivées elles se sont couchées (after arriving they went to bed).

Now try this

SPEAKING

Réponds aux questions en français.
1 Quel est ton rêve?
2 Quels sont les avantages et les inconvénients de travailler en groupe?

Travel

Many people talk about their travel plans, so it is important to learn how to do this in French.

Les voyages

gagner	to win
faire le tour du monde	to go round the world
emprunter	to borrow
promettre	to promise
accompagner	to accompany
pays (m)	country
voyage (m)	trip
voyager	to travel
embarquer	to board (a plane / ship)
avoir l'intention de	to intend to
compter	to plan

Je pense visiter l'Afrique un jour.

Expressing intentions

If you cannot remember how to form or use the future tense, you can talk about your plans and future events using a simple infinitive.

- part of *aller* + the infinitive:
  Je vais beaucoup voyager.
  I'm going to travel a lot.
- part of *avoir* + *l'intention de* + the infinitive:
  J'ai l'intention d'aller au Canada.
  I intend to go to Canada.
- part of *espérer* + the infinitive
  J'espère faire le tour du monde.
  I hope to go round the world.
- *mon rêve / ambition est de* + infinitive
  Mon rêve est de voyager en Australie.
  My dream is to travel to Australia.
- part of *compter / penser* + the infinitive
  Je compte faire beaucoup de voyages.
  I plan to do lots of travelling.

Worked example

Réponds aux questions suivantes:

1 Tu voudrais voyager à l'avenir? Pourquoi (pas)?
   À l'avenir, j'aimerais bien voyager parce que je crois qu'il est important de découvrir d'autres pays et de découvrir des cultures différentes.

2 Quel pays voudrais-tu visiter? Pourquoi?
   Mon rêve est de visiter le Japon parce que je m'intéresse à la technologie et que j'aimerais visiter les entreprises où on fabrique des voitures, des ordinateurs et des jeux électroniques. Je voudrais également faire des visites culturelles là-bas.

3 Où irais-tu si tu gagnais à la loterie?
   Si je gagnais à la loterie, je ferais le tour du monde afin d'élargir mes horizons. Mes copains m'accompagneraient et je payerais tout, l'hôtel, les billets d'avion et les sorties.

Using adjectives in speaking

It is always a good idea to use a variety of adjectives, particularly ones that show you know how to make adjectives agree with the word they describe.

cultures différentes – the way you pronounce différentes shows you that you have made it agree with cultures.

Now try this

Translate these sentences into English.

(7 marks)

1 À l'avenir, je voudrais voyager aux États-Unis avec mes copains.
2 La Suisse est un pays intéressant et varié.
3 J'aimerais passer un mois en Écosse car je n'y suis jamais allée.
4 Mon père a des amis qui habitent à New York.
5 J'ai l'intention de voyager partout dans le monde.

Jobs

Les métiers

agent de police (m)	police officer
caissier / caissière	cashier
charpentier (m)	carpenter
chauffeur (de camion) (m)	(lorry) driver
cuisinier / cuisinière	cook
facteur / factrice	postman / woman
fermier / fermière	farmer
fonctionnaire (m / f)	civil servant
gendarme / policier (m)	police officer
informaticien(ne)	computer scientist
ingénieur(e)	engineer
maçon / maçonne	builder
médecin / docteur (m)	doctor
pharmacien(ne)	pharmacist
plombier (m)	plumber
pompier (m)	firefighter
secrétaire (m / f)	secretary
vétérinaire (m / f)	vet
homme d'affaires	businessman
femme d'affaires	businesswoman

Masculine and feminine forms

Il est infirmier. Elle est infirmière.
He / She is a nurse.
Il est vendeur. Elle est vendeuse.
He / She is a sales assistant.

Il est facteur.
Elle est factrice.

Il est fermier.
Elle est fermière.

This vocabulary will help you talk about the jobs members of your family do.

Look for words like English words (cognates):
infirmier works in an infirmary = nurse
coiffeur/euse is like coiffure (hairstyle) = hairdresser
mécanicien, électricien, journaliste and fleuriste look and sound familiar.

EXAM ALERT!

In tasks like this you **only** need to identify the job. Don't worry about opinions or reasons for liking or disliking the job as these details are not required, even if you hear and understand them.

Worked example

 LISTENING TRACK 39

Listen to these French teenagers talking about jobs. Decide which job they are discussing and put a cross ✗ in the three correct boxes.

(3 marks)

1 J'aimerais devenir médecin mais c'est un métier difficile.

2 Mon père est fonctionnaire mais je pense que c'est une profession ennuyeuse.

3 Moi, je voudrais être maçon comme mon oncle.

☐ **A** architect
☒ **B** civil servant
☐ **C** engineer
☒ **D** doctor
☒ **E** builder
☐ **F** police officer

Listen to the recording

Now try this

  LISTENING TRACK 40

Listen to these people talking about different job choices. What advantages and disadvantages do they give for each job? Answer in English.   **(4 marks)**

Listen to the recording

Job	Advantage	Disadvantage
1 lorry driver		
2 vet		

Part-time jobs

You might be asked about part-time jobs, either yours or someone else's, so the phrases here could help.

Un emploi à temps partiel

Je remplis les rayons.	I stack shelves.
J'ai un job dans un fast-food / une ferme.	I've got a job at a fast-food outlet / farm.
Je livre des journaux et des magazines.	I deliver newspapers and magazines.
Je fais le ménage.	I do housework.
Je travaille dans un centre sportif.	I work in a sports centre.
Je lave les voitures des voisins.	I wash neighbours' cars.
Je travaille comme plongeur / plongeuse.	I am a washer-up.
de temps en temps	from time to time
le soir	in the evening
le lundi	on Mondays
le week-end	at the weekend
chaque matin	every morning
pendant les vacances	during the holidays

Les petits boulots

Give reasons for doing a part-time job if you can.

Je travaille dans un supermarché le week-end. J'ai besoin d'argent supplémentaire parce que je voudrais acheter beaucoup de cadeaux de Noël.
I work in a supermarket at weekends. I need extra money because I'd like to buy lots of Christmas presents.

J'ai un petit job chez un vétérinaire.

Worked example

Tu as un petit job?

> Pour gagner de l'argent, le jeudi soir, je fais du babysitting pour une voisine pendant qu'elle va au cours de yoga. Normalement, je n'ai rien à faire parce que le bébé est déjà endormi, ce qui est fantastique parce que je peux regarder la télé avec canal satellite.

The use of conjunctions, connectives and interesting sentence constructions helps this speech flow – **pendant que** = while, **parce que** = because, **pour gagner de l'argent** = to earn money, **je n'ai rien à faire** = I have nothing to do.

Aiming higher

> Non, mais mon grand frère est à l'université et le week-end il travaille dans un supermarché pour gagner de l'argent. Au début il a dû remplir les rayons, puis il a travaillé à la caisse, mais maintenant il est chef de rayon, et ça c'est mieux payé. Il a besoin d'argent parce que l'année prochaine, il voudrait bien faire un voyage en train pour visiter toutes les grandes villes d'Europe.

Aiming higher

- Talking about someone else and using the third person (he / she) adds variety.
- The use of **past** and **future** tenses as well as the present helps to raise the level.
- il a dû + infinitive (he had to) is a good way to show that you can use more complex structures.

Now try this

Réponds aux questions en français.
1 Tu penses qu'il est important d'avoir un petit job? Pourquoi (pas)?
2 Est-ce que tes amis ont un petit job?

Opinions about jobs

When you are discussing jobs or listening to other people's opinions, there could be positives and negatives to consider.

Opinions sur les emplois

C'est …	It is …
bien payé	well paid
parfait	perfect
tranquille	quiet
intéressant	interesting
facile	easy
varié	varied

C'est …	It is …
mal payé	badly paid
bruyant	noisy
ennuyeux	boring
difficile	difficult
fatigant	tiring
stressant	stressful

Les possibilités d'avancement sont bonnes / mauvaises.	The chances of promotion are good / bad.
Il y a trop de responsabilités.	There is too much responsibility.
Les heures sont trop longues.	The hours are too long.
Les heures sont irrégulières / flexibles.	The hours are irregular / flexible.
On est toujours debout / assis(e)(s).	You are always standing / sitting down.

Small words

Listen carefully for small words that completely change the meaning of a sentence, e.g. the negative words ne … pas.

Ce n'est pas amusant. = It is not funny.

Watch out for these words too:

J'ai peu / beaucoup de responsabilités.	I have little / a lot of responsibility.
J'ai trop de responsabilités.	I have too much responsibility.

Worked example

Léna, Noah and Zoë are discussing their jobs. Who says the following? **(1 mark)**

Listen to the recording

	Léna	Noah	Zoë
A My job is interesting.	☐	☐	☐
B I am well paid.	☒	☐	☐
C I have regular hours.	☐	☐	☐
D I have to stand up all day.	☐	☐	☐
E I've got no prospects.	☐	☐	☐
F I don't get paid much.	☐	☐	☐

– À ton avis, Léna, tu as un bon métier?

– Ah oui, c'est bien payé, mais ce n'est pas très intéressant.

Listening tips

- Here, you need to distinguish between different **opinions** in a listening text. Three people are all using similar vocabulary, but offering different opinions.
- You need to listen to the **whole** extract before you can answer tasks like these. Listen through once to understand the differences of opinion, and then cross the boxes on a second listening.
- Discriminate between opinions such as Léna saying her job is bien payé (well paid) and Noah saying the opposite, mal payé (badly paid).

Now try this

Listen and complete the activity in the worked example. **(5 marks)**

Listen to the recording

Workplaces

Words and phrases about the workplace are always useful, whether it's for discussing part-time jobs, others' professions or your own plans.

Les lieux de travail

atelier (m)	workshop
chantier (m)	building site
hôpital (m)	hospital
salon de coiffure (m)	hairdresser's
bureau (m)	office
banque (f)	bank
cabinet médical (m)	doctor's surgery
commissariat (m)	police station
magasin (m)	shop
école (f)	school
hôtel (m)	hotel
ferme (f)	farm
à l'extérieur	outside / outdoors
à l'intérieur	inside / indoors

Prepositions

Grammar page 110

Prepositions are **small** words that give **big** information about where, how and when things happen.

à	at / to
après	after
avec	with
dans	in
de	from / of
en	in / by
pour	for
sans	without
heures de travail	working hours
dans une usine	in a factory
à domicile	at / from home
en plein air	in the open air
après une semaine	after a week

Worked example

Tu fais un stage dans un bureau. Tu postes cette photo sur un réseau social pour tes copains. Écris une description de la photo et exprime ton opinion sur le travail dans un bureau.

Écris 20–30 mots environ en français. **(12 marks)**

Sur la photo …

on voit le bureau où je fais mon stage. Mes collègues travaillent avec des ordinateurs et ils aiment ça. Je m'entends très bien avec eux car ils sont gentils.

Je voudrais travailler dans une banque.

Writing about a photo

This type of question only asks you to write between 20 and 30 words, so it is not a long task. The photo should give you enough information to write a sentence or two but don't write too much about it. Remember to stick to what you are asked. Here the answer must include your opinion about the work.

This student has added a reason but make sure that what you write is relevant and grammatically accurate.

Now try this

Écoute ces jeunes qui parlent de lieux de travail. Où est-ce qu'ils travaillent?

1 Gina travaille dans un .... **(1 mark)**
2 Didier fait un stage dans une .... **(1 mark)**
3 Lola aimerait travailler dans un .... **(1 mark)**

Listen to the recording

Applying for jobs

You might need to understand a range of vocabulary about jobs in listening and reading activities.

Candidature à un poste

petite annonce (f)	small ad
journal (m)	newspaper
lettre (f)	letter
agence de voyage (f)	travel agency
documentation (f)	information / literature
directeur/trice	manager
gérant/e	manager
disponible	available
dès début (janvier)	from the start of (January)
confiant(e)	confident
responsable	responsible
travailleur/euse	hard-working

Different tenses

If you are writing about yourself, it is all going to be in the first person – but you can use a variety of tenses:

Present je travaille — I work / am working
Perfect j'ai travaillé — I (have) worked
Imperfect je travaillais — I used to work
Pluperfect j'avais travaillé — I had worked
Future je travaillerai — I will work
Conditional je travaillerais — I would work

L'année dernière, j'ai travaillé à Paris.

Worked example

Read this letter from Emma and choose the correct response.

Madame, Monsieur,

J'ai vu votre petite annonce pour le poste de guide touristique dans le journal d'hier et je voudrais poser ma candidature.

J'ai dix-huit ans et je suis anglophone mais j'apprends le français depuis cinq ans et je parle bien l'allemand.

Je suis confiante, responsable et travailleuse et je suis à l'aise avec les adultes.

L'année dernière, j'ai fait un stage de deux semaines dans une agence de voyage.

Je suis disponible pour commencer dès début juin.
…

1 Emma is …   **(1 mark)**
☒ **A** applying for a job
☐ **B** turning down a job offer
☐ **C** writing to a tourist guide

2 Emma …   **(1 mark)**
☐ **A** is German
☒ **B** can speak more than one language
☐ **C** has never studied French

3 She …   **(1 mark)**
☐ **A** cannot relate well to adults
☐ **B** lacks confidence
☒ **C** says she works hard

4 She did work experience …   **(1 mark)**
☐ **A** in a tourist office
☐ **B** two weeks ago
☒ **C** last year

Now try this

Vous écrivez à votre prof car vous allez commencer un petit emploi dans un centre sportif. Mentionnez:
• où vous allez travailler
• les heures de travail
• quand vous devez commencer
• quels sont vos points forts comme employé dans un centre sportif.

Écrivez 40–50 mots en français.   **(16 marks)**

Don't just mention liking sport – dealing with the public might be important, too.

Future study

After school there are many options for further study, including university.

Mes études à l'avenir

université / fac(ulté) (f)	university
apprendre	to learn
étudier	to study
licence (f)	degree
essayer	to try
rêver	to dream
frais (mpl)	expenses
boulot (m)	job
bac (m)	exam equivalent to A levels
chômage (m)	unemployment
dette (f)	debt
emprunter	to borrow
loyer (m)	rent

Verbs followed by à or de + the infinitive.

Here are some verbs you might find useful.

apprendre à	to learn to
commencer à	to start to
consister à	to consist of
réussir à	to succeed in / at
décider de	to decide to
essayer de	to try to
rêver de	to dream of
Je vais apprendre à mieux étudier.	I'm going to learn to study better.

J'ai décidé d'aller à l'université.

Worked example

Lis ce texte.

> De nos jours, les jeunes qui décident d'aller à la fac doivent être certains que c'est le bon choix car cela coûte cher. Bien sûr, les cours universitaires sont moins chers en France qu'en Angleterre, mais il faut payer un loyer et il y aura des frais de nourriture aussi, sans parler des sorties le soir! Après avoir fini leurs études, plein d'étudiants ont des dettes énormes et beaucoup de licenciés sont au chômage.

Complète les phrases. Choisis un mot dans le tableau.

universitaire	simplement	sorties	nourriture
loyer	licence	importante	études

1 Aller à la fac est une décision ..*importante*..

(1 mark)

2 Si on n'habite pas une ville ..*universitaire*.., il faut payer un loyer.   **(1 mark)**

3 À part le loyer, il faut aussi payer la ..*nourriture*...

(1 mark)

4 Plein de gens qui ont une ....*licence*.... sont au chômage.   **(1 mark)**

This must be a feminine noun, which leaves only **nourriture** and **licence** – and only **licence** makes sense.

EXAM ALERT!

Tricky passages can make even cloze (or gap-fill) tasks difficult. The following points may help you.
- Make sure that you read the text carefully and underline words that you don't immediately know.
- Try to work out the meaning of these words from their context.
- Look at the questions and try to translate them, repeating the first two steps.
- Then work out the meanings of the words in the box.
- If you have to guess, at least try to find a word that fits the gap in a grammatical sense (i.e. adjective, noun, etc.).

Now try this

Réponds aux questions en français.
1 Quels sont les avantages et les inconvénients d'aller à l'université?
2 Tu voudrais aller à l'université? Pourquoi (pas)?

Volunteering

There are lots of ways to volunteer – and lots of reasons for doing so.

Le travail bénévole

volontaire (m/f)	volunteer
travail volontaire / bénévole (m)	voluntary work
stage en entreprise (m)	work experience
bénévolement	voluntarily
faire un stage	to do a course / placement
faire du bénévolat	to do voluntary work
développer	to develop
raison (f)	reason
évoluer	to evolve
SDF (sans domicile fixe) (m)	homeless person

Adding a reason

It's always useful to add a reason to explain why you're doing something. There are different ways to do this:

- Use car or parce que (because).
- Use pour or afin de + the infinitive (in order to).
- Use pour que + the subjunctive (in order that).
- Use puisque (seeing that) or comme (as).

Je fais du travail bénévole afin d'aider les animaux en danger.

Worked example

 LISTENING TRACK 43

Listen to the recording

Écoutez ces jeunes qui parlent du travail bénévole. Remplissez les blancs. Choisissez un mot dans le tableau.

> 1 Je travaille comme bénévole pour une petite œuvre caritative où on distribue des aides financières aux personnes sans domicile fixe de la région.
>
> 2 Je viens de faire un stage comme bénévole dans une clinique afin d'acquérir de l'expérience.

Listening for key words

Focus on listening for the words you need to answer the question and try not to be put off by everything else. For example, in the first part of question 1, you know you need the name of a place, and there are only four places included in the list of possible answers.

argent	expérience	restaurant	SDF
chômeurs	association caritative	magasin	hôpital

1 Siana travaille dans un ..une. association. ..caritative... car elle veut aider les ....SDF......
   (2 marks)

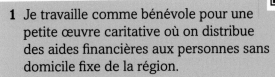 The focus is on the place, association caritative, and the people she wants to help, SDF (sans domicile fixe).

2 Lara a fait un stage dans un ....hôpital.... afin d'acquérir de l'..expérience. **(2 marks)**

 You were listening for a place and you heard dans une clinique – but clinique isn't an option, so you must find a synonym: hôpital.

Now try this

 READING

Read the text and answer the questions.

On fait du bénévolat pour de nombreuses raisons. Certains en font pour des raisons professionnelles, par exemple, pour se familiariser avec le milieu du travail ou pour remplir les exigences de leurs études. Cependant, il existe également des raisons personnelles: pour avoir un sentiment d'appartenance, pour se lancer un défi, ou simplement pour y prendre plaisir.

1 What two professional reasons are given for volunteering? **(2 marks)**
2 Give any two of the personal reasons mentioned for doing voluntary work. **(2 marks)**

Helping others

It's always good to help others – and just as good when someone helps you!

Aider les autres

esprit d'équipe (m)	team spirit
aider	to help
droit (m)	right
coup de main (m)	(helping) hand
sans-abri (m)	homeless person
offrir	to offer
donner	to give
triste / malheureux/euse	unhappy / sad
gentillesse (f)	kindness
utile	useful
soutenir	to support
être conscient(e) de	to be aware of
soigner	to care for
accueillir	to welcome

Using indirect object pronouns

Grammar page 92

te to you
me to me   **indirect object pronouns**   lui to him / her
nous to us   vous to you   leur to them

You use these to replace a noun with à in front of it to say 'to me', 'to him', 'to them', etc.

Remember that these words come **before** the verb (and, in the perfect tense, before the part of avoir).

Je leur explique le problème.
I explain the problem to them.
Je leur ai expliqué le problème.
I explained the problem to them.

Worked example

Read what Sandrine says about helping others and answer the questions in English.

> À mon avis, il est important d'aider les autres, même si ce n'est pas un grand geste. Moi, j'écoute les problèmes de mes copains et je crois que je leur offre de bons conseils. De plus, j'aide mes parents en faisant le ménage et je donne un coup de main à mon petit frère quand il a des difficultés avec ses devoirs.
>
> Néanmoins, moi aussi j'ai besoin d'aide de temps en temps. Mes parents me donnent de l'argent quand je n'en ai plus et mon petit frère m'a aidé la semaine dernière quand je ne pouvais pas faire marcher mon portable.
>
> À l'avenir, je vais faire du travail bénévole dans un logement de sans-abri en ville car j'aimerais faire une différence dans la vie des autres.

1   What does Sandrine offer to her friends?
(1 mark)

good advice

2   In what two ways does she help her family?
(2 marks)

by doing housework and helping her little brother with his homework

3   Name two ways in which her family has helped her. **(2 marks)**

Her parents give her money when she has none and her brother once fixed her mobile

4   Where is she going to do voluntary work and why? **(2 marks)**

at a shelter for the homeless, to make a difference to other people's lives

Answering questions with more than one mark

You will need to supply at least two pieces of information or details in answers that carry two marks, so make sure you answer them as fully as you can. However, don't give too many alternatives or too much information, especially if you are using reasonable guesses or inference, as you might contradict a correct answer.

Now try this

Réponds aux questions en français.
1 Comment est-ce que tu aides tes copains?
2 À l'avenir, tu voudrais faire du bénévolat?

Charities

You might need to listen to or read passages where the helping is on a more formal basis.

Les organisations caritatives

organisation caritative / charitable (f)	charity
vente de charité (f)	charity sale
au profit de	in aid of
donner	to donate
enrichir	to enrich
sentiment (m)	feeling
besoin (m)	need
avoir besoin de	to need
consacrer du temps	to devote time
solitude (f)	loneliness
manque (m)	lack
espoir (m)	hope

Pronouncing similar words

You will have noticed that many French and English words look the same or very similar but sound rather different.

Check the pronunciation of -tion sounds (e.g. organisation) and the vowel sounds in sentiment, where en sounds more like the English 'on'.

Ici on vend des gâteaux au profit d'une association caritative.

Worked example

LISTENING TRACK 44

Listen to the recording

Listen to Florent talking about his charitable work. Choose the correct answer.

> Je travaille pour une organisation caritative deux fois par semaine, après le collège. Je vais à un refuge pour les animaux abandonnés où je retrouve quelques amis qui font aussi du bénévolat. Je promène les chiens, je donne à manger aux chats et s'il y a d'autres bêtes, comme des ânes ou des chèvres, je les soigne. J'ai le sentiment de faire du bien, ce qui me plaît beaucoup. Jeudi dernier, une jeune fille de 12 ans est venue au refuge pour adopter un animal et je lui ai proposé un adorable petit chien.

1   Florent …
- ☐ **A** has worked for a charity for two years
- ☐ **B** works for a charity before school
- ☐ **C** works for his friends
- ☒ **D** works for a charity twice a week   **(1 mark)**

2   At the animal refuge he …
- ☐ **A** feeds the dogs
- ☐ **B** brushes the cats
- ☒ **C** walks the dogs
- ☐ **D** answers the phone   **(1 mark)**

3   He sometimes looks after …
- ☐ **A** horses
- ☒ **B** goats
- ☐ **C** sheep
- ☐ **D** snakes   **(1 mark)**

4   He recently …
- ☐ **A** looked after a donkey
- ☒ **B** helped a girl to choose a pet
- ☐ **C** took in a stray dog
- ☐ **D** adopted a puppy   **(1 mark)**

Now try this

READING

Lis ce texte et mets une croix ✗ dans chaque case correcte.

> Manrouf aide les sans-abri dans la rue. Il travaille le week-end pour une association caritative avec un petit groupe de bénévoles. On donne des vêtements chauds et des couvertures aux SDF et on aborde d'autres problèmes humains, parce que ces gens défavorisées n'ont jamais assez à manger et qu'ils sont souvent seuls et isolés.

Quels problèmes des sans-abri sont mentionnés dans le texte?
- ☐ **A** la solitude
- ☐ **B** la chaleur
- ☐ **C** la violence
- ☐ **D** le froid
- ☐ **E** la faim
- ☐ **F** le chômage   **(3 marks)**

Training

Whatever job you do, you will need training, so here are some useful words and phrases.

La formation

envoyer	to send
formation (f)	training
entreprise (f)	company
carrière (f)	career
professionnel(le)	professional
renvoyer	to dismiss
stage (m)	work placement
pratiquer	to practise
avoir de la chance	to be lucky
avoir raison	to be right
avoir tort	to be wrong
entretien (m)	interview

venir de + infinitive

venir de = to have just done something
Je viens de passer mon bac.
I have just taken my 'bac'.
Elle vient de rentrer.
She has just come back.
Il vient de le dire.
He has just said so.
Nous venons de le faire.
We've just done it.

Elle vient de passer un entretien.
She has just had an interview.

Worked example

Écris au sujet de la formation que tu vas faire avant de commencer un emploi.

Après avoir fini mes études scolaires, j'espère trouver un emploi dans une banque ou dans un bureau. Je ne voudrais pas aller à la fac car ce serait trop cher. Je sais qu'il y aura une formation mais je viens de faire un stage dans le bureau d'un comptable dans ma région et j'ai déjà appris beaucoup de choses.
…

This is just the first paragraph of this student's answer.

Writing about the future

Even if a question asks you to write about the future, this does not stop you using a variety of tenses.

This student managed to use the present, future, conditional and perfect tenses as well as the more complex venir de + infinitive in just the opening paragraph!

Think of ways that you might use past tenses in your answer to this question. For example, you might refer to past ambitions: J'ai toujours voulu devenir comptable (I've always wanted to be an accountant) or Quand j'étais jeune, je voulais être astronaute, mais … (When I was young, I wanted to be an astronaut, but …).

Now try this

 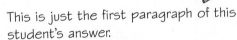

Écoute Samuel qui parle de l'avenir. Mets une croix ✗ dans chaque case correcte.

Listen to the recording

1   Où voudrait-il travailler?

☐ **A** dans une banque

☐ **B** dans un bureau de poste

☐ **C** dans un magasin

☐ **D** dans un hôpital   **(1 mark)**

2   Sa formation va durer combien de temps?

☐ **A** quinze ans

☐ **B** cinq ans

☐ **C** six ans

☐ **D** quatre ans   **(1 mark)**

Future professions

These words and phrases will help you describe the profession you'd like to have in the future – or even a dream job!

Les métiers

métier (m)	profession
qualifié(e)	qualified
directeur / directrice	manager
chercher	to look for
suivre	to follow
choisir	to choose
idéal(e)	ideal
carrière (f)	career
trouver	to find
secteur (m)	sector / field
avoir envie de	to want to
le pour et le contre (m)	pros and cons

Comparing jobs

If you want to say that you like or prefer one profession rather than another, you can use plus / moins ... que (more / less ... than) with an adjective:

Être comptable est plus sécurisant qu'être musicien.

Being an accountant is more secure than being a musician.

Or meilleur / pire ... que (better / worse ... than):

Le métier de médecin est meilleur que celui de facteur.

Being a doctor is better than being a postman.

When talking about professions, you might want to stress the best thing about them:

La meilleure chose, c'est le salaire.

The best thing is the salary.

Le plus important, c'est de gagner beaucoup.
The most important thing is to earn well.

EXAM ALERT!

Even when you are just looking for one-word answers in a listening task, you still need to listen to everything that is said. Try to get into the habit of working out which parts of what you hear are not strictly relevant to the answer for which you are listening closely.

Worked example

Listen to these French teenagers talking about their future professions. Put the number in the box that describes the job sector mentioned. **(3 marks)**

Listen to the recording

> In this particular example, it is the last word that gives you the answer: loisirs, médias and restauration.

1 J'aimerais suivre une carrière dans le secteur des loisirs.

2 Moi, je vais trouver un métier dans le domaine des médias.

3 Quant à moi, c'est dans la restauration.

3	food
☐	IT
☐	science
1	leisure
☐	medicine
2	media

Now try this

Read this text adapted from *Le Petit Prince* by Antoine de Saint-Exupéry.

> C'est ainsi que j'ai abandonné, à l'âge de six ans, une magnifique carrière de peintre. J'ai donc dû choisir un autre métier et j'ai appris à piloter des avions. J'ai volé un peu partout dans le monde.

Which two jobs are mentioned?

(2 marks)

Sporting events

Les évènements sportifs

un évènement sportif (m)	sporting event
Jeux Olympiques / JO (mpl)	Olympic Games
Tour de France (m)	Tour de France (cycle race)
tel(le) que	such as
unir	to unite
encourager	to encourage
touriste (m/f)	tourist
créer	to create
permettre	to allow
individu (m)	individual (person)

Infinitive or subjunctive?

After expressions like il faut (it is necessary / you must), vouloir (to want) or avant (before), you often use an infinitive:

Il faut faire du sport.	You must do sport.
Avant de faire du sport ...	Before doing sport ...
Je veux voir la Coupe du monde.	I want to watch the World Cup.

However, these expressions can also be followed by que and a verb in the subjunctive. You haven't learned this, but you might see it in advanced texts. For example:

Il faut que j'aille au centre sportif.
I must go to the sports centre.

Worked example

Réponds aux questions en français.   **(24 marks)**

1 Décris-moi la photo.

Sur la photo il y a un grand stade de foot. C'est peut-être un match de la Coupe du monde car il y a beaucoup de spectateurs. Le match a lieu le soir et tout le monde s'y intéresse.

2 Je pense que regarder le foot à la télé décourage la participation. Quelle est ton opinion?

Je ne suis pas d'accord. À mon avis, je crois que si on regarde des matchs passionnants à la télé, on va avoir envie de jouer soi-même. Par contre, aller au stade coûte cher, alors pourquoi ne pas regarder des matchs à la maison?

3 Parle-moi d'un événement sportif auquel tu as assisté.

La semaine dernière je suis allé regarder un match de foot au stade de Liverpool car à mon avis, cette équipe est la meilleure du monde. On a gagné 4 à 1 contre Manchester City et c'était vraiment génial.

4 Tu vas regarder les prochains Jeux Olympiques?

Je ne m'intéresse pas à tous les sports olympiques, mais j'adore regarder l'athlétisme et je pense que les athlètes comme Usain Bolt montrent ce qui est possible sans prendre de drogues. Alors, oui, je vais regarder les prochains Jeux Olympiques.

5 Je dis qu'il est ridicule d'encourager la compétition sportive. Quel est ton avis?

Je ne suis pas sûr. Il y a du pour et du contre. Si on encourage la compétition, les joueurs apprennent à mieux jouer mais pour ceux qui ne sont pas forts, ça pourrait être difficile.

EXAM ALERT!

Remember to practise useful responses for the start of your answers: **Je suis d'accord** (I agree); **Je ne suis pas d'accord** (I don't agree); **C'est juste** (That's right); **Vous avez raison** (You're right).

Now try this

Un magazine français cherche des articles sur les évènements sportifs internationaux pour son site Internet. Écrivez un article intéressant sur un événement sportif que vous avez vu.

Mentionnez: • où et quand il s'est passé   • votre opinion sur ce type d'événement
             • ce que vous en pensez   • un événement auquel vous aimeriez assister à l'avenir

Écrivez 130–150 mots environ en français.   **(28 marks)**

Music events

Not all music-lovers can attend music festivals. If you hear or read about them in the exam, be prepared to select specific details or give a general understanding of the meaning of the passages.

La musique

festival de musique (m)	music festival
concert (m)	concert
Il s'agit de …	It's a matter / question of …
J'estime / Je crois / Je pense que …	I feel / believe / think that …
Je suis persuadé(e) que …	I am convinced that …
Je trouve que …	I find that …
bienfait (m)	benefit
valeur (f)	value
carnaval (m)	carnival
musicien(ne)	musician
orchestre (m)	orchestra
groupe (m)	group / band

Perfect, present and near future tenses

Even when you are asked to write in the past, it's possible to introduce other tenses into your written work.

Use these three tenses as much as you can. This table shows five verbs you can fit into almost any speaking or writing task.

present	perfect	near future
je vais	je suis allé(e)	je vais aller
je fais	j'ai fait	je vais faire
je mange	j'ai mangé	je vais manger
je bois	j'ai bu	je vais boire
je visite	j'ai visité	je vais visiter

Sur cette photo, on voit un groupe qui joue en plein air.

Worked example

Écris un email à ton ami(e) français(e) sur une visite récente à un festival de musique.

Mentionne:
• où et quand ça s'est passé
• ce que tu as fait
• ton opinion sur le festival
• tes projets futurs.

Écris 80–90 mots environ en français. **(20 marks)**

Le week-end dernier, je suis allée à un festival de musique à Londres avec ma meilleure copine. Le festival a lieu chaque année dans un parc au centre-ville et il est bien connu. Nous y sommes arrivées tôt et nous avons pu trouver deux places près de la scène. Avant le concert nous avons mangé un sandwich. Les groupes étaient fantastiques et nous nous sommes bien amusées. Moi, j'ai chanté et Annie a dansé!

L'année prochaine, je vais voir un concert de danse folklorique en Bretagne!

And here she has used the near future tense, too.

 EXAM ALERT!

You must cover all four points of the question but you don't have to give equal amounts of space to them all.

 This student has used past tenses from the table above.
Here she uses the present tense.

Now try this

Réponds aux questions en français.
1 Quels sont les avantages d'aller à un festival de musique?
2 Tu préfères des concerts de musique pop ou classique? Pourquoi?

Being green

We can all do our bit to look after the environment. What do you do to be green?

Être écolo

écolo(gique)	green / ecological / environmentally friendly
préoccuper	to preoccupy
réutiliser	to reuse
recycler	to recycle
économiser	to save
eau (f)	water
déchets (mpl)	rubbish
poubelle (f)	dustbin / wastebin
papier (m)	paper
carton (m)	cardboard
plastique (m)	plastic
métal (m)	metal
trier	to sort / separate (rubbish)
verre (m)	glass

The conditional of pouvoir and devoir

To say what you might do or should do, you can use the conditional tense of these two verbs.

You will probably want to use them in one of three forms:

je pourrais I could / might	je devrais I should
on pourrait you / we / people could / might	on devrait you / we / people should
nous pourrions we could / might	nous devrions we should

In all cases they will be followed by an infinitive:

Je pourrais recycler plus.
I could do more recycling.

On devrait se déplacer partout en vélo.

Worked example

 READING

> **Sacha** Je suis très écolo. Je recycle tout et je ne voyage jamais en avion. Mon père vient d'acheter une voiture électrique, alors nous sommes vraiment une famille verte!
>
> **Yannick** Je dois dire que je suis assez paresseux en ce qui concerne le recyclage. Naturellement je trie les déchets mais je recycle seulement les journaux. Je devrais faire plus.
>
> **Nicolas** À l'école c'est un scandale. On ne recycle rien et je viens de me plaindre au directeur mais il n'a pas agi. Mes copains et moi allons essayer d'économiser l'électricité dès aujourd'hui.

Qui parle? Écris S (Sacha), Y (Yannick) ou N (Nicolas).   **(5 marks)**

1 Je ne fais pas assez d'efforts. Y

2 Je vais éteindre la lumière à la fin de chaque cours. N

3 Je recycle beaucoup. S

4 Je ne recycle que le papier. Y

5 Je suis étonné de l'attitude du principal. N

Inferences and deductions

In some reading tasks you might need to work out implied meaning in order to answer a question.

For example, in statement 2 neither the word éteindre or lumière appear in the text, so you must work out that since Nicolas is going to start saving electricity at school it is likely that he will turn off lights.

Likewise, in statement 5 Nicolas thinks the lack of recycling in his school is scandalous and he has had no response to his complaint to the head teacher, so he is likely to be étonné par l'attitude du principal (astonished by the head's attitude).

Now try this

  SPEAKING

Réponds aux questions en français.
1 Tu es écolo?
2 Qu'est-ce que tu as fait récemment pour sauvegarder l'environnement?

Protecting the environment

More than ever before, protecting the environment is crucial, so expect it to be a topic of which you need to be aware.

Protéger l'environnement

environnement (m)	environment
sauver	to save
inondation (f)	flood
planète (f)	planet
terre (f)	earth
pollution (f)	pollution
changement climatique (m)	climate change
réchauffement (m)	warming
espèce (f)	species
déforestation (f)	deforestation
bois (m)	wood
couche d'ozone (f)	ozone layer
effet de serre (m)	greenhouse effect
éviter	to avoid
chauffage central (m)	central heating

Using si

There is a sequence of tenses after si (if) and you will need to be able to recognise them and perhaps use them, too.

si + the present + the future

Si on réduit la pollution, on pourra sauver la planète. If we reduce pollution, we will be able to save the planet.

si + the imperfect + the conditional

Si on pouvait protéger les forêts, il y aurait plus d'habitats pour les animaux sauvages. If we could protect the forests, there would be more habitats for wild animals.

Il faut protéger les animaux en danger de disparition.

Learning vocabulary

There are many skills that can help you solve problems in reading texts but you will always need to learn vocabulary. Try to learn words in context and use them actively in your spoken and written French. If you use them yourself, you might be surprised how many of them you remember and recognise.

Worked example

Read this article about protecting the environment. Answer the questions in English.

> Tout le monde devrait agir. Si on baisse le chauffage central, on pourra réduire la consommation d'énergie. On fera aussi des économies en laissant la voiture au parking pour les trajets courts.
>
> Même de petits gestes pourraient faire une différence, mais au niveau gouvernemental il faut que les pays s'accordent pour qu'on puisse arrêter le réchauffement de la planète qui provoque le changement climatique.

1 What does the article suggest in its first sentence? **(1 mark)**

that everyone should act

For these questions you would need to know **agir** (to act), **chauffage central** (central heating), **baisser** (to lower), **trajet** (journey) and **réchauffement** (warming).

2 What two ways of making savings are suggested? **(2 marks)**

turning central heating down and not using the car for short journeys

3 According to the article, what should happen at an international level? **(1 mark)**

governments must agree to stop global warming.

Now try this

Réponds aux questions en français.
1 Que fais-tu pour sauvegarder l'environnement?
2 Qu'est-ce que tu vas faire pour protéger la planète?

Environmental issues

Some environmental issues are not just local or regional and some issues are not just environmental. You might need to talk about any of them so be prepared!

Les problèmes mondiaux

charbon (m)	coal
énergie renouvelable (f)	renewable energy
pétrole (m)	oil
trou (m)	hole
augmenter	to increase
propre	clean
usine (f)	factory
grave	serious
sale	dirty
jeter	to throw (away)
construire	to build
produits bio	green products
gaspiller	to waste
gaz d'échappement (m)	exhaust fumes
circulation (f)	traffic

Pluperfect tense

Grammar page 105

Formed by the imperfect form of avoir / être + the past participle.

Le gouvernement avait agi …
The government had acted …

j'avais		
tu avais	} fait	had done
il / elle / on avait		

j'étais		
tu étais	} rentré(e)(s)	had returned
il / elle / on était		

Si on avait agi plus tôt, peut-être qu'il n'y aurait pas tant de réchauffement de la terre.
If we had acted earlier, perhaps there wouldn't be so much global warming.

Worked example

SPEAKING

Quels sont les problèmes les plus graves pour la planète, à ton avis?

> À mon avis, le plus grand problème, c'est le réchauffement de la planète. Une des causes principales est la pollution causée par les usines et les voitures.

Aiming higher

> Si on n'arrête pas le réchauffement de la planète, il y aura des conséquences catastrophiques. Si le gouvernement avait agi plus tôt, ce ne serait pas si grave. Moi, j'ai envoyé des emails au gouvernement. Au collège, nous avons encouragé les élèves à utiliser les transports en commun au lieu de venir au collège en voiture.

Aiming higher

To aim for a higher level like the second example, include:
- ✓ a **pluperfect** tense verb: le gouvernement avait agi (the government had acted)
- ✓ a **perfect** tense verb: j'ai envoyé (I sent)
- ✓ a **conditional** verb: ce ne serait pas (it would not be)
- ✓ a **future** tense verb: il y aura (there will be)
- ✓ a **variety** of structures, e.g. au lieu de + infinitive (instead of doing something).

Now try this

LISTENING TRACK 47

Listen to the recording

Écoute ces jeunes qui parlent des problèmes environnementaux. Complète les phrases.

1 Annie pense que le problème le plus grave, c'est …
- ☐ **A** le bruit
- ☐ **B** la circulation
- ☐ **C** la pollution
- ☐ **D** les ordures   **(1 mark)**

2 Selon Paul, le problème le plus sérieux, c'est qu'il y a …
- ☐ **A** trop de bruit
- ☐ **B** trop de véhicules
- ☐ **C** trop de pollution
- ☐ **D** trop de gens   **(1 mark)**

Natural resources

Natural resources are precious and you may need to discuss ways of saving them.

Les ressources naturelles

réfléchir	to think
empreinte carbone (f)	carbon footprint
pauvre	poor
exploiter	to exploit
éteindre	to switch / turn off
robinet (m)	tap
fermer	to shut down / close / turn off
partager	to share
panneaux solaires (mpl)	solar panels
récupérer	to collect
arroser	to water
sécheresse (f)	drought

The passive

Grammar page 108

You might want to use the passive to talk about things that are done (to someone / something). You use être in whichever tense you need, followed by a past participle (which must agree with the subject).

Le coton est cultivé en Afrique.
Cotton is grown in Africa.
Les produits sont transportés en camion.
The products are transported by lorry.
Les ouvriers ont été exploités.
Workers have been exploited.

Le coton est toujours récolté à la main dans certaines régions d'Afrique.

Worked example

READING

Translate this passage into English.   **(7 marks)**

> Dans certains pays africains, la sécheresse est un problème grave et on manque d'eau. Il pleut rarement et il fait toujours très chaud. L'année dernière, j'ai visité le Burkina Faso avec un groupe scolaire et nous avons vu les conditions de vie difficiles des habitants. Après être rentrés en France, mes amis et moi avons essayé d'économiser l'eau.

In certain African countries drought is a serious problem and people lack water. It rarely rains and it's always very hot. Last year I visited Burkina Faso with a school group and we saw the inhabitants' difficult living conditions. Since coming home to France my friends and I have tried to save water.

EXAM ALERT!

Exam tips for translating into English:

- Take care with **on** in French. It can sound clumsy to translate it as 'one' in English. It is usually best translated as 'we', 'you' or 'people'.

- Make sure you put adjectives in the right position when you translate them – they are usually after the noun in French (**pays africains, groupe scolaire, conditions difficiles**).

- Make sure you use the right subject for the verb – it's often **je** but not always (**nous avons vu** – we saw).

- Remember that **il** doesn't always mean 'he'. It can also mean 'it' (**il pleut, il faut**).

Now try this

LISTENING TRACK 48

What ideas for saving natural resources are suggested?
Put a cross ✗ by the correct answers.

☐ **A** collecting rain water
☐ **B** using solar panels
☐ **C** taking showers rather than baths
☐ **D** turning the tap off when brushing teeth
☐ **E** not buying bottled water
☐ **F** turning lights off   **(3 marks)**

Listen to the recording

World problems

Natural disasters and man-made issues could both figure in your exams, so be prepared for them.

Les grandes questions

guerre (f)	war
feu (m)	fire
inondation (f)	flood
marée (f)	tide
mer (f)	sea
paix (f)	peace
pauvreté (f)	poverty
vent (m)	wind
vague (f)	wave
détruire	to destroy
surpeuplé(e)	overpopulated
tuer	to kill
blesser	to injure
dégâts (mpl)	damage
tremblement de terre (m)	earthquake

Prepositions

Grammar page 110

par	by
avec	with
pour	for
sans	without
jusqu'à	until
parmi	among
en dehors de	outside

par un incendie
by a fire

au milieu de la mer
in the middle of the sea

Worked example

Match the news reports to the English headlines.
(5 marks)

1 Certains pays mondiaux sont ravagés par des conflits, ce qui provoque une crise migratoire.
2 Des milliers de personnes ont été tuées par un tremblement de terre en Asie.
3 Des vents forts ont causé la destruction de centaines d'hectares de paysages agricoles en Espagne.
4 Suite à la marée haute, plusieurs villages ont été inondés aux Caraïbes.
5 Un incendie au centre-ville de Lorient a fait des dégâts importants.

Think of synonyms or alternatives for words in the text: a **tremblement de terre** (earthquake) is a natural disaster and **tuées** means 'killed', which relates to 'deaths'.

There may be more than one clue, even in a short passage: here **vents**, **destruction**, **agricoles** (meaning 'farming').

- 5 Fire causes damage
- 2 Deaths following natural disaster
- ☐ Volcanic eruption in Asia causes havoc
- 1 War leading to problems in several countries
- 3 Winds destroy farmland
- 4 High tide causes floods
- ☐ Heavy snow brings down power lines

Now try this

TRACK 49

Écoute ces jeunes qui parlent de problèmes mondiaux.
Mets une croix ✗ dans chaque case correcte.

Listen to the recording

1 Marie décrit …
- ☐ **A** une marée noire
- ☐ **B** une inondation
- ☐ **C** un incendie **(1 mark)**

2 Lucas parle …
- ☐ **A** de la pauvreté
- ☐ **B** des gaz d'échappement
- ☐ **C** du déboisement **(1 mark)**

3 Shona fait mention …
- ☐ **A** d'un tremblement de terre
- ☐ **B** des sans-abri
- ☐ **C** du changement climatique **(1 mark)**

Articles 1

Here you will revise how to say 'the', and 'a' or 'some', in French.

Gender

Every French noun has a gender.
All people, places or things are either masculine (m) or feminine (f).

masculine: le livre (m)   the book
feminine: la table (f)   the table

The words for 'the' and 'a / some' are:

	singular		plural	
	masc	fem	masc	fem
the	le	la	les	les
a / some	un	une	des	des

le livre   the book   un livre   a book
les livres   the books   des livres   some
                                           books

Le and la both become l' if the noun begins with a vowel or silent h:
l'hôpital (m) – hospital
l'église (f) – church

Plurals

Most French nouns make the plural by adding -s but it is not pronounced.

le chat   the cat   ➡   les chats   the cats

- Nouns with the following endings add -x in the plural, and sometimes other letters change too

  -ail   travail   ➡   travaux   works
  -al   animal   ➡   animaux   animals
  -eau   bureau   ➡   bureaux   offices
  -eu   jeu   ➡   jeux   games

- Some nouns that end in -ou add -x in the plural instead of -s. These include bijou, chou, genou, hibou and caillou.

- Nouns ending in -x, -z or -s don't change:

  un os   a bone   deux os   two bones
  un nez   a nose   deux nez   two noses

Masculine or feminine?

If you don't know the gender of a word, you can look it up in a dictionary or on the internet, but here are some tips.

Masculine nouns

male people:	l'homme	the man
male animals:	le chat	the cat
days of the week:	le lundi	Monday
months:	juillet	July
seasons:	l'été	the summer

Most nouns that end in:

-age   le village   the village
-er   le boulanger   the baker
-eau   le bureau   the office

(except eau (f) water)

Feminine nouns

female people: la fille   the girl
female animals: la chatte   the female cat
countries that end in -e: la France
rivers that end in -e: la Seine
(NB an exception is le Rhône)

Most nouns that end in:

-e   la voiture   the car
-ée   une araignée   a spider

All nouns that end in -sion or -tion:

une émission   a programme
la destination   the destination

All nouns ending in -té:

la quantité   the quantity
une identité   an identity

Now try this

Le, la, l' or les? Fill in the missing articles.

.... garçon   .... mère   .... étudiants   .... printemps

.... Espagne   .... Loire   .... condition   .... bleu

.... décision   .... père   .... garage   .... plage

Always try to learn the le or la when you learn a new word.

Articles 2

It is crucial that you can use du, de la, de l' or des to say 'some', and au, à la, à l' or aux to say 'to the'.

How to say 'some'

masculine	feminine	beginning with vowel or silent h	plural
du	de la	de l'	des

le lait   milk   ➡ du lait   some milk

la confiture   jam   ➡ de la confiture   some jam

l'essence   petrol   ➡ de l'essence   some petrol

les animaux   animals   ➡ des animaux   some animals

But after the negative you only use de / d':

Je n'ai pas de pain.   I haven't any bread.

Il n'a pas d'œufs.
He hasn't any eggs.

Using 'some' and 'any'

- We don't always need to use 'some' in English. Sometimes we miss it out altogether, but you **have** to use it in French:

  Veux-tu du lait ou du café?
  Do you want milk or coffee?

- And where we use 'any' in a question in English, French uses 'some':

  Avez-vous des boissons?
  Have you got any drinks?
  Avez-vous du pain?
  Have you got any bread?

How to say 'to the'

masculine	feminine	beginning with vowel or silent h	plural
au	à la	à l'	aux

au bureau   to the office

à la mairie   to the town hall

à l'école   to (the) school

aux toilettes   to the toilets

On va au collège.

Now try this

1 How would you tell someone how to go to these places using **aller**? For example, **Allez au carrefour**.

(a) .... parking (m)

(b) .... toilettes (pl)

(c) .... gare (f)

(d) .... arrêt de bus (m)

(e) .... feux (pl)

(f) .... supermarché (m)

(g) .... château (m)

(h) .... tour Eiffel (f)

2 Translate these phrases into French.

(a)   I want some bread.

(b)   Have you got any milk?

(c)   He hasn't got any petrol.

(d)   I'm going to school.

(e)   Are you going to the town hall?

(f)   He's going to the toilets.

You have all the vocabulary you need on this page.

Adjectives

When using adjectives, you have to think about **agreement** and **position**.

Regular adjectives

Adjectives must agree with the noun they are describing. Regular adjectives add -e for feminine, -s for masculine plural and -es for feminine plural:

singular		plural	
masc	fem	masc	fem
grand	grande	grands	grandes
petit	petite	petits	petites

Some adjectives already end in -e so don't add another:

masc	fem	masc plural	fem plural
timide	timide	timides	timides

And some are a little less regular:

masc	fem	masc plural	fem plural	
long	longue	longs	longues	long
blanc	blanche	blancs	blanches	white
sec	sèche	secs	sèches	dry

A very few adjectives don't change at all e.g:
marron   chestnut
orange   orange

Irregular adjectives

Adjectives that end in -x change their ending to -se in the feminine:

singular		plural	
masc	fem	masc	fem
sérieux	sérieuse	sérieux	sérieuses

Other adjectives like sérieux:
dangereux   dangerous
merveilleux   marvellous
heureux   happy

Adjectives that end in -f change to -ve in the feminine:

singular		plural	
masc	fem	masc	fem
actif	active	actifs	actives

Other adjectives like actif:
sportif   sporty   positif   positive

Adjectives which end in -er change to -ère in the feminine:
premier ➡ première   first
dernier ➡ dernière   last

Adjectives which end in -on, -en or -il double the consonant before adding -e: in the feminine:
mignon ➡ mignonne   nice
gentil ➡ gentille   kind

Position of adjectives

Most adjectives come **after** the noun:
les yeux bleus   les cheveux longs

There are a few common adjectives which come **in front of** the noun:

grand	big	vieux / vieille	old
petit	small	nouveau / nouvelle	new
joli	pretty	meilleur	best

mon meilleur ami
my best friend

ma meilleure amie
my best friend

Now try this

Translate these sentences and phrases into French.
1 a little black dog
2 last week
3 My little brother is very active.
4 My best friend (f) is small and shy.
5 Her brother is tall, sporty but a bit serious.

Possessives

Possessives are used to say 'my', 'your', 'our', etc. They change according to gender and number.

Possessive adjectives

In French the possessive adjective ('my, 'your', etc.) changes to agree with the **gender** and **number** of the noun that follows. There are usually three different words, according to whether the noun is masculine or feminine, singular or plural.

mon frère — my brother (masculine)

ma sœur — my sister (feminine)

mes parents — my parents (plural)

Remember, son / sa / ses mean both 'his' and 'her'.

> **Be careful!** You use mon, ton, son with a feminine noun if it begins with a vowel. For example: mon ami, mon amie – my friend.

masc	fem	plural	
mon	ma	mes	**my**

masc	fem	plural	
son	sa	ses	**his / her**

mon jean   ma veste   mes baskets   son pantalon   sa chemise   ses chaussures

masc	fem	plural	
ton	ta	tes	**your**

ton portable   ta console de jeux   tes jeux

masc	fem	plural	
votre	votre	vos	**your**

votre frère   votre sœur   vos parents

masc	fem	plural	
notre	notre	nos	**our**

notre chat   notre chatte   nos chatons

masc	fem	plural	
leur	leur	leurs	**their**

leur fils   leur fille   leurs enfants

Possessive pronouns

To say, 'It's mine' or 'They're mine', use the following:

masc singular	C'est le mien.	masc plural	Ce sont les miens.
fem singular	C'est la mienne.	fem plural	Ce sont les miennes.

Now try this

Write these in French.

1 my brother ....

2 his friend (m) ....

3 his friends (m and f) ....

4 his bag ....

5 my sister ....

6 her friend (f) ....

7 her friends (m and f) ....

8 her mobile ....

9 my parents ....

10 their friend (m) ....

11 their friends (m and f) ....

12 their car ....

Comparisons

In order to aim for a high grade, you need to be able to use some complex structures such as comparatives and superlatives.

Comparative

You use the **comparative** when you are comparing two things: my house is **taller**.

• Form the comparative by putting plus (more) or moins (less) in front of the adjective.

The adjectives have to agree with the noun they are describing.

Mon frère est grand. Simon est plus grand.	My brother is tall. Simon is taller.
Ma sœur est petite. Nathalie est plus petite.	My sister is small. Nathalie is smaller.

To compare two things:

(taller) than = plus (grand) que

Nathan est plus grand que Tom.   Nathan is taller than Tom.

(smaller) than = moins (grand) que

Ambre est moins grande que sa sœur.   Ambre is smaller than her sister.

as (tall) as = aussi (grand) que

Il est aussi grand que son père.   He is as tall as his father.

Nathan est plus grand que Tom.

Superlative

You use the **superlative** when you are comparing more than two things: my house is **the biggest**.

• Form the superlative by adding the definite article le / la / les as well as plus:

le plus grand / la plus grande / les plus grand(e)s	the biggest
le livre le plus intéressant	the most interesting book
la matière la plus ennuyeuse	the most boring subject

Exceptions to the rule

adjective		comparative		superlative	
bon / bonne	good	meilleur(e)	better	le meilleur / la meilleure	the best
mauvais(e)	bad	pire	worse	le / la pire	the worst

Le film est meilleur que le livre.   The film is better than the book.

le meilleur restaurant   the best restaurant

Now try this

Complete the sentences with the comparative or superlative.

1 L'Everest est la montagne .... du monde. (haut) (*highest*)

2 La veste est .... que la robe. (+ cher) (*more expensive*)

3 Demain il fera .... qu'aujourd'hui. (+ beau) (*nicer*)

4 .... solution est de prendre le train. (bon) (*the best*)

5 Julie est .... que Fabien. (− intelligent) (*less intelligent*)

6 Le TGV est le train .... (rapide) (*the quickest*)

Other adjectives and pronouns

Here you will revise demonstrative and interrogative adjectives and pronouns. Like le, la and les, they have to agree with the noun they are referring to.

Demonstrative adjectives

To say 'this / that', 'these / those':

masc sing	fem sing	masc plural	fem plural
ce	cette	ces	ces

ce livre	this / that book
cette fille	this / that girl
ces livres	these / those books
ces filles	these / those girls

You use cet in front of a masculine noun that begins with a vowel or silent h:

cet hôtel   cet espace

Interrogative adjectives

To ask 'which?':

masc sing	fem sing	masc plural	fem plural
quel	quelle	quels	quelles

Quel enfant?	Which child?
Quelle femme?	Which lady?
Quels garçons?	Which boys?
Quelles filles?	Which girls?

Indefinite adjectives

The words autre (other) and quelque (some) are examples of another important group of adjectives that also agree with the word they describe:

mon autre frère	my other brother
ses autres chaussures	her other shoes
pendant quelque temps	for some time
avec quelques amis	with some friends

This one, that one

These are pronouns. They replace the noun and answer the question, for example: Which book? This one / That one.

masc sing	fem sing	masc plural	fem plural
celui-ci	celle-ci	ceux-ci	celles-ci
celui-là	celle-là	ceux-là	celles-là

ci means 'here', so celui-ci means 'this one (here)'.

là means 'there', so celui-là means 'that one (there)'.

Which one?

These pronouns ask the question 'which one?': lequel?

They agree with the noun they represent.

masc sing	fem sing	masc plural	fem plural
lequel?	laquelle?	lesquels?	lesquelles?

Un livre? Lequel?	A book? Which one?
Ta jupe? Laquelle?	Your skirt? Which one?
Les films? Lesquels?	The films? Which ones?
Les chaussures? Lesquelles?	The shoes? Which ones?

Now try this

Fill in the missing words.

Example:
Je veux **ce** stylo. – I want this pen.
Lequel? – Which one?
Celui-ci. – This one.

1 Noé veut .... veste.
.... (Which one?)
.... (This one.)

2 Je préfère .... portable.
.... (Which one?)
.... (That one.)

3 Manon a choisi .... chaussures.
.... (Which ones?)
.... (These.)

4 Son frère achète .... jeux.
.... (Which ones?)
.... (Those.)

5 On regarde .... film ce soir?
.... (Which one?)
.... (That one.)

Adverbs

An adverb is a word that 'describes' a verb (hence the name). It tells you **how** an action is done: quickly, slowly, loudly, etc.

Using and forming adverbs

You use an adverb when you want to bring your work to life, give more detail and explain or describe how something is done.

In English, a lot of adverbs end in -ly.

In French, a lot of adverbs end in -ment.

• You can form adverbs by adding -ment to the feminine form of an adjective.

heureux ➡ heureuse + -ment ➡
  heureusement   fortunately

doux ➡ douce + -ment ➡
  doucement   quietly

Comparative and superlative of adverbs

Une voiture va vite, un train va plus vite mais un avion va le plus vite.

A car goes fast, a train goes faster but a plane goes fastest.

Some adverbs don't follow this pattern:
vrai ➡ vraiment   really
absolu ➡ absolument   absolutely

Adverbs of time

Some adverbs are useful for a time line when narrating a sequence of events:

d'abord / au début	at the beginning
puis / ensuite / alors	then
maintenant	now
finalement	finally
à l'avenir	in the future
aujourd'hui	today
demain	tomorrow

D'abord j'ai joué au basket puis je suis allé à la piscine.

First of all I played basketball, then I went to the pool.

Adverbs of frequency

Other adverbs tell you how often or when:

rarement	rarely
d'habitude	usually
normalement	normally
souvent	often
de temps en temps	from time to time
régulièrement	regularly
quelquefois	sometimes
tout de suite	straight away
immédiatement	immediately
toujours	always

Adverbs of position

au-dessus	above	en bas	down
en dessous	below	en haut	up
dehors	outside	ici	here
dedans	inside	là-bas	over there
derrière	behind		

Linking adverbs

peut-être	perhaps
par conséquent	as a result
plutôt	rather
probablement	probably
alors	so
seulement	only
en revanche	on the other hand

Now try this

Use as many adverbs as you can to make this passage more interesting.

Notre chat a disparu. Il rentre chaque soir vers six heures. J'ai entendu un bruit. J'ai ouvert la porte et j'ai été surpris de voir Max avec trois petits chatons! Il est entré dans la maison. Max n'est plus Max, mais Maxine!

Object pronouns

You use a pronoun (e.g. it, me, you, them) when you don't want to keep repeating a noun or a name.

Pronouns make your French sound more natural and will help you achieve a higher grade.

Subject and object

The **subject** is the person or thing that is doing the action (verb).

The **object** is the person or thing that is having the action (verb) done to it.

subject	verb	object
Tracey	sends	the email.

subject pronouns		direct object pronouns		indirect object pronouns	
je	I	me	me	me	(to / for) me
tu	you	te	you	te	(to / for) you
il	he / it	le	him / it	lui	(to / for) him / it
elle	she / it	la	her / it	lui	(to / for) her / it
nous	we	nous	us	nous	(to / for) us
vous	you	vous	you	vous	(to / for) you
ils / elles	they	les	them	leur	(to / for) them

Direct object pronouns

In French, the object pronoun comes in front of the verb.

I send it.	Je l'envoie.
He does it.	Il le fait.
We buy them.	Nous les achetons.
They invite us.	Ils nous invitent.

In French, the direct object pronoun 'it' or 'them' is the same as the word for 'the'.

Word order

- In a negative sentence, the pronoun goes after the ne:
  Tu ne la regardes pas?
  Aren't you watching it?
- In the perfect tense, the pronoun comes in front of the **auxiliary** verb (avoir or être):
  Je l'ai déjà regardé(e).   I have already seen it.
  Nous les avons acheté(e)s.   We bought them.

The past participle agrees with the object pronoun, so if the object is feminine or plural the past participle must end in -e, -s or -es.

Indirect object pronouns

You use the indirect object pronoun to replace a noun that has à in front of it.

Sarah envoie un texto à son ami.
Sarah is sending a text to her boyfriend.

Elle lui envoie un texto.
She is sending him a text.

When you have le / la / les and lui / leur in the same sentence, the le / la / les comes first:
Elle le lui envoie.   She sends it to him.
Je le leur ai donné.   I gave it to them.

Now try this

Rewrite the sentences, replacing the object of each sentence with a pronoun.

1 Il a envoyé un message.
2 Je n'ai pas regardé l'émission.
3 Il n'a pas acheté les chaussures.
4 Tu as vu ce film?
5 Sarah a lu ce livre.
6 Mes parents ont acheté la voiture.

More pronouns: y and en

Use y and en in your writing and speaking to demonstrate that you can use a wide range of structures.

y (there)

• You use y to refer to a place which has already been mentioned.

Tu vas à la gare? Oui, j'y vais.   Are you going to the station? Yes, I'm going there.

• You also use it with verbs that take à:

Tu joues au football? Oui, j'y joue.

Do you play football? Yes, I play it.

• y is also used in some common phrases:

il y a   there is / there are   Vas-y!   Go on!

Il y a beaucoup à faire.   There is a lot to do.   Allons-y!   Let's go!

en (of it / of them)

• You use en to replace a noun or du / de la / de l' / des + noun that has already been mentioned.

Tu veux du café? Oui, j'en veux bien.
Do you want some coffee? Yes, I'd like some.

• It is not always translated in English, but you have to include it in French.

Tu manges de la viande? Oui, j'en mange beaucoup.
Do you eat meat? Yes, I eat a lot (of it).

• en is also used with expressions of quantity:

Tu as combien de frères? J'en ai deux.   How many brothers have you got? I've got two (of them).

Tu as acheté des pommes? Oui, j'en ai acheté un kilo.
Did you buy some apples? Yes, I bought a kilo (of them).

• en is also used in the following common phrases:

Qu'est-ce que tu en penses?   What do you think (of it)?

J'en ai marre.   I'm fed up.

Je m'en vais.   I'm going.

Now try this

Rewrite the sentences, replacing the nouns with **y** or **en**.

1 Je suis déjà allé au cinéma.
2 J'ai déjà mangé trop de chips.
3 Je suis allé à Paris hier.
4 Je vais au cinéma de temps en temps.
5 On va souvent au supermarché.
6 Je ne mange jamais de frites.

Other pronouns

Using pronouns in your writing and speaking tasks helps show that you have mastered a wide range of structures.

Relative pronouns qui and que

These are pronouns that relate back to something or someone you have just mentioned.

- Qui (who / which) replaces the **subject** of the sentence. You know this, as you have been using it from the start:

  J'ai un frère qui s'appelle John.
  I have a brother who is called John.

  Ma sœur est la fille qui porte une robe bleue.
  My sister is the girl who is wearing a blue dress.

- Que (whom / which) replaces the **object** of a sentence:

  L'homme que j'ai vu ne portait pas de lunettes.
  The man (whom) I saw didn't wear glasses.

  J'ai acheté le pantalon que j'ai trouvé sur Internet.
  I bought the trousers (which) I found on the internet.

  C'était la même personne que j'avais vue en ville.
  It was the same person (that) I had seen in town.

Emphatic / disjunctive pronouns

These are: moi me, toi you, lui him / it, elle her / it, nous us, vous you, eux them (m), elles them (f).

They are used:

- after **prepositions**: avec moi with me   pour elle for her
- for **emphasis**: Lui, il est paresseux. Him, he's lazy.
- to form a **double subject**: Ma sœur et moi allons en ville. My sister and I are going to town.

où and dont

- Où (where) refers back to a place that has been mentioned previously or is known:

  La ville où j'ai passé mes vacances est vraiment belle.
  The town where I spent my holiday is really beautiful.

  La maison où il habite est très grande.
  The house where he lives is very big.

- Dont means 'whose / of whom / about whom':

  Le monsieur dont j'ai trouvé les lunettes ...
  The gentleman whose glasses I found ...

  La fille dont on a déjà parlé ...
  The girl whom we have already talked about ...

  Le film dont j'ai vu la bande-annonce ...
  The film whose trailer I saw ...

Now try this

Complete these sentences with **qui, que, où** or **dont**.

1 Mon ami .... s'appelle Bruno est fana de football.
2 L'émission .... j'ai vue hier n'était pas passionnante.
3 Le quartier .... ils habitent est vraiment calme.
4 C'est le prof .... je vous ai déjà parlé.
5 Elle a une sœur .... est prof.
6 J'ai accepté le stage .... mon prof m'a proposé.

Present tense: -er verbs

Good news! Most French verbs are -er verbs, and most -er verbs are regular.

Forming the present tense of -er verbs

The endings are:

je	-e	nous	-ons
tu	-es	vous	-ez
il / elle	-e	ils / elles	-ent

Remember that the endings -e, -es and -ent all sound the same when you say these words.

jouer   to play

I play	je joue	we play	nous jouons
you play	tu joues	you play	vous jouez
he / she / one plays	il / elle / on joue	they play	ils / elles jouent

New verbs describing actions connected with technology are all -er verbs:
télécharger (to download)
tchatter (to chat)
bloguer (to blog)

Some common -er verbs

aider	to help	donner	to give	quitter	to leave
aimer	to like	écouter	to listen	rester	to stay
arriver	to arrive	entrer	to enter	téléphoner	to telephone
bavarder	to chat	habiter	to live	travailler	to work
décider	to decide	manger	to eat	trouver	to find
détester	to hate	penser	to think	visiter	to visit

Some -er verbs have spelling changes. These are usually to make them easier to pronounce:

- Verbs that end in -ger in the infinitive (manger, nager, plonger) add -e in the nous form to keep the 'g' sound soft: nous mangeons.
- Verbs that end in -ler and -ter in the infinitive (appeler and jeter) double the l or t in the singular je, tu, il / elle / on and in the third person plural: je m'appelle, je jette.
- Verbs that end in -yer in the infinitive (payer and envoyer) change the y to i in the singular je, tu, il / elle / on and in the third person plural: j'envoie, elle paie.
- Some verbs change e or é to è, for example acheter ➡ j'achète; se lever ➡ je me lève; préférer ➡ je préfère. The change occurs in the je, tu, il / elle / on and ils / elles forms but the nous and vous forms revert to the stem:

je préfère	nous préférons
tu préfères	vous préférez
il / elle / on préfère	ils / elles préfèrent

Now try this

Complete the passage with the correct parts of the verbs in brackets.

Je (s'appeler) Lou. J'ai une sœur qui (s'appeler) Marina et qui (jouer) au tennis. Je (préférer) faire de la danse. Je (chanter) et je (jouer) de la guitare. Le soir nous (rentrer) à cinq heures et nous (manger) un casse-croûte. Puis je (tchatter) avec mes amis, et j'(écouter) de la musique. Quelquefois mon frère et moi (jouer) à der jeux vidéo ou (télécharger) un film à regarder plus tard.

mon frère et moi = we! Which form are you going to use?

Present tense: -ir and -re verbs

There are two groups of -ir verbs: those that take -ss in the plural forms and those that don't.

-ir verbs that take -ss

finir to finish

je finis	nous finissons
tu finis	vous finissez
il / elle / on finit	ils / elles finissent

Verbs like finir:

choisir to choose

By now you will have noticed that the je, tu and il / elle forms of most verbs sound the same **but** they are not all spelled the same, so be careful when you are writing!

-ir verbs that don't take -ss

partir to leave

je pars	nous partons
tu pars	vous partez
il / elle / on part	ils / elles partent

Verbs like partir:

dormir   to sleep (je dors)

sortir   to go out (je sors)

-ir verbs are sometimes referred to as -s -s -t verbs. Can you see why?

-re verbs

répondre   to reply

je réponds	nous répondons
tu réponds	vous répondez
il / elle / on répond	ils / elles répondent

Verbs like répondre:

attendre	to wait
descendre	to go down
entendre	to hear
perdre	to lose
vendre	to sell

Irregular -re verbs

dire   to say

je dis	nous disons
tu dis	vous dites
il / elle / on dit	ils / elles disent

Verbs like dire:

lire	to read	**but** lisons, lisez, lisent
écrire	to write	**but** écrivons, écrivez, écrivent
boire	to drink	**but** buvons, buvez, boivent

Exceptions

The verb prendre (to take) and related verbs like comprendre (to understand) and apprendre (to learn) are regular except for the nous, vous and ils / elles forms:

je prends	nous prenons
tu prends	vous prenez
il / elle / on prend	ils / elles prennent

Now try this

Complete these sentences with the correct part of the verb in brackets.

1 Le matin, je (sortir) à sept heures et demie.
2 Le mardi, les cours (finir) à cinq heures.
3 Mon copain et moi ne (boire) pas de coca.
4 Le train (partir) à 8h20.
5 Nous (apprendre) l'espagnol.
6 Pendant les vacances, nous (dormir) sous la tente.
7 Mes copains (choisir) des frites.

Je dors sous la tente.

Avoir and être

To have (avoir) and to be (être) are two of the most common verbs used in French.
They are both irregular, so you need to learn their different parts really carefully.

Avoir

j'ai	I have
tu as	you have (informal)
il / elle a	he has
nous avons	we have
vous avez	you have (formal)
ils / elles ont	they have

When to use avoir

In French you use avoir to give your age, or to say that you **have** hunger or fear or cold.

J'ai seize ans.	I am 16 years old.
J'ai faim.	I am hungry.
Il a peur des fantômes.	He is afraid of ghosts.
J'ai froid.	I am cold.

Être

je suis	I am
tu es	you are (informal)
il / elle est	he is
nous sommes	we are
vous êtes	you are (formal)
ils / elles sont	they are

The most common mistake with être is to add it when you are using other verbs. Don't just replace 'am' with suis.

I am talking	je parle
we are going	nous allons

Useful phrases with avoir and être

J'ai trois frères.	I have three brothers.
Vous avez tort.	You're wrong.
J'ai mal à la tête.	I have a headache.
J'ai besoin d'un stylo.	I need a pen.
Je suis anglais(e).	I am English.
La table est marron.	The table is brown.
Nous sommes frères.	We are brothers.
Ils sont étudiants.	They are students.

Auxiliary verbs

Avoir and être are both used as **auxiliary verbs**. This means they are used to make other **tenses**. You can use the present tense of avoir and être to make the perfect tense. Don't forget to make agreements with être.

J'ai mangé.	I have eaten.
Nous avons payé.	We have paid.
Elle est allée ...	She has gone ... (or she went ...)
Ils sont partis.	They have left.

Now try this

1 Complete this passage. All the missing words are parts of the verb **avoir**.
Nous .... un petit chaton. Il est tout noir mais il .... les yeux verts.
Il .... toujours faim. Il .... beaucoup de jouets mais j'.......... une balle
de ping-pong qu'il adore et mon petit frère .... acheté un petit oiseau en
fourrure pour lui. .... -tu un animal?

2 Complete this passage. All the missing words are
parts of the verb **être**.

Je .... britannique. Je .... né en Angleterre. Mes parents ....
italiens. Ils .... nés en Italie mais ils habitent ici depuis vingt ans.
Mon frère .... sportif. Il .... champion régional de judo. Ma
sœur .... paresseuse. En revanche je .... charmant!

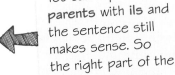

You can replace mes parents with ils and the sentence still makes sense. So the right part of the verb here is mes parents sont.

Reflexive verbs

A reflexive verb is a verb used with an extra little pronoun, for example s'appeler (to be called).

Reflexives and their pronouns

To talk about doing something to yourself, you use a reflexive verb. These verbs need a pronoun, which comes between the subject and the verb.

laver – to wash (the car) ➡ se laver – to get washed (i.e. to wash yourself)

lever – to raise (hand, finger, feet) ➡ se lever – to get up (i.e. to raise yourself out of bed)

Reflexive pronouns:
je + me	nous + nous
tu + te	vous + vous
il / elle / on + se	ils / elles + se

The verb s'appeler

appeler   to call

s'appeler   to call yourself / be called

je m'appelle

tu t'appelles

il / elle / on s'appelle

nous nous appelons

vous vous appelez

ils / elles s'appellent

The verb se laver

laver   to wash

se laver   to get washed (wash yourself)

je me lave

tu te laves

il / elle / on se lave

nous nous lavons

vous vous lavez

ils / elles se lavent

Common reflexive verbs

There are lots of interesting reflexive verbs. The following are useful ones to learn:

s'ennuyer	to get bored je m'ennuie
s'étonner	to be surprised je m'étonne
s'endormir	to fall asleep je m'endors
se reposer	to rest je me repose
se coucher	to go to bed je me couche
se promener	to go for a walk je me promène
se faire bronzer	to sunbathe je me bronze

Perfect tense

In the perfect tense all reflexive verbs take être. So the past participle must **agree** with the subject:

Je me suis lavé(e).   I got washed.

Elle s'est promenée toute seule.
She went for a walk on her own.

Nous nous sommes vite habillé(e)s.
We got dressed quickly.

Vous vous êtes levé(e)(s) trop tard.
You got up too late.

Tu t'es couché(e) de bonne heure?
Did you go to bed early?

Mes parents se sont disputés.
My parents argued.

Now try this

Complete the sentences in this passage with the correct form of the reflexive verb in brackets.

Je ne (s'entendre) pas bien avec mon grand frère. Il (se moquer) de moi. Nous (se disputer) souvent. Je (s'entendre) mieux avec ma sœur. On (s'amuser) bien ensemble. Normalement, nous (se coucher) de bonne heure parce que le matin nous (se lever) à six heures, mais hier mon frère ne (se réveiller) pas avant 8 heures. Quand finalement il (se lever), il ne (se doucher) pas parce qu'il n'a pas eu le temps.

Other important verbs

Many common verbs are irregular so you will have to learn them!

Aller   to go

je vais	nous allons
tu vas	vous allez
il / elle / on va	ils / elles vont

Nous allons à la piscine.

Did you notice the pattern?
The ils / elles form:
aller ➡ vont   faire ➡ font
avoir ➡ ont   être ➡ sont

Faire   to do

je fais	nous faisons
tu fais	vous faites
il / elle / on fait	ils / elles font

Using faire

Faire is used in lots of expressions, especially for talking about the weather:

Il fait beau.	It is fine.
Il fait du vent.	It is windy.
Il fait du soleil.	It is sunny.

It is also used for talking about activities:

Je fais de la natation / de la danse / du VTT.
I do swimming / dancing / mountain biking.

Pouvoir   to be able to

je peux	nous pouvons
tu peux	vous pouvez
il / elle / on peut	ils / elles peuvent

Je peux aller au cinéma.
I can go to the cinema.

Vouloir   to want to

je veux	nous voulons
tu veux	vous voulez
il / elle / on veut	ils / elles veulent

Je veux manger à la pizzeria.
I want to eat at the pizzeria.

Devoir   to have to

je dois	nous devons
tu dois	vous devez
il / elle / on doit	ils / elles doivent

Je dois être à l'heure.
I have to be on time.

Savoir   to know how to

je sais	nous savons
tu sais	vous savez
il / elle / on sait	ils / elles savent

Je sais faire du ski.
I know how to ski.

Now try this

Complete these sentences with the correct parts of the verb and then translate the sentences into English.

1 Je (aller) au collège en car.

2 Nous (faire) du ski en hiver.

3 On (pouvoir) aller au cinéma en ville.

4 Ils (vouloir) aller en Espagne.

5 Tu (devoir) faire tes devoirs.

6 Elle (savoir) jouer du piano

The perfect tense 1

The perfect tense is one of the tenses you use to talk about the past. It is called the passé composé in French. Many verbs use avoir to form the perfect tense.

Formation

The perfect tense of **most** verbs is made up of the verb **to have** (avoir) and the **past participle**.

j'ai	nous avons	+ past
tu as	vous avez	participle
il / elle / on a	ils / elles ont	

J'ai joué au tennis.
I have played tennis / I played tennis.

Use of the perfect tense

You use the perfect tense when you are talking about something that happened at a specific time in the past:

Hier soir j'ai regardé un film.
Last night I watched a film.
L'année dernière, mes parents ont acheté une voiture.
Last year my parents bought a car.

Forming the past participle

For -er verbs, take off the -er and add -é:
manger ➡ mangé
regarder ➡ regardé

J'ai mangé une crêpe.

For -ir verbs, take off the -r:
finir ➡ fini
dormir ➡ dormi

For -re verbs, take off the -re and add -u:
répondre ➡ répondu
attendre ➡ attendu

There are quite a lot of **irregular** past participles and they are the verbs you probably need most – you simply need to learn them.

avoir	➡ eu	savoir	➡ su
être	➡ été	faire	➡ fait
mettre	➡ mis	dire	➡ dit
voir	➡ vu	écrire	➡ écrit
lire	➡ lu	boire	➡ bu
vouloir	➡ voulu	prendre	➡ pris
devoir	➡ dû	comprendre	➡ compris
pouvoir	➡ pu		

Negative sentences

In a negative sentence, you put the ne ... pas round the part of avoir:
Je n'ai pas vu le film.
I haven't seen the film.
Il n'a pas joué au foot.
He did not play football.

Useful phrases

Use these with the perfect tense:

samedi dernier	last Saturday
la semaine dernière	last week
le week-end dernier	last weekend
hier	yesterday

Now try this

Put the infinitives in brackets into the perfect tense to complete the text.
Mercredi dernier j'(prendre) le bus pour aller en ville. J'y (retrouver) un ami. Nous (faire) les magasins. J'(vouloir) acheter des baskets rouges mais elles étaient trop chères. Nous (manger) des burgers et comme boisson j'(choisir) un coca. Mon copain (boire) un milkshake à la fraise. J'(laisser) mon sac au bar. J'(devoir) y retourner et, par conséquent, j'(rater) le bus et j'(devoir) rentrer à pied.

The perfect tense 2

Most verbs form the perfect tense with avoir **but** some verbs use être instead. They are mostly verbs to do with movement.

Verbs that take être

The following 14 verbs take être + the past participle in the perfect tense:

aller / venir	to go / to come
arriver / partir	to arrive / to depart
entrer / sortir	to enter / to go out
monter / descendre	to go up / to go down
rester / tomber	to stay / to fall
naître / mourir	to be born / to die
rentrer / revenir	to return

All reflexive verbs also take être.

MRS VAN DER TRAMP spells out the first letters of the 14 verbs listed above and may be useful in helping you to remember them!

Formation

Être	Past participles
je suis	allé / venu
tu es	arrivé / parti
il / elle / on est	entré / sorti
nous sommes	monté / descendu
vous êtes	né / mort
ils / elles sont	rentré / revenu

Note how the past participle changes according to who is doing the action:

Je suis allé(e).	I went.
Elle est arrivée.	She arrived.
Nous sommes monté(e)s.	We climbed.
Ils sont partis.	They left.

Agreement of the past participle

With verbs that take être, the past participle agrees with the subject of the verb (a bit like adjectives):

Je suis allé(e)
Tu es allé(e)
Il est allé
Elle est allée
Nous sommes allé(e)s
Vous êtes allé(e)(s)
Ils sont allés
Elles sont allées

Aiming higher

- You should be able to use the perfect tense if you are aiming at a higher grade.
- Remember, you use the perfect tense when you are talking about one specific time in the past, so you are likely to start the sentence with a time expression referring to the past.
  For example:
  Samedi dernier …
  Hier …
  Hier soir …
  Il y a deux jours …
  Pendant les vacances …

Now try this

Put the infinitives in brackets into the perfect tense to complete the sentences.
1 Samedi dernier je (partir) de bonne heure.
2 Le matin je (aller) jouer au football.
3 Je (sortir) à dix heures.
4 L'autre équipe (ne pas venir).
5 Nous y (rester) une heure, puis nous (rentrer).
6 Je (arriver) à la maison juste avant midi.

Je suis allée au match.

The imperfect tense

The imperfect is another verb tense you use to talk about the past.

Forming the imperfect

First, take the nous form of the present tense and remove the -ons ending:

nous habit~~ons~~

Then add the following imperfect endings:

je -ais	nous -ions
tu -ais	vous -iez
il / elle / on -ait	ils / elles -aient

habiter to live

j'habitais	nous habitions
tu habitais	vous habitiez
il / elle / on habitait	ils / elles habitaient

> Good news: all verbs except être are regular in the imperfect tense.

Using the imperfect

You use the imperfect tense to describe:

1 What **was happening**:
Il pleuvait.   It was raining.

2 What **used to** happen:
Quand j'étais jeune, je jouais au foot.
When I was young, I used to play football.

3 What was **ongoing** when something else happened:
Je regardais la télévision lorsque quelqu'un a sonné.   I was watching TV when someone rang.

> The key words to look out for are: 'was / were …ing' and 'used to …'.

Some common verbs

These are a few common verbs you should be able to use in the imperfect.

Present	Imperfect	English
voul/ons	je voul+ais	I wanted
av/ons	j'av+ais	I had
all/ons	j'all+ais	I was going
buv/ons	je buv+ais	I was drinking
mange/ons	je mange+ais	I was eating
achet/ons	j'achet+ais	I was buying
finiss/ons	je finiss+ais	I was finishing
dorm/ons	je dorm+ais	I was sleeping

être in the imperfect

The **only** irregular verb in the imperfect tense is être. The stem is ét- and you add the normal imperfect endings to this stem:

j'étais	I was
tu étais	you were
il / elle / on était	he / she / one was
nous étions	we were
vous étiez	you were
ils / elles étaient	they were

Now try this

Complete the text with the imperfect tense of the verbs in the box, then translate it into English.
Why is it written in the imperfect tense?

Quand j'............................ jeune, j'............................ à la campagne.
Nous .... un grand jardin où je .... au foot avec mes frères.
Le samedi, on .... au marché en ville. Il y .... beaucoup de vendeurs de fruits et légumes et un kiosque à journaux où j'............................ des bonbons.
Nous .... des merguez (des saucisses épicées) et nous .... du coca. On .... en bus avec tous nos voisins et nos achats!

avoir être habiter jouer aller acheter manger boire rentrer

The future tense

To aim for a high grade you need to use the future tense as well as the present and past!

Near future tense

When you are talking about what you are **going** to do, use the verb to go (aller) + an infinitive, just as in English:

Je vais aller …   I am going to go …

Ils vont jouer au tennis.
They are going to play tennis.

Mon copain va rentrer à 21h00.
My friend is going to go home at 9 o'clock.

On va se retrouver en ville.
We are going to meet in town.

Remember all the parts of aller (to go):

je vais	nous allons	
tu vas	vous allez	+ infinitive
il / elle / on va	ils / elles vont	

Remember, the **infinitive** is the part of the verb you will find in the dictionary – usually ending in -er, -ir or -re.

For example:

-er: jouer / manger

-ir: finir / choisir / sortir

-re: lire / dire

Future tense

If you are aiming for a top grade, you will need to be able to understand and use the 'proper' future. It is used to say what you **will** do.

The future is made from the **infinitive** + **future tense endings**:

-er verbs	manger	➡ je mangerai	I will eat
-ir verbs	finir	➡ je finirai	I will finish
-re verbs	répondre	➡ je répondrai	I will reply

Remember, -re verbs drop the final e.

The future **endings** are the same as the present tense of avoir except for the nous and vous forms:

je mangerai	nous mangerons
tu mangeras	vous mangerez
il / elle / on mangera	ils / elles mangeront

Which future to use?

Near future (futur proche):
I am going to play football tonight.
This is a simple fact.

Proper future (futur):
I will play football tonight.

You might be:
- expressing an intention.
- responding to a suggestion that you might **not** do something.

Je jouerai au babyfoot au café.

Irregular verbs

Be careful! There are a few common verbs that don't use the infinitive as the stem, but have an irregular stem. The good news is the endings are always the same.

aller	j'irai	I will go
avoir	j'aurai	I will have
être	je serai	I will be
faire	je ferai	I will do
pouvoir	je pourrai	I will be able to
venir	je viendrai	I will come
voir	je verrai	I will see
vouloir	je voudrai	I will want

Now try this

Put all the infinitives in brackets into the future tense to complete the text.

L'année prochaine nous (aller) en France. Nous (prendre) l'Eurostar. On (partir) de Londres et on (arriver) à Paris. Puis on (changer) de train et on (continuer) vers le sud. Nous (faire) du camping. Mes parents (dormir) dans une caravane mais je (dormir) sous une tente. Pendant la journée, nous (aller) à la plage et (jouer) au basket et au tennis. Le soir on (manger) au resto. On (se faire) des amis.

The conditional tense

You should know a few verbs in the conditional and be able to use them in your writing and speaking in order to aim for a higher mark.

The conditional

The conditional is used to say what you **would** do:

je voudrais   I would like
je jouerais   I would play

It is also used for making suggestions:

on pourrait ...   we could ...

The conditional is formed in a similar way to the future. It uses the same stem (usually the infinitive) but then adds the same endings as the imperfect tense:

manger ➡ je mangerais   I would eat
finir   ➡ je finirais   I would finish
vendre ➡ je vendrais   I would sell

You may meet the conditional after si (if):

Si + imperfect tense + conditional

Si tu mangeais correctement, tu n'aurais pas faim.
If you ate properly, you wouldn't be hungry.

Irregular conditionals

Irregular conditionals use the same stems as the irregular future:

Infinitive	Conditional	English
aller	j'irais	I would go
avoir	j'aurais	I would have
être	je serais	I would be
faire	je ferais	I would do
pouvoir	je pourrais	I would be able to
venir	je viendrais	I would come
voir	je verrais	I would see
vouloir	je voudrais	I would like

The endings are always the same, whether the verb is regular or irregular:

je serais   nous serions
tu serais   vous seriez
il / elle serait   ils / elles seraient

Je voudrais aller au concert ce soir.
I'd like to go to the concert this evening.

On pourrait faire du bowling?
We could go bowling?

Now try this

Put the infinitives in the following sentences in the conditional.

1 Je (vouloir) aller en Italie.
2 Si j'avais assez d'argent, j'(aller) en Inde.
3 Nous (pouvoir) faire un long voyage.
4 Tu (aimer) voir ce film?
5 Je (préférer) manger au restaurant.
6 Si j'avais faim, je (manger) une pizza.
7 Il (vouloir) aller en ville samedi.
8 On (pouvoir) aller à la patinoire cet après-midi?
9 Tu (voir) le match si tu restais encore deux jours.
10 Vous (vouloir) quelque chose à boire?

The pluperfect tense

The pluperfect is another past tense; you don't have to **use** it at GCSE but you should be able to **recognise** it. It is used to say what you **had** done.

The pluperfect tense

You use the pluperfect to talk about an event that took place one step further back than another past event.

Whereas the perfect tense means 'I did something' or 'I have done something', the pluperfect is used to say what you **had** done before that.

We **had** finished dinner (pluperfect) when she knocked on the door. (perfect)

J'avais déjà mangé quand je suis allé au cinéma.
I had already eaten when I went to the cinema.

How does it work?

The pluperfect is formed like the perfect tense with the auxiliary (avoir or être) + the past participle.

The difference is that it uses the **imperfect** of the auxiliary:

J'avais déjà mangé.   I had already eaten.
J'étais allé(e) en ville.   I had gone into town.

The verbs that take être in the pluperfect are the same ones that take être in the perfect tense (for a reminder see page 101). Remember MRS VAN DER TRAMP.

Also remember that the past participle of être verbs must agree with the subject.

Mes parents étaient partis en vacances et j'étais seul à la maison.
My parents had gone on holiday and I was alone in the house.

The pluperfect with avoir

Here is an avoir verb in the pluperfect:

j'avais mangé	I had eaten
tu avais mangé	you had eaten
il / elle / on avait mangé	he / she / one had eaten
nous avions mangé	we had eaten
vous aviez mangé	you had eaten
ils / elles avaient mangé	they had eaten

The pluperfect with être

Here is an être verb in the pluperfect:

j'étais allé(e)	I had gone
tu étais allé(e)	you had gone
il / on était allé	he / one had gone
elle / on était allé(e)	she / one had gone
nous étions allé(e)s	we had gone
vous étiez allé(e)(s)	you had gone
ils étaient allés	they had gone
elles étaient allées	they had gone

Now try this

Look at the verbs in the highlighted expressions. What tense are they in: pluperfect, imperfect or perfect?

Pendant les vacances de neige, mes parents (**1**) avaient loué un appartement près des pistes de ski. (**2**) J'avais toujours voulu apprendre à faire du ski. Ma sœur (**3**) avait déjà fait un stage, mais moi, (**4**) je n'en avais jamais fait. (**5**) J'avais passé des heures devant mon ordinateur pour choisir le meilleur matériel. (**6**) J'avais regardé des DVD d'apprentissage du ski. (**7**) Je savais, en principe, comment descendre des pistes de toutes les couleurs, mais le premier jour (**8**) je suis sorti et plouf … (**9**) je suis tombé et (**10**) je me suis cassé la jambe. (**11**) Je ne m'attendais pas à passer les vacances à l'hôpital!

Negatives

You need to be able to understand and use a variety of negatives to aim for a higher grade in all parts of your exam.

Negative expressions

ne ... pas	not
ne ... jamais	never
ne ... plus	no longer, not any more
ne ... rien	nothing, not anything
ne ... personne	nobody, not anybody
ne ... guère	hardly
ne ... aucun(e)	not any
ne ... que	only
ne ... ni ... ni ...	neither ... nor

Formation

You know that negatives are made by making a ne ... pas sandwich around the verb.

The ne is a marker to tell you that a negative is coming ...

ne   verb   pas

Word order

- Personne can also come in front of the verb:
  Personne n'est venu. No one came.
- When the verb has two parts, the negative forms the sandwich around the auxiliary:
  Je ne suis jamais allé(e) en France.
  I have never been to France.
- If there is a pronoun before the auxiliary, it is included in the sandwich:
  Je n'y suis jamais allé(e).
  I've never been there.

- If there are two verbs, the sandwich goes around the first verb:
  Je ne veux pas y aller.
  I don't want to go there.
  Nous ne pouvons pas télécharger l'appli sans mot de passe. We can't download the app without a password.
- If there is a reflexive pronoun, that is included in the sandwich, too:
  Ils ne s'entendent pas bien.
  They don't get on well.

Now try this

1 Match the French negative sentences with the English ones on the right.

1 Il ne mange pas de viande.	**A** We don't want anything else.
2 On m'a dit que tu ne fumes plus.	**B** Manon has never eaten snails.
3 Manon n'a jamais mangé d'escargots.	**C** I didn't see anyone.
4 Nous ne voulons plus rien.	**D** He's only ten.
5 Je n'ai vu personne.	**E** She has no doubts.
6 Elle n'a aucun doute.	**F** Someone told me you don't smoke any more.
7 Il n'a que dix ans.	**G** Where's she from? She's neither Italian nor Spanish.
8 D'où vient-elle? Elle n'est ni italienne ni espagnole.	**H** He doesn't eat meat.

2 Make negative sentences with the expressions provided.
  (a) Tu fais (ne ... rien).
  (b) Tu m'as aidé à la maison (ne ... jamais).
  (c) Tu fais tes devoirs (ne ... plus).
  (d) Tu respectes (ne ... personne).
  (e) Tu fais le nécessaire (ne ... que).
  (f) Tu peux aller au football ou au restaurant ce soir (ne ... ni ... ni).

The perfect infinitive and present participles

If you can use the perfect infinitive or a present participle, you will show greater complexity in your speaking and writing.

The perfect infinitive

The perfect infinitive is used to translate the English, 'after doing something'. It is made up of the infinitive of avoir or être and the past participle of the verb.

après avoir joué au foot — after playing football

après être arrivé(e) — after arriving

Être will still need to have the past participle agree with the subject of the verb, but this is a little more tricky as the subject of the main verb will probably come after the perfect infinitive.

Après être **arrivés, les garçons** ont joué au foot. After arriving, the boys played football.

The perfect infinitive of a reflexive verb needs the appropriate reflexive pronoun and follows the rules for être verbs.

Après **m'**être levé, j'ai pris le petit déjeuner. After getting up, I had breakfast.

The present participle

The English present participle ends in -ing and is used frequently. The French present participle ends in -ant and is far less common. You will, however, often see the present participle used after the word en. In such cases it translates the idea of by, in, on or while doing something.

Il travaille en écoutant de la musique.
He works while listening to music.

To form the present participle, take the -ons off the nous part of the present tense of the verb and simply add -ant:

travailler ➡ travaill~~ons~~ ➡ travaillant working

aller ➡ all~~ons~~ ➡ allant going

There are three exceptions:

avoir ➡ ayant having

être ➡ étant being

savoir ➡ sachant knowing

Now try this

1 Translate these sentences:
   (a) After watching TV, I played football.
   (b) After arriving at the hotel, she had lunch.
   (c) After getting up, he had breakfast.
   (d) After finishing his homework, he went into town.
   (e) After listening to some music, they went to school.

2 Put these verbs into the correct form of the present participle.
   (a) manger
   (b) avoir
   (c) travailler
   (d) finir
   (e) faire

The passive and the subjunctive

You might want to use the passive and you might need to be able to recognise it, too. You might also need to recognise the subjunctive.

The passive

The passive is used to say what is done to someone or something. It is used frequently in English but it is less common in French, although you need to be able to recognise it as well as use it if necessary.

It is formed from a part of être and a past participle. The past participle must agree with the noun.

La maison a été construite.

The house was built.

Les appartements sont vendus.

The flats are sold.

To avoid the passive in French, you can turn the sentence round by using on.

On m'a invité.

I was invited (someone invited me).

The subjunctive

This form of the verb is used to express wishes, thoughts, possibility or necessity. It is often used after a verb followed by que.

Je veux que tu arrives à l'heure.

I want you to arrive on time.

A verb in the subjunctive has the same meaning as in the indicative (all the tenses you have already seen).

To form the subjunctive for all **regular** -er, -ir and -re verbs as well as some irregular verbs, take the 3rd person plural ils form of the present tense, cross off -ent and add the subjunctive endings:

je	-e	nous	-ions
tu	-es	vous	-iez
il / elle / on	-e	ils / elles	-ent

Some verbs are **irregular** in the present subjunctive:

faire je fasse   pouvoir je puisse

aller j'aille   savoir je sache

vouloir je veuille, **but** nous voulions, vous vouliez

Avoir and être are totally irregular and need to be learned separately.

avoir		être	
j'aie	nous ayons	je sois	nous soyons
tu aies	vous ayez	tu sois	vous soyez
il / elle / on ait	ils / elles aient	il / elle / on soit	ils / elles soient

The subjunctive is also used after the following expressions:

bien que / quoique   although

il faut que

you / I / one must / it is necessary

avant que

before (doing something)

à condition que   provided that

bien qu'il soit heureux   although he is happy

il faut que j'y aille   I must go

avant qu'elle parte   before she leaves

à condition que nous travaillions bien

provided that we work well

Now try this

Match up the French and English.

1 Ma maison sera vendue.	**A** I want you to come with me.
2 Je veux que tu m'accompagnes.	**B** You must go.
3 Il faut que tu partes.	**C** before you go out
4 Mon collège a été bâti il y a dix ans.	**D** although he is happy
5 avant que tu sortes	**E** My house will be sold.
6 bien qu'il soit content	**F** My school was built 10 years ago.

Questions

You won't get very far if you can't ask questions, so make sure you know how to!

Ways of asking questions

You can ask a 'yes' and 'no' question in three ways:

1 Change a statement into a question by raising your voice at the end of the sentence:

Tu vas en ville?

This is the most popular way.

2 Put *est-ce que* at the start of the sentence ('is it that ...?').

Est-ce que tu vas en ville?

This is probably the easiest way.

3 Swap around the subject and the verb.

Vas-tu en ville?

Va-t-il en ville?

This is not used as much as it used to be. You should be able to recognise it but you won't be expected to use it.

Qu'est-ce que tu fais?
What are you doing?

Question words

The other way to ask a question is to start with a question word:

Qui?	Who?
Quand?	When?
Où?	Where?
Comment?	How?
Combien de?	How many?
À quelle heure?	At what time?
Pourquoi?	Why?
Que?	What?
Depuis quand?	Since when?

Question words can be followed by *est-ce que*:

Où est-ce que tu habites?
Where do you live?

Comment est-ce que tu vas au collège?
How do you get to school?

À quelle heure est-ce que tu te lèves?
What time do you get up?

Pourquoi est-ce que tu ne te lèves pas plus tôt?
Why don't you get up earlier?

Depuis quand est-ce que tu habites ici?
How long have you lived here?

Qu'est-ce que tu aimes faire?
What do you like doing?

Now try this

Match up the two parts of each question so that they all make sense. Then translate the questions into English.

1 Où   apprends-tu le français?
2 Qui   rentrent tes parents?
3 Comment   voulez-vous faire?
4 Combien   allez-vous?
5 À quelle heure   travaille ton père?
6 Pourquoi   as-tu raté le bus?
7 Que   d'amis as-tu sur Facebook?
8 Depuis quand   va à la fête?

Prepositions, conjunctions and intensifiers

These are all useful little words which can make your work more accurate and complex.

Prepositions

Some prepositions tell you **where** something is:

à côté de	beside
dans	in
derrière	behind
devant	in front of
dehors	outside
en face de	opposite
entre	between
loin de	far from
près de	near / close to
partout	everywhere
sous	under
sur	on
vers	towards

Note that the de changes to du, de la, de l' or des, depending on the noun that follows:

à côté du cinéma	next to the cinema
en face de la gare	opposite the station
près de l'école	near the school
près des magasins	near the shops

Others are just useful little words:

à	at / to
avec	with
chez	at the house of …
en	in / at
environ	about
jusqu'à	up to / until
sans	without
sauf	except

Verbs with prepositions

Some common verbs take a preposition before another infinitive:

décider de (sortir)   to decide to (go out)

apprendre à (conduire)   to learn to (drive)

réussir à (faire) …   to succeed in (doing) …

oublier de (faire) …   to forget to (do) …

Useful conjunctions

Use conjunctions to combine short sentences.

d'abord	at first	aussi	also / as well
au début	at the start	donc	so / then
alors	then	à la fin	in the end
puis	then	et	and
ensuite	next	mais	but
ou	or		

Intensifiers

très	very
Il est très grand.	He is very tall.
un peu	a bit
Elle est un peu timide.	She's a bit shy.
trop	too
Nous sommes trop fatigués.	We are too tired.
assez	quite
J'ai assez mangé.	I'm full. (I've eaten enough.)
beaucoup	much / many
Merci beaucoup.	Many thanks.

Now try this

Choose a suitable preposition or conjunction from the box to fill each gap.

Je me sentais triste. Mon chat avait disparu! J'avais cherché (**1**) .... J'avais cherché (**2**) .... le lit, (**3**) .... le placard, (**4**) .... la porte. (**5**) .... j'ai eu une idée, je suis allé (**6**) .... et j'ai cherché (**7**) .... le jardin, mais (**8**) .... succès. (**9**) .... je suis rentré (**10**) .... ma chambre. Je suis allé (**11**) .... lit. Je l'ai vu! Il était (**12**) .... les draps.

sous   puis   dans   au   sans   partout   à la fin   dehors   dans   sous   dans   derrière

Vocabulary

This section starts with general terms that are useful in a wide variety of situations and then divides vocabulary between the five main topics covered in this revision guide.

1 High-frequency language   **2** Identity and culture   **3** Local area, holiday and travel

4 School   **5** Future aspirations, study and work   **6** International and global dimension

Sections marked **Aiming higher** are only needed if you are studying for the Higher tier paper.

Learning vocabulary is essential preparation for all four skills of reading, writing, listening and speaking but don't try to learn too much at once – concentrate on learning and testing yourself one page at a time.

1 High-frequency language

Question words

à quelle heure?	(at) what time?
comment?	how?
combien de ...?	how much ...?, how many ...?
de quelle couleur?	what colour?
où?	where?
pourquoi?	why?
quel / quelle ...?	what / which ...? (singular item m/f)
quels / quelles ...?	what / which ...? (plural item m/f)
que ...?	what ...?
quoi?	what?
qu'est-ce qui ...?	what? (as subject)
qu'est-ce que ...?	what? (as object)
quand?	when?
qui?	who?

Quantities

assez de	enough
beaucoup de	a lot of / many
demi	half
encore de	more
moins de	less
moitié (f)	half
pas mal de	quite a few
plein de	a lot of
plus de	more
plusieurs	several
quelques	some / a few
trop de	too many / much
un kilo de	a kilo of
un litre de	a litre of
un morceau de	a piece of
un paquet de	a packet of
un peu de	a little of
un pot de	a jar of
un tiers de	a third of
une boîte de	a tin / box of
une bouteille de	a bottle of
une douzaine de	a dozen
une tranche de	a slice of

Connecting words

alors	then
aussi	also
car	because
d'abord	first
donc	so
enfin	finally / at last
ensuite	then
et	and
finalement	finally
mais	but
même si	even if
ou	or
parce que	because
puis	then
puisque	since
si	if
tout d'abord	first of all

Days of the week

lundi	jeudi
mardi	vendredi
mercredi	samedi
	dimanche

Months of the year

janvier	January
février	February
mars	March
avril	April
mai	May
juin	June
juillet	July
août	August
septembre	September
octobre	October
novembre	November
décembre	December

Other expressions

à moi	mine / my turn
à mon avis	in my opinion
avec plaisir	with pleasure
bien sûr	of course
bof	don't care!
bonne chance	good luck
ça dépend	it depends
ça m'énerve	it annoys me
ça m'est égal	I don't mind
ça me fait rire	it makes me laugh
ça me plaît	I like it
ça ne fait rien	it doesn't matter
ça ne me dit rien	that doesn't interest me
ça s'écrit comment?	how do you spell that?
ça suffit	that's enough
ça va	I'm fine
d'accord	okay
d'habitude	usually
défense de	you are not allowed to
encore une fois	once again
être en train de	to be in the middle of
être sur le point de	to be about to
il est interdit de	it is forbidden to / you are not allowed to
il faut	it is necessary to / you must
il y a	there is / there are
j'en ai assez / marre	I've had enough
personnellement	personally
quel dommage	what a shame
tant mieux	all the better
tant pis	too bad
voici	here you are
voilà	there you are

Now try this

Practise days and months by translating the birthdays of family and friends into French.

High-frequency language

Prepositions

à	at / to
à cause de	because of
à côté de	next to
après	after
au bout de	at the end of
au-dessus de	above
au milieu de	in the middle of
autour de	around
avant	before
avec	with
chez	at (someone's house)
contre	against
dans	in
de	from
derrière	behind
devant	in front of
en	in / by
en face de	opposite
entre	between
environ	about
jusqu'à	until
loin de	far from
nulle part	nowhere
par	through / by
parmi	among
pendant	during
pour	for / in order to
près de	near
sans	without
sauf	except
selon	according to
sous	under
sur	on
vers	towards

Adverbs of place

dedans	inside
dehors	outside
devant	in front
derrière	behind
en haut	at the top
ici	here
là	there
là-bas	over there
là-haut	up there
partout	everywhere
quelque part	somewhere

Time expressions

à l'heure	on time
à partir de	from
après	after
après-demain	the day after tomorrow
après-midi (m)	afternoon
au début	at the start
aujourd'hui	today
avant	before
avant-hier	the day before yesterday
bientôt	soon
de bonne heure	on time / early
de temps en temps	from time to time
déjà	already
demain	tomorrow
depuis	since
deux fois	twice
en même temps	at the same time
hier	yesterday
hier soir	last night
jour (m)	day
journée (f)	day('s activity)
lendemain (m)	the next day
maintenant	now
matin (m)	morning
minuit	midnight
minute (f)	minute
nuit (f)	night
pendant	during / for
plus tard	later
prochain	next
quinzaine (f)	a fortnight
quinze jours	a fortnight
semaine (f)	week
soir (m)	evening
soirée (f)	evening / party
toujours	always
tous les jours	every day
tout à l'heure	just now / in a little while
une fois	once
veille (f)	the night before
week-end (m)	weekend

Verbs A–D

accepter	to accept
accompagner	to accompany
acheter	to buy
adorer	to love
aider	to help
aimer	to like
ajouter	to add
allumer	to switch on / light
améliorer	to improve
annuler	to cancel
appeler	to call
apprendre	to learn
arriver	to arrive
attendre	to wait for
atterrir	to land
avoir	to have
bavarder	to chat
boire	to drink
changer	to change
charger	to load / charge
choisir	to choose
cliquer	to click
coller	to stick
commander	to order
commencer	to begin
comprendre	to understand
compter	to count / intend
conduire	to drive
connaître	to know (be familiar with)
conseiller	to advise
contacter	to contact
coûter	to cost
croire	to think / believe
décider	to decide
décrire	to describe
demander	to ask
dépenser	to spend
descendre	to go down
désirer	to want / desire
détester	to hate
devoir	to have to
dire	to say
discuter	to discuss
donner	to give
dormir	to sleep
durer	to last

Now try this

Test yourself on the time expressions above by covering up the English column and then writing down the English translations yourself. Compare your answers with the list above. How many have you got right?

① High-frequency language

Verbs E–P

écouter	to listen
écrire	to write
empêcher	to prevent
emprunter	to borrow
entendre	to hear
entrer	to enter / go in
envoyer	to send
espérer	to hope
essayer	to try
être	to be
étudier	to study
fermer	to close / switch off
finir	to finish / end
frapper	to knock / hit
gagner	to win / earn
garer	to park
habiter	to live
informer	to inform
introduire	to introduce
inviter	to invite
jeter	to throw
laisser	to leave (an object)
louer	to rent / hire
manger	to eat
manquer	to miss
marcher	to walk
mériter	to deserve
mettre	to put
monter	to climb / go up
monter dans	to get on / in
montrer	to show
neiger	to snow
noter	to note
offrir	to give (presents)
organiser	to organise
oublier	to forget
ouvrir	to open
pardonner	to forgive
parler	to speak
partir	to leave
passer	to pass (by)
passer	to take (an exam)
penser	to think
perdre	to lose
permettre	to allow

Verbs P–S

plaire	to please
pleurer	to cry
poser une question	to ask a question
pousser	to push
pouvoir	to be able to
préférer	to prefer
prendre	to take
présenter	to present
prêter	to lend
prévenir	to warn
produire	to produce
quitter	to leave (a place)
raconter	to tell
rater	to miss / mess up
recevoir	to receive / host
rechercher	to research
recommander	to recommend
regretter	to regret / be sorry
rembourser	to refund
remercier	to thank
remettre	to put back
remplacer	to replace
remplir	to fill
rencontrer	to meet
rendre visite à	to visit (a person)
rentrer	to return
réparer	to repair
répéter	to repeat
répondre	to answer / reply
réserver	to reserve / book
ressembler à	to look like / resemble
rester	to stay
retourner	to return
réussir	to succeed / to pass (an exam)
réviser	to revise
rire	to laugh
rouler	to go along (in a car)
s'adresser à	to speak to
s'amuser	to enjoy oneself
s'appeler	to be called
s'arrêter	to stop

Verbs S–Z

s'asseoir	to sit down
s'échapper	to escape
s'ennuyer	to be bored
s'intéresser à	to be interested in
s'occuper de	to look after
sauter	to jump
sauver	to save
savoir	to know (a fact / how to)
se débrouiller	to manage / deal with things
se dépêcher	to hurry
se disputer	to argue
se fâcher	to get angry
se promener	to go for a walk
se rappeler	to remember
se servir de	to use
se souvenir de	to remember
se taire	to be quiet
se terminer	to end
se trouver	to be located
sembler	to seem
servir	to serve
signer	to sign
sonner	to ring
souhaiter	to wish
sourire	to smile
stationner	to park
suivre	to follow
surfer sur Internet	to surf the internet
taper	to type
téléphoner	to phone
tenir	to hold
tirer	to pull
tomber	to fall
toucher	to touch
travailler	to work
trouver	to find
utiliser	to use
vendre	to sell
venir	to come
vérifier	to check
visiter	to visit (a place)
vivre	to live
voir	to see
voler	to steal / fly
vouloir	to want

Now try this

Pick five verbs from each column and put them into the present, perfect and future tenses for the je form.
Check your answers by looking at pages 95–103.

High-frequency language

Most adjectives take -e in the feminine: bruyant ➡ bruyante, petit ➡ petite, **except** if they already end in an unaccented -e (e.g. juste, facile). Endings for irregular adjectives are shown.

Adjectives A–G

affreux/euse	awful
ancien(ne)	old / former
autre	other
beau / bel / belle	beautiful
bon(ne)	good / correct
bref / brève	brief
bruyant	noisy
cadet(te)	younger
cassé	broken
chaud	hot
cher / chère	expensive / dear
chouette	great
comique	comical
compliqué	complicated
confiant	confident
confortable	comfortable
content	happy / pleased
correct	correct
court	short
dégoûtant	disgusting
dernier/ière	last
désolé	sorry
difficile	difficult
dur	hard
dynamique	dynamic
éducatif/ive	educational
embêtant	annoying
en colère	angry
énervant	annoying
ennuyeux/euse	boring
énorme	enormous
étonné	surprised
fâché	angry
facile	easy
faible	weak
fatigant	tiring
fatigué	tired
faux / fausse	false
favori(te)	favourite
fermé	closed
formidable	great / marvellous
fort	strong
génial	great / brilliant
grand	big / tall
gratuit	free
gros(se)	fat

Adjectives H–R

haut	high
heureux/euse	happy
incroyable	unbelievable
injuste	unfair
inquiet / inquiète	worried
insatisfait	dissatisfied
inutile	useless
jeune	young
joli	pretty
juste	fair
laid	ugly
léger / légère	light
libre	free
long(ue)	long
lourd	heavy
magnifique	magnificent
malheureux/euse	unhappy
mauvais	bad
merveilleux/euse	marvellous
moche	ugly / rotten
mûr	mature
nécessaire	necessary
neuf / neuve	new (brand new)
nombreux/euse	numerous
nouveau / nouvel / nouvelle	new
nul(le)	rubbish
ouvert	open
parfait	perfect
pas cher / chère	cheap
perdu	lost
pessimiste	pessimistic
petit	small
préféré	favourite
premier/ière	first
pressé	in a hurry
prêt	ready
prochain	next
proche	close
propre	clean / own
récent	recent
recherché	sought after
reconnaissant	grateful
reconnu	recognised / well known
réel(le)	real
responsable	responsible
rigolo(te)	funny

Adjectives S–Z

sale	dirty
satisfait	satisfied
sensass	sensational / terrific
seul	alone
sévère	strict
silencieux/ieuse	silent
simple	easy
super	great
sûr (de moi etc.)	confident
surpris	surprised
tranquille	calm / quiet
travailleur/euse	hardworking
triste	sad
typique	typical
utile	useful
valable	valid
vieux / vieil / vieille	old
vrai	true

Adverbs

d'habitude	usually
déjà	already
encore	more / again
ensemble	together
heureusement	fortunately
ici	here
immédiatement	immediately
là	there
là-bas	over there
là-haut	up there
longtemps	(for a) long time
malheureusement	unfortunately
normalement	usually
peut-être	perhaps
plutôt	rather
pourtant	however
presque	almost
quelquefois	sometimes
rarement	rarely
récemment	recently
souvent	often
surtout	especially
toujours	always / still
tout de suite	straight away
très	very
trop	too
vite	quickly
vraiment	really

Now try this

Pick five adjectives from each column and see if you can write a sentence in French using each word.

114

② Identity and culture

Family

aîné	eldest (brother/ sister)
ami (m) / amie (f)	friend
amoureux/euse	in love
animé	lively
anniversaire (m)	birthday
baiser (m)	kiss
beau-fils (m) / belle-fille (f)	son-in-law / daughter-in-law (also stepson / stepdaughter)
beau-frère (m) / belle-sœur (f)	brother-in-law / sister-in-law
bébé (m)	baby
cadeau (m)	present / gift
célèbre	famous
célibataire	single
copain (m) / copine (f)	friend (also boyfriend / girlfriend)
correspondant (m) / correspondante (f)	pen friend
cousin (m) / cousine (f)	cousin
demi- (e.g. demi-sœur)	half- (e.g. half-sister)
demi- / (e.g. demi-frère)	step- (e.g. step-brother)
divorcé	divorced
divorcer	to get divorced
enfant (m/f)	child
faire du babysitting	to babysit
famille (f)	family
femme (f)	wife / woman
fête (f)	party
fêter	to celebrate
fiancé	engaged
fiancé (m) / fiancée (f)	fiancé(e)
fille (f)	daughter / girl
fils (m)	son / boy
fils unique (m) / fille unique (f)	only child
frère (m)	brother
frères et sœurs (mpl)	brothers and sisters / siblings
(frères) jumeaux (mpl)	(twin) brothers
garder	to care for / look after
grand-mère (f)	grandmother
grand-père (m)	grandfather
grands-parents (mpl)	grandparents

homme (m)	man
intelligent	intelligent
jumeau (m) / jumelle (f)	twin
lieu de naissance (m)	birthplace
maman	mum
mamie (f) / mémé (f)	grandma / granny
mari (m)	husband
marié	married
membre de la famille (m)	member of the family
mère (f)	mother
moi-même / toi-même, etc.	myself / yourself, etc.
mort	dead
multiculturel	multicultural
(date de) naissance (f)	(date of) birth
né	born
neveu (m)	nephew
nièce (f)	niece
nom de famille (m)	surname
oncle (m)	uncle
papa (m)	dad
papy (m) / pépé (m)	grandad
parents (mpl)	parents
paresseux/euse	lazy
père (m)	father
petit-fils (m) / petite-fille (f)	grandson / granddaughter
plus âgé	older
prénom (m)	first name
respecter	to respect
s'appeler	to be called
se marier	to get married
séparé	separated
séparer	to separate / split up
sœur (f)	sister
surnom (m)	nickname
surprise-partie (f)	party
tante (f)	aunt
vie (f)	life
voisin (m) / voisine (f)	neighbour

Pets

animal domestique (m)	pet
chat (m)	cat
chien (m)	dog
cochon d'Inde (m)	guinea pig
hamster (m)	hamster

lapin (m)	rabbit
poisson rouge (m)	goldfish
poisson tropical (m)	tropical fish
tortue (f)	tortoise

Describing where you live

appartement (m)	flat / apartment
bureau (m)	study / desk
chaise (f)	chair
chambre (f)	bedroom
chez moi	at home / at my house
confortable	comfortable
cuisine (f)	kitchen
démodé	old-fashioned
domicile (m)	place of residence
en désordre	untidy
fauteuil (m)	armchair
garage (m)	garage
grenier (m)	loft / attic
idéal	ideal
immeuble (m)	block (of flats)
invitation (f)	invitation
jardin (m)	garden
maison (f)	house
maison jumelée (f)	semi-detached house
maison mitoyenne (f)	terraced house
meubles (mpl)	furniture
normal	normal
salle à manger (f)	dining room
salle de bain(s) (f)	bathroom
salle de séjour (f) / séjour (m)	living room
salon (m)	lounge
canapé (m)	sofa / settee
vieux / vieille	old
visite (f)	visit

Family celebrations

Bon anniversaire	Happy birthday
fête (f)	celebration / party
fête des mères (f)	Mother's Day
fiançailles (fpl)	engagement

cochon d'Inde (m) guinea pig

poisson rouge (m) goldfish

Now try this

To help you learn family vocabulary, draw a family tree and label the relationships in French. You could even add your pets!

② Identity and culture

Personality adjectives

amiable	friendly
autoritaire	bossy
aventureux/euse	adventurous
bavard	chatty
charmant	charming
égoïste	selfish
gentil/le	nice / kind
honnête	honest
insupportable	unbearable
méchant	mean / nasty
optimiste	optimistic
pessimiste	pessimistic
raisonnable	reasonable / sensible
rangé	tidy / neat
sage	well-behaved
sérieux/euse	serious
seul	alone
sportif/ive	sporty
sympa	nice / likeable
vilain	naughty

Describing character

agacer	to annoy
amitié (f)	friendship
bavarder / tchatter	to chat / chatter
caractère (m)	character
être de bonne / mauvaise humeur	to be in a good / bad mood
humeur (f)	mood
personnalité (f)	character / personality
rapports (mpl)	relationship
religion (f)	religion
s'entendre (bien) avec	to get on (well) with
se disputer	to argue / quarrel
avoir de l'humour (m)	to have a sense of humour
sentiment (m)	feeling

Aiming higher

à l'aise	comfortable (at ease)
adopté	adopted
agaçant	annoying
au chômage	unemployed
bande (f)	gang
bouton (m)	spot / pimple
cabinet de travail (m)	study / home office
carrière (f)	career
célibataire (m/f)	single person

compréhensif/ive	understanding
confiant	self-confident
connaissance (f)	acquaintance
curé (m)	priest
déprimé	depressed
désavantager	to disadvantage
discrimination (f)	discrimination
dispute (f)	argument
effronté	cheeky
équilibré	well-balanced
expérimenter	to experience \ to test
fiable	reliable
fiançailles (fpl)	engagement
fidèle	loyal / faithful
foi (f)	faith (religious)
fou / folle	mad / crazy
gâté	spoilt
généreux/euse	generous
genre (m)	gender / sex
hall d'entrée (m)	hall (in house) / lobby
harceler	to pick on / harass / bully
indépendant	independent
jaloux/ouse	jealous
maison de retraite (f)	old people's home
mariage (m)	marriage / wedding
marié (m) / mariée (f)	bridegroom / bride
mère / père célibataire	single parent
meublé	furnished
mineur	underage
modèle (m)	role model
noces (fpl)	marriage ceremony / wedding
parent / parente (m/f)	relative / relation
prétentieux/euse	pretentious
prêtre (m)	priest
raciste	racist
retraité (m) / retraitée (f)	pensioner / senior citizen
réunion (f)	meeting
sensible	sensitive
sexe (m)	gender / sex
sexiste	sexist
similaire	similar
soutenir	to support
sûr de soi	self-confident
têtu	stubborn
trait (m)	character trait
troisième âge (m)	old / third age
bonne action (f)	good deed
vaniteux/euse	conceited

vrais jumeaux (mpl) / vraies jumelles (fpl)	identical twins

Describing appearance

adolescent (m) / adolescente (f) / ado (m/f)	adolescent
adulte (m/f)	adult / grown-up
âge (m)	age
avoir l'air	to look (e.g. angry / happy)
barbu	bearded
beau / belle	beautiful
bouche (f)	mouth
bouclé	curly
célébrité / star (f)	celebrity
cheveux (mpl)	hair
frisé	curly
gens (mpl)	people
image (f)	picture
jeunesse (f)	youth (i.e. the time of life)
laid	ugly
mec (m)	guy / dude / bloke
mince	thin / slim
moche	ugly
personne (f)	person
piercing (m)	body piercing
raide	straight (hair)

Dress and style

à la mode	fashionable
bague (f)	ring
baskets (fpl)	trainers
bijouterie (f)	jeweller's / jewellery
bijoux (mpl)	jewels
blouson (m)	casual jacket
bottes (fpl)	boots
cabine d'essayage (f)	changing / fitting room
caleçon (m)	boxer shorts / leggings
casquette (f)	cap
ceinture (f)	belt
chapeau (m)	hat

chauve bald

lunettes (fpl) glasses

yeux (mpl) eyes

boucle d'oreille (f) earring

visage (m) face

moustache (f) moustache

barbe (f) beard

116

Now try this

To help you learn personality adjectives, write out the French words in three lists: positive, negative and neutral. Then memorise six adjectives that could describe you, members of your family and a friend.

② Identity and culture

chaussette (f)	sock	blanc / blanche	white	chanteur (m) /	singer
chaussure (f)	shoe	bleu	blue	chanteuse (f)	
chemise (f)	shirt	brun	brown (of hair)	clarinette (f)	clarinet
chemise de	nightdress	châtain	chestnut	classique	classical / classic
nuit (f)		(invariable)		clavier (m)	keyboard
collant (m)	tights	clair	light	concert (m)	concert
collier (m)	necklace	foncé	dark	dessin animé (m)	cartoon
costume (m)	suit	gris	grey	disque compact /	CD
coton (m)	cotton	marron	brown	CD (m)	
cravate (f)	tie	(invariable)		flûte (f)	flute
cuir (m)	leather	noir	black	flûte à bec (f)	recorder
culotte (f)	pants	rose	pink		(instrument)
de taille	medium (size)	rouge	red	groupe (m)	band / group
moyenne		vert	green	guitare (f)	guitar
démodé	old-fashioned	violet/te	violet	jeu vidéo (m)	computer game

Colours

Going out

Music and reading

Sport

écharpe (f)	scarf
fringues (fpl)	clothes (slang)
gant (m)	glove
habillé	dressed
jupe (f)	skirt
laine (f)	wool (woollen)
(en laine)	
lin (m) (en lin)	linen (made of linen)
maillot de bain (m)	swimming costume
manteau (m)	coat
maquillage (m)	make-up
marque (f)	make / brand
mode (f)	fashion
montre (f)	watch
pantalon (m)	trousers
pantoufle (f)	slipper
parapluie (m)	umbrella
pointure (f)	size (of shoes)
pull (m)	sweater / jumper
rayé	striped
rétro	retro
robe (f)	dress
rouge à lèvres (m)	lipstick
sac à main (m)	handbag
slip (m)	briefs / underwear
soutien-gorge (m)	bra
survêtement (m)	tracksuit
taille (f)	size (general)
tatouage (m)	tattoo
tenue de sport (f)	sports kit
tricot (m)	sweater / jumper
veste (f)	jacket
vêtements (mpl)	clothes
vêtu (de)	dressed (in)

Going out

activité (f)	activity
appareil photo (m)	camera
argent de poche (m)	pocket money
boîte de nuit (f)	nightclub
club (m)	club
club des jeunes (m)	youth club
collection (f)	collection
collectionner	to collect
compétition (f)	competition
concours (m)	competition
console de jeux (f)	games console
disco(thèque) (f)	disco
échecs (mpl)	chess
équipement (m)	equipment
fana(tique) de	fanatical about
jeu d'échecs (m)	chess set
jouet (m)	toy
joueur (m) / joueuse (f)	player
loisirs (mpl)	leisure
maison des jeunes (f)	youth club
passe-temps (m)	hobby / leisure activity
plaisir (m)	pleasure / amusement
portable (m)	mobile phone
série (f)	series
temps libre (m)	free time
vie (f)	life

Music and reading

batterie (f)	drums
BD (f)	comic (book / magazine)
chaîne hi-fi (f)	stereo system / music centre
chanson (f)	song
chanteur (m) / chanteuse (f)	singer
clarinette (f)	clarinet
classique	classical / classic
clavier (m)	keyboard
concert (m)	concert
dessin animé (m)	cartoon
disque compact / CD (m)	CD
flûte (f)	flute
flûte à bec (f)	recorder (instrument)
groupe (m)	band / group
guitare (f)	guitar
jeu vidéo (m)	computer game
lecture (f)	reading
livre (m)	book
magazine (m)	magazine
lecteur mp3 (m)	mp3 player
musique (f)	music
musique folk (f)	folk music
musique pop (f)	pop music
orchestre (m)	orchestra
piano (m)	piano
rap (m)	rap
revue (f)	magazine
rock (m)	rock music
roman policier (m)	detective novel
romantique	romantic
saxophone (m)	saxophone
scène (f)	stage
trompette (f)	trumpet
violon (m)	violin

Sport

aller à la pêche	to go fishing
alpinisme (m)	mountaineering
arbitre (m)	referee
arts martiaux (mpl)	martial arts
athlétisme (m)	athletics
badminton (m)	badminton
ballon (m)	ball
basket (m)	basketball
boules (fpl)	boules
boxe (f)	boxing
canoë-kayak (m)	canoeing
course (f)	race / racing
cyclisme (m)	cycling
danse (f)	dance / dancing
équipe (f)	team
équitation (f)	horse-riding
escalade (f)	(rock) climbing
foot(ball) (m)	football
gymnastique (f)	gymnastics
handball (m)	handball
hockey (m)	hockey
jeu (m)	game
judo (m)	judo
karaté (m)	karate
musculation (f)	body-building

Now try this

Choose five activities for you and five for your best friend, and memorise them. Write sentences to describe what you do and what your friend does. Then use each one in a sentence in either the past or the future.

② Identity and culture

natation (f)	swimming	émission (f)	TV programme		
parachutage (m)	parachuting	feuilleton (m)	soap (opera)		
parapente (m)	paragliding	film d'aventure	adventure /action		
patinage (m) /	ice skating	/ d'action (m)	film		
patin à glace (m)		film d'épouvante	horror film		
pétanque (f)	boules	/ d'horreur (m)			
planche à	windsurfing	film	spy film		
voile (f)		d'espionnage (m)			
roller (m)	rollerblading	film	fantasy film		
rugby (m)	rugby	fantastique (m)			
skate (m)	skateboarding	film de science-	science fiction		
ski (m)	skiing	fiction (m)	film		
ski nautique (m)	water skiing	film de	thriller		
sport (m)	sport	suspense (m)			
(court de)	tennis (court)	film romantique	romantic film /		
tennis (m)		(m)	rom com		
assister à	to attend	informations /	news		
	(match, etc.)	infos (fpl)			
danser	to dance	jeu télévisé (m)	quiz show		
faire de	to go horse-	pièce de	play (theatre)		
l'équitation /	riding	théâtre (f)			
du cheval		spectacle (m)	show (theatre,		
faire de	to exercise		etc.)		
l'exercice		western (m)	Western (film)		

Using social media

blog (m)	blog
charger	to load
connexion (f)	connection
copier	to copy
courrier	email
électronique (m)	
cyber	cyber bullying
harcèlement (m)	
écran (m)	screen
effacer	to erase / delete
email (m)	email
forum (m)	chatroom
graver	to burn (disk)
Internet (m)	internet
lien (m)	link
logiciel (m)	software
mél (m)	email
mettre en ligne	to upload
mot de	password
passe (m)	
numérique	digital
ordinateur (m)	computer
page	homepage
d'accueil (f)	
page	internet page
Internet (f)	
page web (f)	web page
réseau	social network
social (m)	
risque (m)	risk
sauvegarder	to save / back up
sécurité (f)	security
site Internet /	website
web (m)	
surfer sur	to surf (the net)
Internet	
taper	to type
tchatter	to chat (online)
(en ligne)	
télécharger	to download
toile (f)	web
virus (m)	virus
web (m)	web
webcam (f)	webcam

faire de la	to do
gymnastique	gymnastics
faire de la	to swim
natation	
faire de la	to sail
voile	
faire des	to hike / ramble
randonnées	
faire du bowling	to go bowling
faire du patin	to roller-skate
à roulettes	
faire du skate	to skateboard
faire du sport	to do sport
faire partie de	to be a member of
faire une	to go for a walk
promenade	
féliciter	to congratulate
marquer un but	to score a goal
nager	to swim
participer (à)	to take part (in)
pêcher	to fish
promener	to take out for
	a walk (dog)
s'entraîner	to train
se promener	to go for a walk
tirer	to shoot

Aiming higher

bricolage (m)	DIY
câble (m)	cable TV
canne à pêche (f)	fishing rod
comédie de	sitcom
situation (f)	
comédie	drama (TV etc.)
dramatique (f)	
comédie	musical (show)
musicale (f)	
connaissances	knowledge
(fpl)	
doublé	dubbed (film)
écouteurs (mpl)	earphones
film policier (m)	detective /
	police film
jeu de société (m)	board game
jeu	electronic game
électronique (m)	
mélodie (f)	melody / tune
polar (m)	detective /
	police film
sous-titres (mpl)	subtitles
spectateur (m) /	viewer /
spectatrice (f)	audience
	member
télécommande (f)	remote control
télévision par	cable TV
câble (f)	
télévision	satellite TV
satellite (f)	
version	original version
originale (f)	(i.e. not
	dubbed)

Film and television

actualités (fpl)	news
affiche (f)	poster
chaîne (f)	(TV) channel
divertissement	entertainment
(m)	
documentaire (m)	documentary

Aiming higher

articles de	sports
sport (mpl)	equipment
aviron (m)	rowing
but (m)	goal
caméra (f)	camcorder /
	video camera
championnat (m)	championship
escrime (f)	fencing
ligue (f)	league /
	division (sports)
mi-temps (f)	half-time
plongée	scuba diving
sous-marine (f)	
tir à l'arc (m)	archery
tournoi (m)	tournament
voilier (m)	sailing boat

Now try this

List five activities you like doing and
five you don't, then memorise them all!

③ Local area, holiday and travel

Local area

agent de police (m)	policeman
agricole	agricultural
animé	lively
campagne (f)	countryside
circulation (f)	traffic
coin (m)	corner
colline (f)	hill
embouteillage (m)	traffic jam
endroit (m)	place
feu (m)	traffic lights
fleuve (m)	river (that flows into sea)
habitant (m) / habitante (f)	inhabitant / local
industriel/le	industrial
lieu (m)	place
ouvert	open
passage piéton (m)	pedestrian crossing
piéton (m)	pedestrian
place (f)	square (in town)
policier (m)	policeman
pont (m)	bridge
poubelle (f)	litter / rubbish bin
public / publique	public / municipal
rivière (f)	river
route (f)	road
rue (f)	road / street
sens unique (m)	one-way street
zone piétonne (f)	pedestrian area

Shops and buildings

aire de jeux (f)	playground
banlieue (f)	suburb / outskirts of town
banque (f)	bank
bar (m)	bar
bâtiment (m)	building
bibliothèque (f)	library
boîte de nuit (f)	nightclub
boucherie (f)	butcher's
boulangerie (f)	bakery / baker's
bowling (m)	bowling alley
café (m)	cafe
caisse (f)	till / cash desk
cathédrale (f)	cathedral
centre commercial (m)	shopping centre
centre de loisirs (m)	leisure centre

centre sportif (m)	sports centre
centre-ville (m)	town centre
château (m)	castle
cinéma (m)	cinema
commerce (m)	business / trade
commercial	commercial
commissariat (m)	police station
disco(thèque) (f)	disco
droguerie (f)	household goods shop (cleaning materials, etc.)
église (f)	church
(magasin d')électroménager (m)	electrical goods (retailer)
épicerie (f)	grocery / grocer's
ferme (f)	farm
galerie (d'art) (f)	art gallery
grand magasin (m)	department store
hôpital (m)	hospital
hôtel de ville (m)	town hall (in large town / city)
hypermarché (m)	hypermarket
industrie (f)	industry
jardin public (m)	park
kiosque à journaux (m)	newspaper stall
lac (m)	lake
magasin (m)	shop
marché (m)	market
mairie (f)	town hall (in small town / village)
monument (m)	monument
mosquée (f)	mosque
musée (m)	museum
parc (m)	park
patinoire (f)	ice rink
piscine (f)	swimming pool
poste (f)	post office
quartier (m)	area (in town)
rayon (m)	department (in a shop)
stade (m)	stadium
supermarché (m)	supermarket
(bureau de) tabac (m)	tobacconist's
terrain de jeux (m)	playground
théâtre (m)	theatre
usine (f)	factory
village (m)	village
ville (f)	town

 Aiming higher

caisse d'épargne (f)	savings bank
distributeur (m)	ATM / cash point
environs (mpl)	surrounding area / vicinity
espace vert (m)	park / green space
feux d'artifice (m)	fireworks
fontaine (f)	fountain
gendarme (m)	policeman
gendarmerie (f)	police station
grande surface (f)	hypermarket
laverie automatique (f)	launderette
nettoyage à sec (m)	dry cleaning
passage à niveau (m)	level crossing
poids lourd (m)	heavy goods vehicle (HGV)
pressing (m)	dry cleaner's
quincaillerie (f)	hardware shop

Public holidays

Janvier 1

Bonne année!	Happy New Year!
Carême (m)	Lent
Fête des rois (f)	Twelfth Night / Epiphany (6 January)
jour férié / de fête (m)	public holiday
lundi de Pâques (m)	Easter Monday
Noël (m)	Christmas
Nouvel An (m)	New Year
Pâques	Easter
veille de Noël (f)	Christmas Eve
vendredi saint (m)	Good Friday

Now try this

List all the amenities in your area in French, then try to learn them all. Can you tell someone how to get there? If not, make sure you work through Directions (see page 38).

❸ Local area, holiday and travel

Tourism

agence de voyage (f)	travel agency
attraction (f)	tourist attraction
brochure (f)	brochure / leaflet
excursion (f)	outing / trip
fermé	closed
fermeture (f)	closing
fête (f)	holiday / fair / festival
historique	historic
office de tourisme (m)	tourist information office
ouvert	open
ouverture (f)	opening
palais (m)	palace
région (f)	region
site touristique (m)	tourist attraction
spectacle (m)	show
tour (f)	tower
tour (m)	tour
touriste (m/f)	tourist
touristique	tourist (adjective)
visite guidée (f)	guided tour

Accommodation

allumer	to turn / switch on
ascenseur (m)	lift
auberge de jeunesse (f)	youth hostel
baignoire (f)	bath (thing)
bain (m)	bath (activity)
balcon (m)	balcony
bloc sanitaire (m)	shower block (e.g. on campsite)
brosse à dents (f)	toothbrush
bureau d'accueil /de renseignements (m)	information office
camping (m)	campsite
chambre (f)	(bed)room (in a hotel)
chambre à deux lits (f)	twin-bedded room
chambre pour une / deux personne(s) (f)	single / double room
chauffage (m)	heating
clef / clé (f)	key
client (m)	guest (in a hotel) / customer
climatisation (f)	air conditioning
colonie de vacances (f)	summer camp
complet	full (hotel, etc.)
douche (f)	shower

drap (m)	sheet
emplacement (m)	pitch (for tent)
enregistrement (m)	registration
étage (m)	floor (1st, 2nd etc.)
éteindre	to turn / switch off
étoile (f)	star
faire du camping	to camp
fenêtre (f)	window
gîte (m)	rented holiday cottage
hôtel (m)	hotel
inclus	included
lavabo (m)	washbasin
liste des prix (f)	price list
lit (m)	bed
oreiller (m)	pillow
rez-de-chaussée (m)	ground floor
sac de couchage (m)	sleeping bag
salle de bain(s) (f)	bathroom
savon (m)	soap
tarif (m)	price list / rate
tente (f)	tent
toilettes (fpl)	toilets
valise (f)	suitcase

Holidays

à l'extérieur	outside
à l'intérieur	inside
accueil (m)	reception
au bord de la mer	(at the) seaside
Bon séjour!	Enjoy your stay!
calme	calm / peaceful
confortable	comfortable
de luxe	luxurious
défaire une valise	to unpack
défense de	(it is) forbidden to
demi-pension (f)	half board
dentifrice (m)	toothpaste
distractions (fpl)	entertainment / things to do
en avance	in advance
en plein air	outside / open-air
entrée (f)	entrance
escalier (m)	staircase
faire une valise	to pack
interdit de	(it is) forbidden to
location (f)	hire / rent (e.g. house)

location (de vélos) (f)	(bike) hire
louer	to hire
mer (f)	sea
montagne (f)	mountain
papier hygiénique (m)	toilet paper
pension complète (f)	full board
pièce d'identité (f)	identity document
piscine couverte (f)	indoor swimming pool
plage (f)	beach
poste de télévision (m)	television (set)
potable	suitable for drinking
problème (m)	problem
réception (f)	reception
réceptionniste (m/f)	receptionist
réservation (f)	booking
saison (f)	season
salle de jeux (f)	games room
situé	situated
sortie (f)	way out / exit
sous-sol (m)	basement
souvenir (m)	souvenir
spacieux/euse	spacious
téléviseur (m)	television (set)
tranquille	calm / peaceful
vitrine (f)	(shop) window
vue (f) (sur)	view (over)

Aiming higher

avoir lieu	to take place
chambres d'hôtes (f)	B&B
défilé (m)	procession
draps de lit (m)	bed linen
exposition (f)	exhibition
hospitalité (f)	hospitality
logement (m)	accommodation
loger	to put up / accommodate
loyer (m)	rent / rental
panneau (m)	sign
pittoresque	picturesque
séjourner	to stay (for a holiday)
spectacle son et lumière (m)	sound and light show
station balnéaire (f)	seaside resort
station de ski (f)	ski resort
vacances d'hiver (fpl)	winter holidays
vacances de neige (fpl)	winter / skiing holiday
voyage organisé (m)	package holiday

salle de jeux (f)
games room

Now try this

Choose 10 words that describe your dream holiday and memorise them. Practise using them to describe what you would like to do/have done on a holiday.

③ Local area, holiday and travel

At the border

à l'étranger	abroad
carte postale (f)	postcard
contrôle des passeports (m)	passport control
côte (f)	coast
degré (m)	degree
étranger (m) / étrangère (f)	foreign / foreigner
fiche (f)	form
frontière (f)	border
navire (m)	ship
passeport (m)	passport
pays (m)	country (i.e. nation)
voyage (m)	journey / trip
voyageur (m)	traveller

On the road

autoroute (f)	motorway
bicyclette (f)	bicycle
camion (m)	lorry
car (m)	coach
caravane (f)	caravan
carrefour (m)	crossroads
carte (f)	map (of country)
carte routière (f)	road map
essence (f)	petrol
essence sans plomb (f)	unleaded petrol
gasoil (m)	diesel (fuel)
mobylette (f)	moped
moto (f)	motorbike
parking (m)	car park
permis de conduire (m)	driving licence
piste cyclable (f)	cycle path
plan (de la ville) (m)	map (of the town)
priorité (f)	priority
route (f)	road
station-service (f)	garage / service station / petrol station
taxi (m)	taxi
urgence (f)	emergency
vélo (m)	bike
voiture (f)	car

La limitation de vitesse.

Public transport

aéroport (m)	airport
aller-retour (m)	return ticket
aller simple (m)	single ticket
arrêt (m)	stop (bus / tram, etc.)
arrêt de bus (m)	bus stop
arrivée (f)	arrival
autobus (m)	bus
avion (m)	plane
bagages (mpl)	luggage
bateau (m)	boat
billet (m)	(train) ticket
bruit (m)	noise
buffet (m)	snack bar / buffet (on train)
bureau des objets trouvés (m)	lost property office
(en) bus (m)	(by) bus
carnet (m)	book of tickets
chemin de fer (m)	railway
compartiment (m)	compartment
conducteur (m) / conductrice (f)	driver
consigne (f)	left-luggage office / locker
contrôleur (m)	ticket inspector
correspondance (f)	connection
délai (m)	waiting period / time limit
départ (m)	departure
destination (f)	destination
direct	direct / fast
direction (f)	direction
ferry (m)	ferry
gare (f)	(railway) station
gare routière (f)	bus / coach station
guichet (m)	ticket office
horaire (m)	timetable
libre	free / available / vacant
ligne (f)	line / route
métro (m)	underground (railway)
occupé	occupied / taken / engaged
passager (m) / passagère (f)	passenger
port (m)	port
quai (m)	platform
réduction (f)	reduction
retard (m)	delay
salle d'attente (f)	waiting room

sortie (f)	exit
station de métro (f)	underground station
supplément (m)	supplement
tarif (m)	fare
ticket (m)	(tram / bus or metro) ticket
train (m)	train
trajet (m)	(short) journey
tramway (m)	tram
transports en commun (mpl)	public transport
traversée (f)	crossing (ferry)
vol (m)	flight
wagon-lit (m)	sleeping car (in a train)

Aiming higher

aire (de repos) (f)	motorway services
canal (m)	canal
ceinture de sécurité (f)	seat belt
composter	to validate a ticket (e.g. train / tram)
douanes (fpl)	customs
doubler	to overtake
écraser	to run over (traffic accident)
embarquer	to board (plane / ship)
en provenance de	coming / arriving from (planes / trains)
événement (m)	event
(train) express (m)	fast train
freiner	to brake
freins (mpl)	brakes
hélicoptère (m)	helicopter
heures de pointe (fpl)	rush hour
intersection (f)	junction
péage (m)	toll
portière (f)	door (of train, etc.)
rond-point (m)	roundabout (in road)
sens interdit (m)	no entry (road)
sortie de secours (f)	emergency exit
stationnement interdit (m)	no parking
véhicule (m)	vehicle
vitesse (f)	speed

Now try this

Choose 10 words that describe a journey you have recently made, or make regularly. Learn them well, and practise using them by exchanging journey descriptions with a friend.

③ Local area, holiday and travel

Asking / getting directions

à droite	(on the) right
à gauche	(on the) left
à pied	on foot
c'est tout près / à 100 mètres	it is very close / 100 metres away
continue / continuez	continue
grande-rue (f)	high street / main street
jusqu'à	as far as
pour aller à ...?	how do I get to ...?
prends / prenez la première rue à gauche	take the first road on the left
tourne / tournez à droite / gauche	turn right / left
traverse / traversez	cross (over)
va / allez tout droit	go straight on
vous êtes à pied / en voiture?	are you on foot / in a car?

Dealing with problems

accueil (m)	customer services
adresse (f)	address
adresse email (f)	email address
cassé	broken
client (m) / cliente (f)	customer
délai d'attente (m)	waiting time
dommages (m)	damage
échanger	to exchange
erreur (f)	mistake
facture (f)	bill / invoice
faute (f)	mistake
faux numéro (m)	wrong number
formulaire (m)	form
garantie (f)	guarantee
garantir	to guarantee
livraison (f)	delivery
livrer	to deliver
marcher / fonctionner	to work / function
note (f)	bill
numéro de telephone (m)	telephone number
panne (f)	breakdown

portefeuille (m)	wallet
porte-monnaie (m)	purse
(faire une) réclamation (f)	(to make a) complaint
reçu (m)	receipt
remplacer	to replace
réparation (f)	repair
se plaindre	to complain
service (m)	service
taille (f)	size
vol (m)	theft

Aiming higher

assurance (f)	insurance
assurer	to insure
mode d'emploi (m)	instructions
plainte (f)	complaint
produit de remplacement (m)	replacement (part)
ramener / rapporter	to bring / take back / return (a product)
rendre	to return / give back

The weather

beau	nice (weather)
briller	to shine
brouillard (m)	fog
brume (f)	mist
chaleur (f)	heat
chaud	hot
ciel (m)	sky
clair	bright
climat (m)	climate
couvert	overcast
dans / à l'est	in the east
dans / à l'ouest	in the west
dans le / au nord	in the north
dans le / au sud	in the south
degré (m)	degree (temperature)
ensoleillé	sunny
froid (m)	cold
geler	to freeze
il gèle	it is freezing
il neige	it is snowing
il pleut	it is raining
il y a des éclairs	there's lightning
il y a du soleil	the sun is shining
il y a du tonnerre	there's thunder
il y a un orage	it is stormy
mauvais	bad
météo (f)	weather report

neige (f)	snow
neiger	to snow
nuage (m)	cloud
nuageux	cloudy
orage (m)	storm
pleuvoir	to rain
pluie (f)	rain
saison (f)	season
sec	dry
soleil (m)	sun
température maximale (f)	highest temperature
température minimale (f)	lowest temperature
tempête (f)	storm
temps (m)	weather
vent (m)	wind

Aiming higher

température moyenne (f)	average temperature
averses (fpl)	showers
brumeux	misty
éclaircie (f)	bright spell
grêle (f)	hail
grêler	to hail
incertain	changeable
orageux	stormy
pluvieux	rainy
prévisions météo (fpl)	weather forecast
s'éclaircir	to brighten up
température basse (f)	low temperature
température élevée (f)	high temperature
variable	changeable

Languages / nationalities

allemand	German
américain	American
anglais	English
écossais	Scottish
espagnol	Spanish
français	French
gallois	Welsh
grec / grecque	Greek
indien / indienne	Indian
irlandais	Irish
italien / italienne	Italian
pakistanais	Pakistani
russe	Russian
suisse	Swiss
tunisien / tunisienne	Tunisian
turque	Turkish

Now try this

Test your knowledge of weather vocabulary, and of tenses, by trying to describe the weather yesterday, the weather today and what you hope the weather will be like tomorrow.

③ Local area, holiday and travel

Eating out / shopping

addition (f)	bill
appétit (m)	appetite
argent (m)	money
assiette (f)	plate
Bon appétit!	Enjoy your meal!
carte (f)	menu
choix (m)	choice
client (m) / cliente (f)	customer
commander	to order
couteau (m)	knife
couvert (m)	place setting
cuillère (f)	spoon
cuit	cooked
déjeuner (m)	lunch
délicieux/euse	delicious
dîner (m)	dinner / evening meal
doux / douce	sweet
entrée (f)	starter
fermé	closed
fourchette (f)	fork
goûter	to taste
goûter (m)	afternoon snack
journée de repos (f)	rest day / day off
menu à prix fixe (m)	fixed-price menu
nappe (f)	tablecloth
petit déjeuner (m)	breakfast
petite cuiller / cuillère (f)	teaspoon
plat du jour (m)	dish of the day
plat principal (m)	main course
pourboire (m)	tip (money)
repas (m)	meal
restaurant (m)	restaurant
salle à manger (f)	dining room
salon de thé (m)	tea room
savoureux/euse	tasty
self(-service) (m)	self-service restaurant
serveur (m) / serveuse (f)	waiter / waitress
service (m)	service
serviette (f)	napkin
servir	to serve / wait at table
snack (m)	snack bar
spécialité (f)	speciality
sucré	sweet (taste)
végétarien/ne	vegetarian

Food

agneau (m)	lamb
alimentation (f)	food
baguette (f)	baguette
beurre (m)	butter
bifteck (m)	steak
biscuit (m)	biscuit
bœuf (m)	beef
bonbon (m)	sweet
brochette (f)	kebab
casse-croûte (m)	snack
céréales (fpl)	cereals
chips (fpl)	crisps
confiture (f)	jam
côtelette (f) (de porc / d'agneau)	(pork / lamb) chop
crème (f)	cream
escargots (mpl)	snails
frites (fpl)	chips
fromage (m)	cheese
gâteau (m)	cake
glace (f)	ice cream
huile (f)	oil
jambon (m)	ham
lait (m)	milk
mélangé	mixed
morceau (m)	piece
moutarde (f)	mustard
nourriture (f)	food
œuf (m)	egg
pain (m)	bread
part (f)	piece (e.g. of cake)
pâtes (fpl)	pasta
petit gâteau (m)	biscuit
plat cuisiné (m)	ready meal
poisson (m)	fish
poivre (m)	pepper (i.e. seasoning)
pot (m)	jar
potage (m)	soup
poulet (m)	chicken
riz (m)	rice
rôti (m)	roast
salé	salty / savoury
sandwich (m)	sandwich
sauce vinaigrette (f)	salad / French dressing
saucisse (f)	sausage
saucisson (m)	sausage eaten cold in slices (e.g. salami)
sel (m)	salt
soupe (f)	soup
steak (m)	steak
sucre (m)	sugar

tartine (f)	slice of bread (with butter / jam)
thon (m)	tuna
tranche (f)	slice
vanille (f)	vanilla
viande (f)	meat
viande hachée (f)	mince
vinaigre (m)	vinegar

Drinks

bière (f)	beer
boisson (f)	drink
bouteille (f)	bottle
café (m)	coffee
cafetière (f)	pot of coffee
chocolat chaud (m)	hot chocolate
eau minérale (f)	mineral water
jus de fruit / d'orange (m)	fruit / orange juice
tasse (f)	cup
thé (m)	tea
verre (m)	glass

Fruit and vegetables

abricot (m)	apricot
ananas (m)	pineapple
banane (f)	banana
carotte (f)	carrot
cerise (f)	cherry
champignon (m)	mushroom
chou (m)	cabbage
chou-fleur (m)	cauliflower
choux de Bruxelles (mpl)	Brussels sprouts
citron (m)	lemon
concombre (m)	cucumber
fraise (f)	strawberry
framboise (f)	raspberry
haricot (m)	bean
haricots verts (mpl)	green beans
légume (m)	vegetable
pamplemousse (m)	grapefruit
pêche (f)	peach
petits pois (mpl)	peas
poire (f)	pear
pomme (f)	apple
pomme de terre (f)	potato
prune (f)	plum
raisins (mpl)	grapes
salade (f)	lettuce / salad
tomate (f)	tomato

Now try this

Think about what you have eaten and drunk today. Check that you can say it in French.

School

General words

bibliothèque (f)	library
bulletin scolaire (m)	report
cantine (f)	canteen
car de ramassage (m)	school bus
cartable (m)	school bag
chorale (f)	choir
collège (m)	secondary school (11–15 yr olds)
concierge (m/f)	caretaker
conseiller (m) / conseillère (f) d'orientation	careers adviser
couloir (m)	corridor
cour de récréation (f)	playground
cours (m)	lesson
cravate (f)	tie
directeur (m) / directrice (f)	headteacher
(école) maternelle (f)	kindergarten / nursery school
école primaire (f)	primary school
école privée (f)	private school
école publique (f)	state school
éducation (f)	education
élève (m/f)	pupil
emploi du temps (m)	timetable
enseigner	to teach
équipe (f)	team
état (m)	state
étudiant (m) / étudiante (f)	university / higher education student
excursion scolaire (f)	school trip
fort (en)	good at (subject)
grande salle (f)	school hall
grandes vacances (fpl)	summer holidays
groupe scolaire (m)	school group / party
gymnase (m)	gym
heure (f)	lesson / hour
heure du déjeuner (f)	lunch break

journée scolaire (f)	school day
laboratoire (m)	laboratory
laboratoire de langues (m)	language lab
livre scolaire (m)	school book
lycée (m)	sixth form
lycée d'enseignement professionnel / LEP (m)	vocational / technical college
mi-trimestre (m)	half-term
mixte	mixed
prof(esseur) (m/f)	teacher
pupitre (m)	desk
récré(ation) (f)	break
redoubler	to repeat a year
règle (f)	rule
remplaçant (m) / remplaçante (f)	supply teacher
rentrée (f)	first day back at school
résultat (m)	result
retenue (f)	detention
réussi	successful
salle de classe (f)	classroom
salle de sport (f)	sports hall / gym
salle des profs (f)	staff room
semestre (m)	semester
sérieux/ieuse	serious (hard working)
strict / sévère	strict
succès (m) / réussite (f)	success
terrain de sport (m)	sports field
travailler dur	to work hard
trimestre (m)	term
uniforme (m)	uniform

School years

année scolaire (f)	school year
sixième (f)	yr 7
cinquième (f)	yr 8
quatrième (f)	yr 9
troisième (f)	yr 10
seconde (f)	yr 11
première (f)	yr 12
terminale (f)	yr 13

vacances (scolaires) (fpl)	(school) holidays
vestiaires (mpl)	changing room

In the classroom

absent	absent
bloc-notes (m)	(note) pad
cahier (m)	exercise book
calculatrice (f)	calculator
calculer	to calculate
ciseaux (mpl)	scissors
colle (f)	glue
contrôle (m)	test / assessment
copie (f)	copy / (exam) paper
corriger	to correct
crayon (m)	pencil
devoirs (mpl)	homework
dictionnaire (m)	dictionary
exercice (m)	exercise / practice
expérience (f)	experiment
faire attention	to pay attention / be careful
feutre (m)	felt-tip (pen)
fiche de travail (f)	worksheet
gomme (f)	rubber
injuste	unfair
intelligent	clever
juste	fair
livre (m)	book
niveau (m)	level / performance
note (f)	mark / grade
page (f)	page
pratiquer	to practise / do
présent	present (in school)
projecteur (m)	projector
question (f)	question
règle (f)	ruler
répéter	to repeat
réponse (f)	answer
stylo (m)	ballpoint (pen)
tableau (noir / blanc) (m)	(black / white) board
taille-crayon(s) (m)	sharpener
travailleur/euse	hard-working
trousse (f)	pencil case

Now try this

Think about all the people in your school. Can you describe in French what they do and what they are like?

School

Subjects and qualifications

allemand (m)	German
anglais (m)	English
art dramatique (m)	drama
arts ménagers (mpl)	food technology
bac(calauréat) (m)	A levels equivalent
biologie (f)	biology
brevet (m)	GCSE equivalent
bulletin scolaire (m)	school report / certificate
chimie (f)	chemistry
contrôle (m)	test
dessin (m)	art
diplôme (m)	qualification
échange (m)	exchange
éducation physique / EPS (f)	PE
espagnol (m)	Spanish
études des médias (fpl)	media studies
examen (m)	exam
faible (en)	weak / bad at (subject)
français (m)	French
géographie (f)	geography
groupe théâtral (m)	drama group
gymnastique (f)	gymnastics
histoire (f)	history
histoire-géo (f)	history-geography / humanities
informatique (f)	ICT
l'enseignement moral et civique (EMC)	personal, social health and economic (PSHE) education
italien (m)	Italian
langues (vivantes) (fpl)	(modern) languages
langues étrangères (fpl)	foreign languages
mathématiques / maths (fpl)	maths
matière (f)	subject
musique (f)	music
oral (m)	oral
passer un examen	to sit / take an exam
physique (f)	physics

progrès (m)	progress
projet (m)	plan / project
projets (mpl)	future plans
religion (f)	religion / religious studies
réussir	to succeed / pass (exam)
réviser	to revise
sciences (fpl)	sciences
sociologie (f)	sociology
technologie (f)	design technology / DT
technologie (f)	technology

Aiming higher

accepter	to agree
appel (m)	class register
assistant (m) / assistante (f) (de français, etc.)	(French etc.) assistant
autorisation (f)	permission
cartouche (d'encre) (f)	(ink) cartridge
centre de formation (m)	training centre
certificat de fin d'études (m)	school leaving certificate
commerce (m)	business studies
copier des lignes	to do lines (punishment)
doué	gifted
échouer	to do badly / fail
économie (f)	economics
enseigner	to teach
épeler	to spell
être annulé	to be cancelled
être d'accord	to agree
être collé / en retenue	to have a detention
études (fpl)	studies
examen final (m)	final exam

facultatif/ive	optional (subject)
laisser tomber	to drop (a subject)
internat (m)	boarding school
latin (m)	Latin
licence (f)	degree (university)
matière obligatoire (f)	core / compulsory subject
passer (en classe supérieure)	to move up (to the next form / year)
pensionnat (m)	boarding school
perfectionner	to improve (one's knowledge / skills in)
perte de temps (f)	waste of time
pression (f)	pressure
principal (m)	headteacher of college
prononcer	to pronounce
prononciation (f)	pronunciation
proviseur (m)	headteacher
rédaction (f)	essay
rencontre parents-professeurs (f)	parents' evening
réunion (f)	meeting / discussion
sciences nat(urelles) (fpl)	biology
sciences physiques (fpl)	physics and chemistry
sécher les cours	to skip lessons
sociologie (f)	sociology
stylo-bille (m)	ballpoint pen
surveillant (m) / surveillante (f)	supervisor
traduction (f)	translation
traduire	to translate

maths ●
English ●
history ●
art ●
chemistry ●
music ●

mathématiques
anglais
histoire
dessin
chimie
musique

Now try this

What GCSEs are you and your friends taking? Check that you can translate them all into French.
If you're thinking of doing A levels, can you translate these too?

⑤ Future aspirations, study and work

Jobs

acteur (m) / actrice (f)	actor
agent de police (m)	police officer
agriculteur (m) / agricultrice (f)	farmer
boucher (m) / bouchère (f)	butcher
boulanger (m) / boulangère (f)	baker
caissier (m) / caissière (f)	cashier
chauffeur (m)	driver
couture (f)	sewing / tailoring
cuisinier (m) / cuisinière (f)	cook
dentiste (m/f)	dentist
dessinateur (m) dessinatrice (f)	designer
directeur (m) / directrice (f)	manager
docteur (m)	doctor
électricien (m) / électricienne (f)	electrician
employé (m) / employée (f) (de banque)	(bank) employee
étudiant (m) / étudiante (f)	student
fermier (m) / fermière (f)	farmer
fonctionnaire (m/f)	civil servant
gérant (m) / gérante (f)	manager
hôtesse de l'air (f)	air hostess / cabin crew
infirmier (m) / infirmière (f)	nurse
informaticien (m) / informaticienne (f)	computer scientist
ingénieur (m) / ingénieure (f)	engineer
instituteur (m) / institutrice (f)	(primary school) teacher
maçon (m)	builder
mécanicien (m) / mécanicienne (f)	mechanic
médecin (m/f)	doctor

pharmacien (m) / pharmacienne (f)	pharmacist
plombier (m)	plumber
policier (m)	police officer
pompier (m)	firefighter
professeur (m/f)	(secondary school) teacher
programmeur (m)	programmer
représentant (m) / représentant (f)	(sales) rep(resentative)
serveur (m) / serveuse (f)	waiter / waitress
steward (de l'air) (m)	steward / cabin crew
technicien (m) / technicienne (f)	technician

Working

à l'heure	per hour
à mi-temps / temps partiel	part-time
au chômage	unemployed
bénévolement	voluntarily / without pay
bien payé	well paid
pause-café / thé / déjeuner (f)	coffee / tea / lunch break
chômage (m)	unemployment
classer	to file
classeur (m)	file (for paper)
collègue (m/f)	colleague
compétences (fpl)	skills
conditions de travail (fpl)	terms of employment
conférence (f)	conference
demande d'emploi (f)	job application
dossier (m)	folder
emploi (m)	job
entretien (m)	interview (job)
entrevue (f)	interview
expérimenté	experienced
fichier (m)	(computer) file
mal payé	badly paid
occupé	busy
organiser	to organise
prévu	planned
projet (m)	plan / project
répondeur (m)	answerphone
réunion (f)	meeting
salaire (m)	salary
taper	to type

Ambitions

ambition (f)	ambition
annonce (f)	advertisement
apprentissage (m)	apprenticeship
éducatif/ive	educational
faire des études	to study
faire un stage	to do a course, or work placement
formation (f)	training
formulaire (m)	form
imprimer	to print
langue (f)	language
licence (f)	degree (university)
mode (f)	fashion
poser sa candidature	to apply for a job
publicité (f)	advertisement
remplir un formulaire	to fill in a form

Businesses / organisations

agence de voyages (f)	travel agency
commerce (m)	business / shop
informatique (f)	computer science
marketing (m)	marketing
organisation caritative (f)	charity
société (f)	society / company
théâtre (m)	drama
université (f)	university

un infirmier

un plombier

une fermière

Now try this

To help you learn the jobs vocabulary, make a list of five jobs that you would like to do and five that you would not like to do, and then memorise them.

⑥ International and global dimension: bringing the world together

Environmental issues

animaux (mpl)	animals
avantages (mpl)	advantages
campagne (f)	campaign / countryside
catastrophe (f)	disaster
charbon (m)	coal
climat (m)	climate
commerce équitable (m)	fairtrade
contre	against (not in favour of)
déchets (mpl)	rubbish
désastre (m)	disaster
désavantages (mpl)	disadvantages
eau potable (f)	drinking water
économiser (l'eau)	to save (water)
électricité (f)	electricity
énergie (f)	energy / power
environnement (m)	environment
faim (f)	hunger
famine (f)	famine
forêt (tropicale) (f)	(rain)forest
gaz (m)	gas
gens (mpl)	people
guerre (f)	war
inondation (f)	flood / flooding
international	international
manque (de) (m)	lack (of)
monde (m)	world
mondial	global / worldwide
mourir	to die
ordures (fpl)	rubbish
ouragan (m)	hurricane
pauvreté (f)	poverty
pays (m)	country
pétrole (m)	oil
planète (f)	planet
polluer	to pollute
pollution (f)	pollution
population (f)	population
pour	for (in favour of)
protection (f)	protection
protéger	to protect
recycler	to recycle
ressources naturelles (fpl)	natural resources

sécheresse (f)	drought
terre (f)	earth
vivre	to live

Aiming higher

affamé	starving
bénéficier	to benefit
climatique	climate (adjective)
contaminer	to contaminate
droits de l'homme (mpl)	human rights
eau douce (f)	fresh water
eau salée (f)	salt water
espèce (f)	species
espionnage (m)	spying
faire du compost	to (make) compost
instantané	instant (adjective)

l'énergie solaire

centrale nucléaire

qui souffre de malnutrition	malnourished
malheureux	unfortunate / in need
manquer	to lack
menacer	to threaten
réchauffement de la terre / planète (m)	global warming
sauvegarder	to protect
sauver	to save
sécurité (f)	security
survivre	to survive
tremblement de terre (m)	earthquake
trier	to sort / separate (e.g. rubbish)

Il faut toujours trier ses déchets.

Now try this

List the major problems facing the world in French and try to learn them.

Answers

The answers to the Speaking and Writing activities below are sample answers – there are many ways you could answer these questions.

Identity and culture

1. Physical descriptions

Mon ami, qui s'appelle Paul, a le même âge que moi. Il a les yeux noisette et les cheveux courts, raides et blonds. Il est assez grand et très mince et tout le monde pense qu'il est beau. Son visage est rond et il a un petit nez.

2. Character descriptions

sympa, drôle, effronté

3. Describing family

1 spoilt / unbearable / gets on her nerves [any 2]
2 (a bit) selfish
3 helps her with her homework
4 lives a long way away / in Switzerland [either]

4. Friends

A, D, E, F

5. Role models

Mon modèle est mon oncle Louis. Il est modeste, honnête, très généreux et me traite toujours en adulte. Je m'entends bien avec lui et je le trouve sympa aussi.

6. Relationships

Je m'entends bien avec la plupart des élèves de mon école car ils sont assez gentils et agréables, mais on se dispute de temps en temps. Quant aux profs, ils sont en général compréhensifs et travailleurs, donc je les respecte.

Il y a quelques jours, un élève a volé le portable de mon copain et ils se sont battus, mais heureusement les incidents violents sont rares parce que les rapports entre profs et élèves dans mon école sont bons. L'année prochaine, je vais rester à la même école car j'ai beaucoup d'amis ici.

7. When I was younger

Listen to the recording

Quand j'étais plus jeune, je jouais au foot et je faisais du judo. J'étais très heureuse parce que ma vie était simple et que mes parents étaient toujours là pour moi.

8. Peer group

B, D, E

9. Money

1 found a part-time job in a chemist's   2 to have extra money
3 buy a (new) mobile

10. Customs

1 Pouvez-vous (me) recommander un bon hôtel?
2 Qu'est-ce que tu aimes faire le week-end? / Qu'est-ce que tu veux / vas faire ce week-end?

11. Everyday life

Listen to the recording

Après m'être levé, je m'habille et je prends le petit déjeuner avant d'aller au collège. Une fois rentré le soir, je fais mes devoirs, je regarde un peu de télé et je dîne. Plus tard, je promène le chien ou je sors de temps en temps avec mes copains. Je me couche assez tard.

12. Meals at home

Le matin, je mange des céréales et le soir, je préfère prendre un repas léger comme une salade verte ou des pâtes. Ma mère prépare des repas délicieux, surtout le week-end quand elle a plus de temps libre, donc on mange bien.

Hier soir, j'ai mangé de la soupe de tomates et une tranche de gâteau au chocolat avant de sortir avec mes copains. Demain, mon père va préparer le repas du soir, de l'agneau avec des pommes de terres rôties.

13. Food and drink

1 sa mère   2 sa sœur   3 Lysette

14. Shopping

1 link MP3 player to receiver in hat   2 pocket / bag
3 not more than 12 metres away   4 none

15. Shopping for food

1 Je voudrais un paquet de biscuits.
2 Nous avons assez de légumes.
3 Il y a beaucoup / plein de pêches.

16. Social media

Listen to the recording

1 J'aime bien les réseaux sociaux car je peux rester en contact avec mes amis, mais je peux aussi me renseigner sur toutes sortes de choses.
2 Je passe environ deux heures en ligne par jour. Je surfe sur le web afin de trouver des renseignements pour mon travail scolaire, je tchatte avec mes copains et je télécharge souvent de la musique.
3 Je préfère Facebook parce qu'on peut y poster des photos et rester en contact avec tout le monde. C'est tout un monde virtuel.

17. Technology

nothing / it's free

18. Internet advantages and disadvantages

Listen to the recording

1 Moi, j'utilise Internet car cela m'aide avec mon travail scolaire et c'est rapide et facile. Naturellement, je surfe sur le web pour m'amuser et j'aime les réseaux sociaux parce qu'on peut rester en contact avec ses amis, même à l'étranger.
2 Selon moi, Internet permet d'élargir ses horizons puisqu'on peut s'informer, faire des achats sans devoir quitter la maison

et tchatter avec des copains. Néanmoins, il faut surveiller les enfants en ligne et il ne faut pas passer trop de temps devant un écran car on risque de devenir moins actif.

19. Arranging to go out

1 sports centre   **2** swimming   **3** has to do homework

20. Hobbies

Comme passe-temps, j'aime surtout jouer de la batterie et j'en joue tous les soirs parce que c'est relaxant. De temps en temps je regarde la télé ou j'écoute de la musique, mais j'aime aussi tchatter avec mes amis en ligne.

Le week-end dernier, je suis allé à un concert avec quelques copains et c'était génial parce que c'était mon groupe préféré. Dimanche j'ai déjeuné en ville avec ma famille.

Le week-end prochain, je vais faire de la planche à voile au bord de la mer avec mon frère. On va bien s'amuser.

21. Music

pop / nul / instruments

22. Sport

Listen to the recording

1 J'aime jouer au foot dans le parc avec mes copains le week-end, mais mon sport préféré c'est le volley. J'y joue pour un club le mercredi et je trouve ça passionnant. De temps en temps, je fais du VTT à la campagne et la semaine dernière j'ai joué au rugby.

2 Je voudrais essayer le ski nautique parce que c'est un sport intéressant et technique et, puisque je nage bien, je n'aurais pas de problèmes si je tombais.

23. Reading

A, B, D

24. Films

Sur la photo il y a un groupe de jeunes dans un cinéma. Tout le monde rit car le film est marrant. J'adore aller au cinéma parce que j'aime le grand écran.

25. TV

Je préfère regarder les documentaires.
Hier j'ai regardé un dessin animé avec mon frère.
Demain je vais regarder mon feuilleton préféré.

26. Celebrations

In France, 1 November is a popular religious celebration. All the schools are shut and everyone spends the day with their family. You think of members of the family who have died and you go to church, where people take lots of flowers. In the evening you often have a big meal together.

27. Festivals

1 the second Sunday in May   **2** flowers
3 a card   **4** wrote a poem

Local area, holiday and travel

28. Holiday preferences

1 to the seaside   **2** active
3 to the mountains   **4** camping

29. Hotels

Listen to the recording

1 En général, les hôtels sont confortables même s'ils coûtent cher. On n'a pas besoin de préparer les repas car il y a souvent un restaurant où on peut dîner le soir et prendre le petit déjeuner le matin.

2 L'hôtel de mes rêves serait au bord de la mer et donnerait sur la plage. Il y aurait une piscine en plein air et la vue de mon balcon serait impressionnante. Le personnel serait poli et serviable. Les repas dans le restaurant seraient délicieux!

30. Campsites

I like going camping because I like nature and love being in the open air. Unfortunately my family prefers to stay in a hotel or holiday home, so usually we don't go camping. When I'm older, I'm going to go camping with my friends in Wales and that will be great.

31. Accommodation

1 dans une auberge de jeunesse   **2** dans une caravane
3 sale   **4** deux semaines

32. Holiday destinations

1 a villa
2 three rooms / running water / electricity
3 terrible food
4 the villa / the South of France / where Dad/Mum wants

33. Travel

1 abroad   **2** France / he has friends there
3 New Zealand

34. Holiday activities

1 Il y a un homme et trois enfants. Ils font du ski. Il neige et ils ont froid.
2 Je n'ai jamais fait de ski mais je voudrais skier un jour parce que ce serait amusant.
3 Je préfère les vacances d'été car j'aime le beau temps. J'adore tous les sports nautiques.
4 Je suis allé en Espagne avec ma famille et c'était vraiment génial.
5 Mes vacances idéales seraient en Australie car je voudrais voir les animaux sauvages là-bas.

35. Holiday plans

1 Elle y va pour la première fois.
2 chic / cher / à Tokyo [any 2]
3 sa famille et ses copains

36. Holiday experiences

1 du ski   **2** à la patinoire
3 au tennis de table

37. Transport

Listen to the recording

1 Je préfère prendre le train car c'est pratique et assez facile. On peut dormir, lire, écouter de la musique ou même faire du travail quand on voyage.

2 J'ai peur de prendre l'avion. Je sais que c'est un moyen de transport rapide, mais je ne peux pas prendre l'avion.

38. Directions

1 straight on **2** second left **3** cross the bridge

39. Holiday problems

1 a queue at the ticket office **2** bang on time
3 a seat on the train

40. Asking for help

Listen to the recording

1 Je veux échanger cette robe, s'il vous plaît.
2 La robe est trop petite.
3 Je l'ai achetée hier.
4 Vous avez une robe plus grande?
5 C'est combien?

41. Eating out in a café

Delphine: B, D Marcus: A, C

42. Eating out in a restaurant

Hier, je suis allé(e) en ville à un nouveau restaurant italien avec mon copain qui s'appelle Lionel. J'ai pris une pizza qui était délicieuse et il a choisi du poulet au citron avec des légumes et il l'a trouvé vraiment savoureux. Selon moi, le restaurant était fantastique car le service était excellent et le repas très bien préparé. Normalement on va au restaurant en famille pour fêter un anniversaire. Par exemple, le mois prochain, on va aller à un restaurant français car mon frère va fêter ses dix ans. J'espère que le repas sera excellent.

43. Buying gifts

a pink leather belt

44. Opinions about food

Listen to the recording

1 Je préfère manger des pâtes car j'adore la cuisine italienne. Hier, j'ai mangé des spaghettis avec une sauce tomate à l'ail et c'était délicieux.
2 Comme boisson, j'aime bien le coca mais je sais que c'est mauvais pour la santé. De temps en temps, je bois du thé au lait et le soir, je prends toujours deux verres d'eau parce que c'est bon pour la peau.

45. Weather

A, C, F, H

46. Tourism

Listen to the recording

1 J'aime assez faire du tourisme mais je ne m'intéresse pas à l'histoire, alors je trouve les monuments et les musées un peu ennuyeux. Cependant, j'aime bien admirer la campagne et j'adore faire des excursions en bateau.
2 Ma ville est historique et des touristes viennent ici pour admirer la belle cathédrale gothique et les ruines du château. On peut également aller au musée d'art moderne, et pour ceux qui aiment la nature, la ville est entourée de belles collines et de lacs.

47. Describing a town

1 C **2** B

48. Countries

Selon moi, les vacances sont importantes parce qu'on peut se détendre et oublier les soucis de la vie de tous les jours, alors je pars en vacances au moins une fois par an.
L'été dernier, ma famille a décidé d'aller au Canada car mon grand-père y habite et les vacances étaient magnifiques. Après être arrivés à Montréal, nous nous sommes installés dans notre hôtel qui était vraiment confortable. Ensuite mon grand-père est venu à l'hôtel et on a pris un repas ensemble.
Un jour on a visité les chutes du Niagara qui m'ont plu énormément. J'ai aussi apprécié les montagnes et les lacs où j'ai fait du ski et de la planche à voile pour la première fois.
À l'avenir je voudrais aller aux États-Unis car ma meilleur copine vient d'aller y vivre et elle me manque beaucoup. J'aimerais bien lui rendre visite.

49. Places to visit

A, C, E

50. Describing a region

Listen to the recording

1 Je vois un village à la montagne, peut-être en France. Il y a plein de maisons et une église à droite. Puisqu'il n'y a pas de neige sur les montagnes, je pense que c'est l'été.
2 Moi, j'aime habiter en Angleterre car mes copains et ma famille habitent ici, mais je voudrais habiter en Espagne un jour parce qu'il y fait plus chaud.
3 Je préfère habiter en ville car il y a plus de distractions, comme le bowling ou les boîtes de nuit. Je trouve la campagne assez ennuyeuse puisque c'est trop tranquille.
4 À l'avenir, je voudrais habiter au bord de la mer parce qu'il y fait chaud en été et moi, j'aime les sports nautiques.
5 Quand j'étais plus jeune, j'habitais à Londres mais on a déménagé il y a dix ans, ce qui m'a déplu car tous mes copains habitent là-bas.

School

51. Subjects

Lucas: IT like / easy; Manrouf: PE dislike / (too) tiring; Kévin: History like / fascinating

52. School life

1 opinion positive **2** opinion positive et négative
3 opinion négative

53. School day

L'après-midi à mon collège ne dure que deux heures, heureusement! On a deux cours sauf le mercredi où on a deux heures de sport, ce que je déteste parce que je ne suis pas du tout sportive et que je préférerais lire ou faire du dessin. Les cours finissent à trois heures quarante et, après avoir pris le car, j'arrive chez moi vers quatre heures et demie, souvent épuisée!

54. Comparing schools

1 A **2** C **3** B

55. Describing schools

A, D, F

66. School rules

Listen to the recording

À mon avis, le règlement de mon collège est plutôt juste, mais je n'aime pas mon uniforme scolaire parce qu'il est inconfortable et démodé.
Je voudrais pouvoir porter du maquillage car ça me donnerait plus de confiance en moi. J'aimerais aussi porter mes propres vêtements au collège parce que je les trouve plus confortables.

67. Problems and pressures

not being able to finish homework
A room is to be set aside for her in school (1) so that she can work after lessons (1).

68. Primary school

Listen to the recording

Mon école primaire était toute petite mais en général, les instituteurs étaient gentils et je m'amusais bien. Il y avait une cour où je jouais au foot et au basket avec mes copains et tout le monde était content.
Bien que j'aime mon collège, j'ai toujours préféré mon école primaire parce qu'il y avait moins de stress et de contrôles et la vie était plus facile.

69. Success at school

, B, F

70. School trips

, E, F

71. School activities

Je joue au foot pour mon collège / lycée / école..
Je chante dans la chorale.
Je voudrais / J'aimerais participer à une pièce (de théâtre).
Mon équipe de basket a gagné un match hier.
Il y a un festival de musique au collège lycée / école chaque année et c'est super.

Exchanges

Oui, je suis allé en France avec mon collège il y a deux ans.
Mon correspondant était sympa et sa famille m'a accueilli chaleureusement.
Le voyage était un peu pénible à cause de la mer agitée, mais une fois arrivé en France, j'étais vraiment heureux. J'ai réussi à parler français presque tout le temps et j'ai visité la région avec la famille de mon correspondant.

Future aspirations, study and work

73. Future plans

take a gap year
study for (A level) exams / the baccalauréat and do some voluntary work
three years

64. Languages beyond the classroom

Listen to the recording

1 Si on sait parler une autre langue, on peut trouver plus facilement un bon emploi dans un autre pays. En plus, on peut mieux connaître les gens et la culture d'un pays étranger.
2 Je trouve les cours assez difficiles mais utiles. J'ai laissé tomber l'espagnol mais j'ai continué mes études de français et j'ai souvent de bonnes notes.

65. Looking to the future

Listen to the recording

1 Mon rêve est de devenir joueur de foot professionnel mais je sais que ce sera difficile. Je vais quand même faire tout ce que je peux pour réussir.
2 Si on travaille en groupe, on peut entreprendre de plus grands projets. Par contre, il faut partager les profits, et il faut bien s'entendre avec les autres membres de l'équipe.

66. Travel

1 In the future I'd like to travel to the USA with my friends.
2 Switzerland is an interesting and varied country.
3 I'd like to spend a month in Scotland as I've never been there (before).
4 My father has (some) friends who live in New York.
5 I intend to travel all over the world.

67. Jobs

1 well paid, long hours
2 help animals, training/qualification hard

68. Part-time jobs

Listen to the recording

1 À mon avis, il est important d'avoir un petit emploi si on a besoin d'argent supplémentaire. De plus, quand on travaille, on a un peu plus d'indépendance, ce qui est essentiel dans le monde d'aujourd'hui.
2 Quelques copains travaillent à temps partiel. Il y en a qui n'ont pas de petit job parce qu'ils ont trop de travail scolaire, mais leurs parents leur donnent de l'argent de poche.

69. Opinions about jobs

A Zoë   C Noah   D Léna   E Zoë   F Noah

70. Workplaces

1 supermarché   2 ferme   3 salon de coiffure

71. Applying for jobs

Je viens de trouver un petit job dans un centre sportif en ville.
La journée commence à dix heures et on finit à dix-sept heures.
Je devrai commencer dans une semaine. On me dit que je suis responsable et confiant, alors je vais pouvoir bien communiquer avec les clients.

72. Future study

1 Si on va à la fac, on obtient un diplôme, ce qui permettrait de trouver un emploi bien payé. Par contre, aller à l'université coûte cher et on aura des dettes à la fin de ses études.
2 Moi, je ne sais pas ce que je voudrais faire, mais j'irai peut-être à l'université car j'aimerais être dentiste et il faut continuer les études pendant plusieurs années.

73. Volunteering

1 to become familiar with the world of work / to fulfil the requirements of their studies
2 to enjoy a sense of belonging / as a challenge / for fun [any 2]

74. Helping others

1 J'écoute mes copains quand ils ont des soucis. Par exemple, hier j'ai parlé avec ma meilleure copine qui était triste car ses parents sont en train de se séparer et je lui ai dit qu'elle pouvait compter sur moi.
2 Je voudrais faire du travail bénévole l'année prochaine, dans un centre sportif où on organise des activités pour les personnes défavorisées. J'espère faire du bien.

75. Charities

A, D, E

76. Training

1 D   2 B

77. Future professions

painter, pilot

International and global dimension

78. Sporting events

L'année dernière, j'ai passé une semaine en France à regarder le Tour de France. J'ai vu le départ à Rennes, dans le nord-ouest de la France, avec mon père qui adore le cyclisme, et ensuite on a suivi cinq étapes jusqu'à Poitiers.
À mon avis, c'était super parce que j'ai pu voir les cyclistes de près et le soir, je discuté de ce qui s'était passé pendant la journée avec mon père dans un café.
Selon moi, les évènements sportifs internationaux permettent aux gens de passer un bon moment. De plus, ils attirent plein de touristes et unissent les gens, tout en encourageant la fierté nationale.
À l'avenir, j'aimerais surtout assister aux Jeux Olympiques parce que l'athlétisme me passionne et je voudrais également voyager à l'étranger pour pouvoir élargir mes horizons.

79. Music events

1 On peut rencontrer des gens de différents pays et se faire de nouveaux amis. De plus, on a l'occasion d'écouter des chanteurs ou des groupes célèbres en live et c'est vraiment génial.

2 Je préfère les concerts live de musique pop parce que la musique classique ne me dit rien et qu'en plus, il faut écouter la musique classique en silence et je déteste ça.

80. Being green

1 Je suis assez écolo. Je recycle le verre et le papier tous les jours et j'économise l'eau et l'énergie, mais je pourrais faire plus. Je vais essayer d'utiliser les transports en commun ou de me déplacer à pied.
2 J'ai décidé de prendre des douches plutôt que des bains. Je viens aussi d'acheter un nouveau vélo car je veux me déplacer plus souvent en vélo au lieu de demander à mes parents de me conduire partout.

81. Protecting the environment

1 Je fais ce que je peux. Par exemple, le week-end dernier, je suis allé en ville à pied et j'ai dit à mes parents de baisser le chauffage central afin d'économiser le gaz.
2 Plus tard, je ne vais pas acheter une grosse voiture avec un moteur énorme et je vais faire partie d'un groupe écolo comme Greenpeace car je m'inquiète pour le futur.

82. Environmental issues

1 C   2 B

83. Natural resources

A, B, E

84. World problems

1 C   2 C   3 B

Grammar

85. Articles 1

le garçon   **la** mère
les étudiants   **le** printemps
l'Espagne   **la** Loire
la condition   **le** bleu
la décision   **le** père
le garage   **la** plage

86. Articles 2

1 (a) Allez **au**   (b) Allez **aux**   (c) Allez **à la**
   (d) Allez **à l'**   (e) Allez **aux**   (f) Allez **au**
   (g) Allez **au**   (h) Allez **à la**
2 (a) Je veux **du** pain.   (b) Avez-vous **du** lait?
   (c) Il n'a pas **d'**essence.   (d) Je vais **à l'**école.
   (e) Est-ce que tu vas **à la** mairie?   (f) Il va **aux** toilettes.

87. Adjectives

1 un petit chien noir
2 la semaine dernière
3 Mon petit frère est très actif.
4 Ma meilleure amie est petite et timide.
5 Son frère est grand, sportif mais un peu sérieux.

88. Possessives

1 mon frère   2 son ami   3 ses amis
4 son sac   5 ma sœur   6 son amie
7 ses amis   8 son portable   9 mes parents
10 leur ami   11 leurs amis   12 leur voiture

89. Comparisons

L'Everest est la montagne **la plus haute** du monde.
La veste est **plus chère** que la robe.
Demain il fera **plus beau** qu'aujourd'hui.
La meilleure solution est de prendre le train.
Julie est **moins intelligente** que Fabien.
Le TGV est le train **le plus rapide**.

90. Other adjectives and pronouns

Noé veut cette veste. Laquelle? Celle-ci.
Je préfère ce portable. Lequel? Celui-là.
Manon a choisi ces chaussures. Lesquelles? Celles-ci.
Son frère achète ces jeux. Lesquels? Ceux-là.
On regarde ce film ce soir. Lequel? Celui-là.

91. Adverbs

Notre chat a disparu. **D'habitude**, il rentre chaque soir, **toujours** vers six heures. **Soudain**, j'ai entendu un bruit. **Très doucement** j'ai ouvert la porte et j'ai été **vraiment** surpris de voir Max avec trois petit chatons! **Finalement,** il est entré dans la maison. **Évidemment**, Max n'est plus Max, mais Maxine!

92. Object pronouns

Il l'a envoyé.
Il ne les a pas achetées.
Sarah l'a lu.

2 Je ne l'ai pas regardée.
4 Tu l'as vu?
6 Mes parents l'ont achetée.

93. More pronouns: *y* and *en*

J'y suis déjà allé.
J'y suis allé hier.
On y va souvent.

2 J'en ai déjà mangé trop.
4 J'y vais de temps en temps.
6 Je n'en mange jamais.

94. Other pronouns

Mon ami **qui** s'appelle Bruno est fana de football.
L'émission **que** j'ai vue hier n'était pas passionnante.
Le quartier **où** ils habitent est vraiment calme.
C'est le prof **dont** je vous ai déjà parlé.
Elle a une sœur **qui** est prof.
J'ai accepté le stage **que** mon prof m'a proposé.

95. Present tense: *-er* verbs

Je m'appelle Lou. J'ai une sœur qui **s'appelle** Marina et qui **joue** au tennis. Je **préfère** faire de la danse. Je **chante** et je **joue** de la guitare. Le soir nous **rentrons** à cinq heures et nous **mangeons** un casse-croûte. Puis je **tchatte** avec mes amis, et j'**écoute** de la musique. Quelquefois mon frère et moi **jouons** à des jeux vidéo ou **téléchargeons** un film à regarder plus tard.

96. Present tense: *-ir* and *-re* verbs

Le matin je **sors** à sept heures et demie.
Le mardi les cours **finissent** à cinq heures.
Mon copain et moi ne **buvons** pas de coca.
Le train **part** à 8h20.
Nous **apprenons** l'espagnol.
Pendant les vacances nous **dormons** sous la tente.
Mes copains **choisissent** des frites.

97. *Avoir* and *être*

Nous **avons** un petit chaton. Il est tout noir mais il **a** les yeux verts. Il **a** toujours faim. Il **a** beaucoup de jouets mais j'**ai** une balle de ping-pong qu'il adore et mon petit frère acheté un petit oiseau en fourrure pour lui. **As**-tu un animal?
Je **suis** britannique. Je **suis** né en Angleterre. Mes parents **sont** italiens. Ils **sont** nés en Italie mais ils habitent ici depuis vingt ans. Mon frère **est** sportif. Il **est** champion régional de judo. Ma sœur **est** paresseuse. En revanche je **suis** charmant!

98. Reflexive verbs

Je ne **m'entends** pas bien avec mon grand frère. Il **se moque** de moi. Nous **nous disputons** souvent. Je **m'entends** mieux avec ma sœur. On **s'amuse** bien ensemble. Nous **nous couchons** de bonne heure parce que le matin nous **nous levons** à six heures – mais hier mon frère ne **s'est réveillé** pas avant 8 heures.. Quand finalement il **s'est levé** il ne **s'est douché** pas parce qu'il n'a pas eu le temps.

99. Other important verbs

1   vais / I go to school by bus.
2   faisons / We go skiing in winter.
3   peut / You can go to the cinema in town.
4   veulent / They want to go to Spain.
5   dois / You must do your homework.
6   sait / She knows how to play the piano.

100. The perfect tense 1

Mercredi dernier j'**ai pris** le bus pour aller en ville. J'y **ai retrouvé** un ami. Nous **avons fait** les magasins. J'**ai voulu** acheter des baskets rouges mais elles étaient trop chères. Nous **avons mangé** des burgers et comme boisson j'**ai choisi** un coca. Mon copain **a bu** un milkshake fraise. J'**ai laissé** mon sac au bar. **J'ai dû** y retourner et, par conséquent, j'**ai raté** le bus et j'**ai dû** rentrer à pied.

101. The perfect tense 2

1   Samedi dernier je **suis parti(e)** de bonne heure.
2   Le matin je **suis allé(e)** jouer au football.
3   Je **suis sorti(e)** à dix heures.
4   L'autre équipe **n'est pas venue**.
5   Nous y **sommes restés** une heure, puis nous **sommes rentrés**.
6   Je **suis arrivé(e)** à la maison juste avant midi.

102. The imperfect tense

It's written in the imperfect because it's about what someone used to do.
Quand j'**étais** jeune, j'**habitais** à la campagne. Nous **avions** un grand jardin où je **jouais** au foot avec mes frères. Le samedi on **allait** au marché en ville. Il y **avait** beaucoup de vendeurs de fruits et légumes et un kiosque à journaux où j'**achetais** des bonbons. Nous **mangions** des merguez (des saucisses épicées) et nous **buvions** du coca. On **rentrait** en bus avec tous nos voisins et nos achats!

103. The future tense

L'année prochaine nous **irons** en France. Nous **prendrons** l'Eurostar. On **partira** de Londres et on **arrivera** à Paris. Puis on **changera** de train et on **continuera** vers le sud. Nous **ferons** du camping. Mes parents **dormiront** dans une caravane mais je **dormirai** sous une tente. Pendant la journée nous **irons** à la plage et **jouerons** au basket et au tennis. Le soir on **mangera** au resto. On **se fera** des amis.

104. The conditional tense

1   Je **voudrais** aller en Italie.
2   Si j'avais assez d'argent, j'**irais** en Inde.
3   Nous **pourrions** faire un long voyage.
4   Tu **aimerais** voir ce film?
5   Je **préférerais** manger au restaurant.
6   Si j'avais faim, je **mangerais** une pizza.
7   Il **voudrait** aller en ville samedi.
8   On **pourrait** aller à la patinoire cet après-midi?
9   Tu **verrais** le match si tu restais encore deux jours.
10 Vous **voudriez** quelque chose à boire?

105. The pluperfect tense

pluperfect verbs: 1–6; imperfect verbs: 7, 11; perfect verbs: 8, 9, 10

106. Negatives

1   1H, 2F, 3B, 4A, 5C, 6E, 7D, 8G
2   **(a)** Tu ne fais rien.

(b) Tu ne m'as jamais aidé à la maison.
   (c) Tu ne fais plus tes devoirs.
   (d) Tu ne respectes personne.
   (e) Tu ne fais que le nécessaire.
   (f) Tu ne peux aller ni au football ni au restaurant ce soir.

107. The perfect infinitive and present participles

1 (a) Après avoir regardé la télé, j'ai joué au foot.
   (b) Après être arrivée à l'hôtel, elle a déjeuné.
   (c) Après s'être levé, il a pris le petit déjeuner.
   (d) Après avoir fini ses devoirs, il est allé en ville.
   (e) Après avoir écouté de la musique, ils/elles sont allé(e)s à l'école.

2 (a) en mangeant   (b) en ayant   (c) en travaillant
   (d) en finissant   (e) en faisant

108. The passive and the subjunctive

1 E   2 A   3 B   4 F   5 C   6 D

109. Questions

Où travaille ton père? Where does your father work?
Qui va à la fête? Who is going to the party?
Comment allez-vous? How are you?
Combien d'amis as-tu sur Facebook? How many friends do you have on Facebook?
À quelle heure rentrent tes parents? What time are your parents coming home?
Pourquoi as-tu raté le bus? Why did you miss the bus?
Que voulez-vous faire? What do you want to do?
Depuis quand apprends-tu le français? How long have you been learning French?

110. Prepositions, conjunctions and intensifiers

1 partout	2 sous	3 dans	4 derrière
5 puis	6 dehors	7 dans	8 sans
9 à la fin	10 dans	11 au	12 sous

Published by Pearson Education Limited, 80 Strand, London, WC2R 0RL.

www.pearsonschoolsandfecolleges.co.uk

Copies of official specifications for all Pearson qualifications may be found on the website: qualifications.pearson.com

Text and illustrations © Pearson Education Limited 2016
Produced, typeset and illustrations by Cambridge Publishing Management Ltd
Cover illustration by Miriam Sturdee

The rights of Stuart Glover and Rosi McNab to be identified as authors of this work have been asserted by them in accordance with the Copyright, Designs and Patents Act 1988.

First published 2016

19

10 9 8 7 6 5

British Library Cataloguing in Publication Data
A catalogue record for this book is available from the British Library

ISBN 9781292132082

Acknowledgements

The publisher would like to thank the following for their kind permission to reproduce their photographs:

(Key: b-bottom; c-centre; l-left; r-right; t-top)

123RF.com: Alfred Hofer 103, Cathy Yeulet 53, Garry518 88c (a), My Make OU 60, stockbroker 57r; **Alamy Images**: Directphoto.org 104l, John Morris 67l, Kevin Foy 49, Leonid Nyshko 88cl, Peter Stone 47, Photos 12 24t, Pixoi Ltd 69l; **Corbis**: 67r, photolibrary.com / Randy Faris 62; **Creatas**: 82, 84l; **Fotolia.com**: alexandre zveiger 79, Anton Gvozdikov 10r, Bart Kowski 97, Dasha Petrenko 10, ivanmateev 41cl, lilechka75 41br, Maksim Shebeko 44, Mikael Damkier 78, Monkey Business 24c, 56, 70, oneinchpunch 8, pixamo 80, Sondem 7, sveta 88c, Tyler Olson 51, utkamandarinka 57l, VadimGuzhva 68, violet711 27, yanlev 35; **Getty Images**: commerceandculturestock 83, Gerry Ellis 73, Handout 84r, Ryan McVay 40; **Grand Canyon National Park**: 96; **Images of France**: 102; **Masterfile UK Ltd**: Classic Stock 89; **Pearson Education Ltd**: Sophie Bluy 9, 54, 69r, 86, 87l, 87r, Jules Selmes 41, 100, 105; **Photolibrary.com**: Kevin Arnold 34, Stockbroker / Monkey Business Images Ltd 104r; **Rex Shutterstock**: Nils Jorgensen 2; **Shutterstock.com**: Alexander Studentschnig 50, Andrey_Popov 76, EdBockStock 1l, Elena Eliseeva 28, Featureflash Photo Agency 64, Gemenacom 88l, Gregory Gerber 93cl, Hung Chung Chih 81, Iakov Filimonov 43, IM_photo 22l, Kjuuurs 33, Maxisport 22r, 93tr, Monkey Business Images 6, Nikonaft 71, Odua Images 17, Ortodox 93bl, Paul Cowan 12, Przemyslaw Ceynowa 88r, Shebeko 93tl, SnowWhiteImages 1r, Sorbis 36, Valentyn Volkov 13, vinz89 77, vovan 88cr; **Sozaijiten**: 109

All other images © Pearson Education

We are grateful to the following for permission to reproduce copyright material

Extract on page 32 adapted from *Le Petit Nicolas en Vacances*, Editions Gallimard (Sempé, J.J. and Goscinny, R. 1962); Quote on page 77 adapted from *Le Petit Prince* (de Saint-Exupéry, A. 1943), © Editions GALLIMARD Tous les droits d'auteur de ce texte sont reservés. Sauf autorisation, toute utilisation de celui-ci autre que la consultation individuelle et privée est interdite. www.gallimard.fr, Copyright 1943 by Houghton Mifflin Harcourt Publishing Company. Copyright © renewed 1971 by Consuelo de Saint-Exupéry. Reprinted by permission of Houghton Mifflin Harcourt Publishing Company.

Notes from the publisher

1. In order to ensure that this resource offers high-quality support for the associated Pearson qualification, it has been through a review process by the awarding body. This process confirms that this resource fully covers the teaching and learning content of the specification or part of a specification at which it is aimed. It also confirms that it demonstrates an appropriate balance between the development of subject skills, knowledge and understanding, in addition to preparation for assessment.

Endorsement does not cover any guidance on assessment activities or processes (e.g. practice questions or advice on how to answer assessment questions), included in the resource nor does it prescribe any particular approach to the teaching or delivery of a related course.

While the publishers have made every attempt to ensure that advice on the qualification and its assessment is accurate, the official specification and associated assessment guidance materials are the only authoritative source of information and should always be referred to for definitive guidance.

Pearson examiners have not contributed to any sections in this resource relevant to examination papers for which they have responsibility.

Examiners will not use endorsed resources as a source of material for any assessment set by Pearson.

Endorsement of a resource does not mean that the resource is required to achieve this Pearson qualification, nor does it mean that it is the only suitable material available to support the qualification, and any resource lists produced by the awarding body shall include this and other appropriate resources.

2. Pearson has robust editorial processes, including answer and fact checks, to ensure the accuracy of the content in this publication, and every effort is made to ensure this publication is free of errors. We are, however, only human, and occasionally errors do occur. Pearson is not liable for any misunderstandings that arise as a result of errors in this publication, but it is our priority to ensure that the content is accurate. If you spot an error, please do contact us at resourcescorrections@pearson.com so we can make sure it is corrected.